IN THE LANDS OF FIRE AND SUN

In the LANDS *of* FIRE *and* SUN

Resistance and Accommodation in the Huichol Sierra, 1723–1930

MICHELE MCARDLE STEPHENS

University of Nebraska Press | Lincoln and London

Portions of chapter 4 previously appeared as "'As Long as They Have Their Land': The Huichol of Western Mexico, 1850–1895" in *Ethnohistory* 62, no. 1 (January 2015): 39–60. DOI: 10.1215/00141801-2681777.

Library of Congress Cataloging-in-Publication Data
Names: McArdle Stephens, Michele, author.
Title: In the Lands of Fire and Sun: Resistance and Accommodation in the Huichol Sierra, 1723–1930 / Michele McArdle Stephens.
Description: Lincoln: University of Nebraska Press, [2018] | Includes bibliographical references and index.
Identifiers: LCCN 2017041403
ISBN 9780803288584 (cloth: alk. paper)
ISBN 9781496205902 (epub)
ISBN 9781496205919 (mobi)
ISBN 9781496205926 (pdf)
Subjects: LCSH: Huichol Indians—History. | Huichol Indians—Ethnic identity. | Huichol Indians—Cultural assimilation.
Classification: LCC F1221.H9 M223 2018 | DDC 305.897/4544—dc23 LC record available at https://lccn.loc.gov/2017041403

Set in Merope by E. Cuddy.

For my grandparents
And to the Wixáritari

CONTENTS

ILLUSTRATIONS

Following page 84

MAPS

FIGURES

ACKNOWLEDGMENTS

This project has been a labor of love for more than a decade, and many people have helped support my work since its inception. Deep gratitude is extended to the staff at a number of archives in Mexico, the United States, and Europe. In Mexico: Gaby and staff at the Archivo Histórico del Estado de Jalisco; the Archivo General de la Nación (Mexico); the Archivo de la Mitra del Arzobispado de Guadalajara; and a note of special appreciation to Fray Carlos Badillo at the Archivo Histórico Franciscano de Zapopan. While the staff at all of the archives were friendly and helpful, Fray Carlos was an endless source of information and wonderful conversation, sharing books and documents without which this project would be considerably less rich. In Seville: the archivists at the Archivo General de Indias could not have been more helpful, particularly because studying sixteenth-century documents is outside of my comfort zone. And in Berlin: the multilingual staff of the Ibero-Amerikanishes Institut and the Bureau of Ethnology in Berlin were very patient with me. In the United States: the staff in the Prints and Photographs Reading Room at the Library of Congress; the Smithsonian Institute's National Anthropology Archives; the archivists at the American Museum of Natural History (New York); and Allison Colborne and Diana Bird at the Laboratory of Anthropology in Santa Fe. I am so grateful to have worked with such kind and professional individuals throughout the world.

I have had the great fortune to be well-funded during my time at West Virginia University. I received a Senate Grant for Faculty Research in 2014, which funded the final stages of my research. I also received a Riggle Summer Fellowship in 2015, which allowed me time to write and think about how to reframe certain aspects of my manuscript. My department has also helped ensure that I have the resources I need to attend the numerous annual conferences where I have sharpened my arguments. I am so grateful for the support.

Projects like these are made all the more rich because of an author's friends and family. So many people have provided advice, wisdom, critiques, and friendship over the years, and it is impossible to name all of the wonderful people I have met on this journey. The following friends and colleagues have had a deep, lasting impact on my scholarship and my personal life and may never know how much I value their companionship and advice, even from afar. In Norman: the faculty and staff in the Department of History at the University of Oklahoma, especially Terry Rugeley and my graduate committee; many thanks to Emily Wardrop, Mandy Taylor-Montoya, Abby Wightman, Patrick Bottiger, Margarita Peraza-Rugeley, Catherine Kelly, and Rich Hamerla for being great friends. In Granville: the faculty and staff at Denison University, especially Trey Proctor in the Department of History; much appreciation to my friends Lauren Araiza, Olivia Aguilar, Nilay Ozok-Gundogan, and Jo Tague. In Morgantown: my colleagues in the Department of History, and a special note of thanks to Martha May and Rebecca Warnke for patiently answering my many questions; to my dear friends Victoria Garrett, Edward Chauca, Ángel Tuninetti, Shauna Fisher, Christina Fattore Morgan, Tania de Miguel Magro, Matthew Titolo, Mason Moseley, Kim Welch, and Ari Bryan. In Mexico and elsewhere: Bruno Calgaro Sandi, Susan Deeds, Tracy Goode, David Rex Galindo, Martin Nesvig, Gabriel Martínez-Serna, Pete Sigal, Ben Fallaw, and Fernando Calderón. I am a better person, colleague, and scholar because of all of you.

I also extend a sincere note of appreciation to my enormous family. I cannot name you all, but know that I value your support and affection. I have been mostly absent from my family since 2000, but their support has been unyielding as I pursued my education and career. First, thanks to Tim for pushing me to get through graduate school, dealing with my very long and frequent absences, and taking care of our dogs. Jen O'Brien, my long-time best pal, never fails to make me giggle like a schoolgirl during our chats. My sister Lisa, my brother-in-law Seth, and my nephews are constant sources of laughter and fun, particularly when they force me to take breaks, lest I get more "academic wrinkles." My sister Stephanie and her family warmly welcome me whenever I visit. My mother, Barbara McArdle, and her partner, Mary Banks, have been my biggest champions and always forgive my time away from them. My dad, Stephen McArdle, never fails to mention how proud he is of me. (I am certain his coworkers tire of hearing about me.) Finally, special thanks to two uncles: Joe Reali and Tom McArdle. My family always encouraged me to be bold, be brave, and be happy, three requirements to complete such a long project.

Finally, there is one other person who has read this manuscript more than I, and he deserves tremendous thanks. I could not have completed this book without the friendship, critiques, and suggestions of Laurent Corbeil, who knows more about the Huichols than most. Thank you for making this a better project.

A special note of thanks to the anonymous reviewers and to the wonderfully supportive staff at the University of Nebraska Press, especially Matt Bokovoy and Heather Stauffer. This project would not have been possible without the indomitable spirit of the Huichols of the past and the Wixárika of the present. I hope to someday repay the communities I have studied from the distance of time.

PROLOGUE

According to Huichol oral culture, in the distant past a Huichol ancestor named Kauyaumari journeyed to Wirikuta to fulfill religious obligations that his gods required of him. Wirikuta, infused with mystical power, was the home of Tamatsi Maxa Kwaxí (Elder Brother Deer Tail) and the birthplace of Tayaupá (Our Father the Sun).[1] While on his pilgrimage Kauyaumari encountered an enemy group in the area; in an attempt to pass through unmolested, Kauyaumari described to them his beliefs and his purpose for visiting Wirikuta. Despite this explanation, Kauyaumari's adversaries attacked and his people fled into the desert. The pilgrims were helpless in the harsh terrain of the northern deserts and were forced to abandon their cooking utensils and drinking gourds as they escaped. Their enemies destroyed all of their supplies, and Kauyaumari and his people had no means to survive the dry climate. Observing the plight of their supplicants, the gods, especially Tamatsi Maxa Kwaxí, pitied the pious travelers and provided them with a life-saving gift of peyote, sprouted from the horns of the deer. Kauyaumari and his followers discovered that the cactus could help them survive hunger and thirst for days at a time.[2]

Although the Huichols have had to adapt to modern issues like highways, buses, and fenced ranches along the route to Wirikuta, they nevertheless continue to adhere to the guidelines passed down from the gods. Pilgrims undertake a series of rituals before embarking on their journey and observe particular behaviors that are important to a successful pilgrimage and a bountiful year.

Today, in preparation for the journey to Wirikuta, the leader of the *peyoteros* (peyote-hunters) guides his followers through their required tasks. First, pilgrims pay homage to Tatewarí (Our Grandfather Fire) at his primary temple site near Santa Catarina, and attendants remain behind to care for the fire.[3] Failure to maintain the fire properly at home could endanger the pilgrims.[4] Next, all individuals participating in the peregrination confess their sins to the *mara'akame* (Hu: singer, holy person; pl. *mara'akate*). This binds the Huichols to one another in solidarity and guarantees that no secrets exist between members. These "sins" are different from what westerners might expect; most are of a sexual nature, as opposed to transgressions involving theft or violence. The ceremony is typically light-hearted; sins are knotted into a rope and then cast into the fire at the conclusion of the confessional ceremony. The oldest participants receive praise, in a manner of speaking, for their lifetime of prowess, while youngsters are teased for their lack of experience.[5]

Once pilgrims decide to undertake the journey, participants abstain from certain actions and behaviors. For instance, pilgrims are prohibited from eating salt and "are pledged to abstinence," as otherwise they will endanger their compatriots and the entire undertaking.[6] During the journey itself, pilgrims fast at specific times and only eat ritually prepared foods.[7] These rules are not meant to punish Huichol pilgrims, but instead are symbolic: in fasting, pilgrims recreate the suffering that Kauyaumari and his followers experienced in ancient times, which connects Huichols in the modern age to their ancestors and gods.[8]

After a long and arduous trek, the pilgrims begin their rituals designed to please the gods and ensure a plentiful hunt in Wirikuta. When the group is within five days of reaching Wirikuta, they begin their five days of fasting to commemorate Kauyaumari's suffering.[9] Once placated through the proper rituals, Elder Brother Deer Tail reveals his precious gift of peyote to his Huichol supplicants and then the hunt may proceed.

Stealthily, like a hunter stalking his prey, each pilgrim searches the ground in anticipation. They move eastward toward Re'unar or 'Unaxa, the "Burnt Mountain Where the Sun Was Born" and slow their movements when they approach the foot of the mountains, "for peyote was more likely to be found" near there.[10] Upon locating the tiny god-cactus, sprung from the tracks that Elder Brother Deer Tail left behind, the mara'akame hunts it, just as the men might pursue deer back home in the Sierra. The mara'akame shoots the peyote with his ceremonial arrows and then speaks quietly to it so as to prevent its "escape."[11] He is careful not to remove the roots (bones), so that next year Huichols might be blessed with the life-giving cactus.[12] After giving thanks to the gods and consuming a bit of this first piece of peyote, the pilgrims set out to hunt peyote on their own; having "at last become one with the landscape" they "become the gods whose names they bore."[13] Before taking leave of Wirikuta, their beloved holy land, *jicareros* (Hu: *xukurikate*, peyote gatherers) gather enough of the tiny gods to ensure a steady supply for personal and family use and more to sell or trade.[14]

Why the Huichols maintain this custom, in spite of the hardships and dangers (particularly in the twenty-first century), is critical to understanding the history of the peoples who call themselves Huichol. The pilgrimage and its relevance to Huichol culture and history has existed since long before Europeans ever conceived of the Americas.[15] The worship of the cactus ties Huichols to the beginning of time, giving them rights to specific places in the modern Mexican landscape. Because nearly everything in the Huichol world is imbued with both mundane and spiritual purposes, including geography, loss of their lands and their access to their peyote-centered religion means that the Huichols would cease to exist. The Huichols had experienced the effects of alien cultures in the past and had managed to adapt to their changing surroundings. However, in the late nineteenth century, as land pressures became an increasing concern, the Huichols faced the possibility of not only the end of their existence in the Sierra, but also the loss of their cultural identity.

This story, the legacy of the primordial peyote hunt, is an important cultural tool that scholars can use to understand elements of Huichol history. From ancient times, peyote and deer were bound together within the complex Huichol cosmology, as it was Elder Brother Deer Tail who gave the primordial Huichols peyote to survive their ordeal in the desert. The relationship between Tamatsi Maxa Kwaxí and Kauyaumari became a sacred one, inextricably intertwined between the hunting of the cactus and the worship of the deer. To obtain peyote in an appropriate manner, however, Tamatsi Maxa Kwaxí passed on explicit instructions to Kauyaumari and his followers (or contemporary Huichols). If precisely adhered to, these commands would ensure Huichol survival.

The peyote story also provides a map to the Huichol homeland and illuminates a complex ritual universe that extends in the four cardinal directions; it provides a backdrop for the past several centuries of history. Physical locations within this space are important because the Huichols' gods have imbued them with religious significance.[16] When mestizo ranchers stole that land to graze their cattle, they were not just taking Huichol land, they were depriving the Huichols of religiously important territory. Since at least the conquest of the Sierra in 1722–23, Huichol leaders have defended their lands from their Spanish and Mexican neighbors by moving deeper into the mountains. They insulated their culture by assimilating aspects of alien societies as they saw fit and vehemently defying the desires of priests, friars, and politicians.

The Huichols' imprint has been on the landscape since long before Europeans arrived. No one knows with certainty from where Kauyaumari and his followers began their journey or where they ended; whether they came from the east and settled in the west sometime in the distant past is immaterial in the grand scheme of things.[17] Regardless of the Huichols provenance, the peyote tale explains the importance of their presence around Real de Catorce, and historical documentation places their homeland in the Sierra Madre Occidental. Thus, Huichol cosmology blankets the landscape, firmly placing them within a vast west Mexican landscape that the Huichols consider their home and Holy Land. This helps explain the relationship between the Huichols and the wider world surrounding them.[18]

INTRODUCTION

The Huichols' physical world comprises varying landscapes and, at first glance, the environment appears rugged, wild, and desolate. Alongside the highways that weave through the state of San Luis Potosí, soaring peaks rise above the valley floor and the sun scorches the dry, dusty earth. The most common sights are cows, goats, and *remolinos*, whirlwinds of dust kicked up from the desert floor. A narrow, two-lane, cobblestone road brings residents, visitors, and supplies into Wirikuta, known more commonly as Real de Catorce, the small mountain town nearly 9,000 feet above sea level.

Wirikuta is a special location both because peyote grows there and also because the Huichols consider the area to be the birthplace of the Sun. According to the Huichols, the Sun was born at El Quemado, the Burned Mountain, also known as 'Unaxa or Re'unar. From the top of this mountain, facing west back toward the Huichol heartland of Teakata, the desert meets the horizon.[1]

About two hundred miles west-southwest of Wirikuta, the Huichols make their homes, farms, and lives in the high mountains of the Sierra Madre Occidental. Canyons plunge hundreds of feet to the valley floors below, and rivers that may be a trickle during the dry season turn into raging torrents after the rains arrive. This part of Mexico, where Jalisco, Zacatecas, Durango, and Nayarit intersect, forms some of the most rugged terrain in the country, providing sanctuary for native peoples for millennia. It is vast, expansive, isolating, and yet, the area has never been "isolated" from neighboring regions. A retreat from danger, the western Sierra Madre Occidental has served as the Huichols' home, a "region of refuge" for centuries, helping them maintain their culture, identity, and land.[2]

Who are the Huichols and what can the struggles of this small, little-known group tell us about indigenous peoples in Mexico and elsewhere? During the period under study, the total population ranged from about 2,000 at the end of the eighteenth century to roughly 4,000 recorded in an 1894 Mexican census.[3] More recent data compiled by the government of Jalisco and published in 2010 provides a better picture of the contemporary population size. Currently in Jalisco, the Huichols number around 13,000, with about 10,000 speaking at least some Spanish.[4] As observers have noted, there has been considerable out-migration in recent decades, and some Huichols live in the neighboring states of Nayarit, Durango, and Zacatecas (see map 1).[5] So, while the Huichols were a relatively small group during the eighteenth and nineteenth centuries, their population has grown much larger over the course of the twentieth century.

The Huichols worship a vast cosmology of deities that help to define and determine many elements of their daily lives. Grandfather Fire, Grandmother Creator, Elder Brother Deer Tail, and myriad other deities provide guidance to the Huichols, in addition to spiritual and physical sustenance.[6] The centrality of their religious culture, which revolves around pilgrimage and seasonal agricultural festivals, influences the organization of their lives and is depicted on various sorts of Huichol material culture. With the arrival of Spaniards in the sixteenth and seventeenth centuries, some elements of Catholic belief infiltrated the Huichol cosmology; however, despite hundreds of years of evangelization, Catholic influence has not destroyed Huichol religiosity.[7]

The rugged mountain areas in which the Huichols live have distinct wet and dry seasons, which the Huichols exploit to maximize agricultural output. They continue to practice slash-and-burn agriculture with whatever tools are available to them; farming is spiritually important in addition to its obvious nutritional value.[8] Corn, beans, squash, and deer made up the traditional diet of the Huichols in the Sierra until the deer population dwindled at some point (though the animal has since been reintroduced). Deer and corn have dictated the Huichol spiritual calendar, with specific tasks permissible only after the hunt or the harvest.[9]

The Huichols refer to themselves as Wixáritari (sing. Wixárika, also used for their language), as opposed to Huichol.[10] Though I use the term Huichol to refer to the peoples and their language, an important point to consider is that the label is problematic, both because it implies a political unity that is nonexistent and also because outsiders imposed the term upon them. Until very recently, most indigenous groups in Mexico have viewed themselves in a very local sense; while there may be cultural and linguistic affinity and geographic proximity, there is generally no overarching identity. For the sake of semantic ease, Huichol will be used.

Why study the Huichols? Their narrative illuminates some clear behavioral patterns similar to some indigenous histories in Mexico, while contradicting others. According to all available evidence, the Huichols rarely fell under the control of any imperial groups (indigenous or European) and only succumbed to Spanish subjugation in the 1720s. In previous centuries the Huichols claimed that their ancestors were not unduly influenced or burdened by the Toltecs, nor were they tributaries of the Aztecs or the P'urhépechas (Tarascans). The Huichols, it seems, were a culturally affiliated group bound by common language, culture, and geography, but bound politically to no one but their gods.[11]

In light of this, what did conquest and colonization mean to the Huichols? How did they meet these challenges and in what ways did such trials transform their culture? If the Huichols simply adapted their culture to fit more neatly in a changing and globalizing Mexico, how did they do so and why? Was it necessity or desire? Are those mutually exclusive? Did prolonged contact create a wholly new Huichol identity, or did communities turn inward on themselves? Again, could they have done both, depending on individual circumstances? And how did the Huichols learn to combat the

Spanish imperial and Mexican national governments to protect their lands and cultural hallmarks and ensure the survival of future generations? Finally, why did the Huichols appropriate certain elements, such as the legal system, while resisting others? These questions form the heart of this book.

I argue that despite the changing political, social, and cultural contexts around them, most Huichols successfully defended their culture and communities through a series of reactions and adaptations to external threats. They navigated these stressors not through a complete rejection of alien peoples and ideas, but instead through an ongoing process of selective appropriation and contestation. It is rare that native communities had the opportunity to meet such challenges head on, and I suggest that their late conquest and geographical location helped. By exploring these questions more fully, a picture of a small slice of Mexico emerges that has implications for how indigenous groups throughout the world can and do thrive despite ever-increasing state and international presences in their lives. The Huichols demonstrate the potential for the existence of distinct indigenous identities in spite of homogenizing state and global programs.

In the Huichols we see a microcosm of important themes in Mexican history since its inception as a Spanish colony. The Huichols have survived, persisted, and culturally evolved in response to an increasingly powerful state over the course of the Mexican national period, something that all indigenous groups experienced to one degree or another. Their history demonstrates currents common in the history of the place we now know as Mexico. Theirs is a part of Mexico's history that remains hidden if one focuses solely on the heart of Mexico or on the big events (independence, revolution, assimilation) that historians have emphasized in past decades; the Huichols exemplify the spirit of independence and defiance that existed on Mexico's peripheries. They refused to be subjugated, and it took more than a century for the Spanish to conquer them. Catholic priests never converted them in a uniform way, though that is not to suggest that Huichols rejected wholesale all elements of Catholicism.

The reforms of the nineteenth century only hardened their resolve, and Liberal and Porfirian policies did not dislodge them from their lands. At each turn outsiders' decisions and actions affected the Huichols, yet they met these challenges in ways that served to benefit them in the best ways possible, often by selectively incorporating elements of Mexican sociocultural norms. Thus, this project examines a micro- and macro-historical treatment of Mexico over the *longue durée*. It sheds light on the forgotten (or ignored) history of a small, heretofore obscure native group, while simultaneously contextualizing problems that affected the lives of *all* poor Mexicans in this era.

For much of its modern history, Mexico has been and remains geographically and politically separated between center and periphery, city versus rural, mestizo and indigenous.[12] Most of the recent literature addressing Mexican history necessarily juxtaposes this periphery-center dichotomy in a way that pits native populations (periphery) against mestizos (or Spaniards/Mexicans [center]). This study fits in this model, examining the Huichols vis-à-vis Spaniards and later Mexicans. It is also a distinctly rural study, providing a glimpse of how indigenous towns in outlying areas have been influenced by the fixtures and processes of government in the metropole.[13] During the colonial period Spanish conquistadors and colonists in search of gold traveled near the Huichol homelands but found only silver in the areas surrounding Zacatecas. This brought outsiders into reasonably close contact with the Huichols, but not on the day-to-day basis that was more common either further south or later in the nineteenth and twentieth centuries. Thus during the period of Spanish dominion, Huichol land was not a commodity, and only small haciendas emerged in the colonial period that would challenge Huichol territorial claims.[14] In this particular part of the Sierra Madre Occidental, land—though imperfect for agricultural pursuits—was reasonably abundant for grazing.[15] Thus silver mining did not affect the Huichols, but the agricultural activities that supported the silver economy in Spain's colonies (i.e., farming, cattle ranching) eventually did.

The relationship between land and value is critical if we are to understand why the Huichols maintained such a steadfast attitude throughout the centuries. The Huichols have a different value system for the land on which they live and work. As underscored in the prologue, the deer gods instructed the Huichols' ancestors to settle in the western Sierra. Despite this, throughout their history, the Huichols have fought with Spaniards and Mexicans over land to maintain their spiritual ties to the land, while others sought to obtain dominion for other reasons.

As Mexico transformed from colony into nation, it attempted to legitimize its territory by mapping the land. This also helped solidify the idea of Mexico as a nation.[16] But the act of mapping territory imposed national (and sometimes international) boundaries on indigenous communities that meant very little to them. Over the course of the mid-nineteenth century, surveying and delimiting Mexican territory became linked to government modernization and centralization projects. Simultaneously, indigenous peoples, increasingly viewed by political elites as barriers to progress, found themselves having their lands surveyed out from under them.[17] For the Huichols, the potential loss of land threatened not only their physical survival but also their ability to maintain their religion and existence as an ethnic group.

The construction of identity and ethnicity has been an important topic of study for scholars of indigenous Mexico. What constitutes an indigenous group in Mexico (and elsewhere, for that matter)? How has a group's identity, or sense of itself, shifted over time? What forces help shape indigenous identity? How does the definition of a group's identity change in response to modernization? Are indigenous peoples actively choosing to be indigenous in the modern era and, if so, why?[18] Scholars have tackled these questions in their studies of a few important indigenous groups that have helped define this study of the Huichols.

Of particular relevance to the Huichol story, in terms of defining "indigenous" in modern Mexico, is the history of the Lacandon Mayas. Deep in the Lacandon jungle of the state of Chiapas, the Lacandons live, similar to the

Huichols, almost entirely separated from their nonindigenous neighbors. This is a process of choice. The landscape of the Chiapan highlands allows for such separation, and as the Huichols have used the Sierra Madre Occidental as a region of refuge, the Lacandon Mayas moved deeper into the jungle to avoid contact with mestizos and other outsiders.[19] For decades the common assumption was that the Lacandons were merely fossils of their Classic-era ancestors, existing in a modern, though "degraded" form.[20] However, through ethnographic and ethnohistorical analyses, the Lacandons' links to the Classic Mayas have emerged, though the modern peoples exist as any other indigenous groups do: as a result of transformative processes that began with the upheavals of the colonial period and continued through the nineteenth and twentieth centuries.[21] In this way, the Lacandons are comparable to the Huichols; neither group presents as timeless fossils, but as living communities who adapt "and define themselves in terms of their cultural struggles against foreign cultural forces."[22] Such contact with outside forces has helped shape modern indigenous peoples in many cases, not destroy them.[23]

The creation of identity in spite of external upheavals is key to understanding how indigenous peoples worked within the confines of a hegemonic empire or state. Frequently, identifying labels like "Maya" or "Aztec" are imposed on groups by outsiders who have little understanding of the identity politics of the native people themselves. This is particularly true in the case of the Mayas and the Huichols, and it presents challenges to ethnohistorians. Yucatec speakers generally rejected overarching ethnic identities and did not refer to themselves as Maya, the way scholars and laypeople do today.[24] In fact, the word Maya rarely appeared in colonial texts, and if it did, it generally referred to language, not people.[25] Similarly, as I pointed out earlier, the Huichols have rarely viewed themselves as politically unified, and while some use the term "Huichol," they prefer their own word: Wixárika.

The maintenance of ethnic identities within the confines of a hegemonic empire and state is another theme that some historians have emphasized in their examinations of Mexican indigenous groups. The acceptance or rejection of outside influences has helped to shape some native identities, as in the case of the Yaquis in northwestern Mexico. Fiercely opposed to conquest by the Spanish, the Yaquis accepted Jesuit missionaries in the early seventeenth century. The Jesuits brought with them both religion and their policy of "reducing" semisedentary and nonsedentary peoples into missions that dotted the frontier of New Spain.[26]

The temporal and thematic scope of this book is vast, with each chapter addressing some form of Huichol reaction to an external threat or potential hazard. Throughout this study of the Huichols, three underlying themes emerge: defense of lands, defense of religion, and understanding Huichol ethnicity. I believe we can envision these topics like a triad in which none is more important than the other. However, in the case of the Huichols, the defense of land is most evident in the context of existing literature. Ultimately this historical study of the Huichols is dependent upon sources. As a result, elements of the Huichols (culture, for example) fade in and out of this story because evidence is either thin, nonexistent, or unavailable owing to the ravages of time. What emerges is a history that is at times political, cultural, and/or social, as evidence dictates.

In the first chapter, the menace facing the Huichols is the arrival of the Spanish in western Mexico. While Spaniards were uncommon in the Sierra Madre Occidental until the very late sixteenth century, their presence in other parts of the area created conditions to which the Huichols had to react. As their homelands were a region of refuge, it appears as though refugees from the midcentury wars of conquest moved into the mountains, and conquistadors ranged through the area searching for gold and silver in points north. More Spaniards, especially Franciscan friars, traversed the Sierra throughout the seventeenth and into the eighteenth centuries, forcing the Huichols to adapt to newcomers and their language, religious practices, and social customs.

The transition from colony to nation required the Huichols to adjust yet again, as legal definitions of landholding practices changed. Thus the focus of chapter 2 is Huichol reactions to the nascent, albeit chaotic, nation of Mexico. Huichol participation in the Mexican War for independence was neither uniform nor broad-based, demonstrating an interesting, though not unique, element of Huichol culture: their lack of overarching political unity.

This absence of "Huichol-ness" becomes more clearly defined in chapter 3, during a period in which the Huichols experienced intense scrutiny by different elements of the Catholic Church. Franciscan missionaries, who had mostly fled the region during the violence of the Independence era, returned during the 1820s to evangelize the reticent Huichols. Their reaction to the threat Catholicism posed to their belief system comprises this section of the book. Some Huichols embraced Catholicism more readily than did others; on the whole, however, Franciscan friars were frustrated in their efforts to convert the Huichols away from their ancient ways. By the 1850s the Franciscans abandoned their efforts once more, as political tides turned against them in a series of anticlerical measures that also had important implications for indigenous groups.

The rise of Liberalism in Mexico dramatically transformed relationships between native peoples and the state, particularly regarding land rights. Land increasingly became commodified, and many groups that had been mostly left alone now experienced the presence of the state in new ways. The Huichols reacted in a number of ways to this legal and literal encroachment, including minor participation in the Lozada Rebellion (1850s–70s). Mostly, however, the Huichols used legal measures between the 1850s and the 1890s to protect their lands, which simultaneously safeguarded their cultural traditions. Constantly fomenting armed rebellion, I argue, would only have brought disaster (as it did to the Yaquis in the last quarter of the nineteenth century). Their actions and reactions during this period are the focus of chapter 4.

As Mexico stabilized after many decades of political conflict, foreigners increasingly found Mexico to be an enticing place of scholarly pursuit. For budding anthropologists and ethnographers, the race to document Mexico's indigenous populations before they "disappeared" began in earnest in the 1890s. Several prominent ethnographers traveled through the Huichol Sierra, documenting their culture. Normally reserved and sometimes hostile to outsiders, how did the Huichols cope with these foreign strangers, with their questions, mestizo porters, and cameras? Chapter 5 examines the relationships between the Huichols and three European ethnographers, who spent more than a decade combined studying the Huichols between 1895 and 1912.

The outbreak of violence brought an end to scientific research in western Mexico. Huichol villages once again demonstrated that all politics—including identity politics—are local. During the revolution Huichol villages chose sides or remained neutral based on what suited their needs. Unfortunately, evidence depicting their participation is scant for both the Mexican Revolution and the Cristero Rebellion. Nevertheless, there is enough anecdotal data to illustrate how the Huichols faced the threats of the horrific violence of the revolution. Chapter 6 will analyze the Huichols during this dreadful period in Mexican history.

But what of the modern people? As mentioned at the beginning of this introduction, many Huichols have been forced out of their homelands in the Sierra Madre Occidental and into surrounding cities, where they maintain their language, connections to the Sierra, and material culture. While my intent is not to explain the out-migration that occurred in the second half of the twentieth century, I would like to illuminate briefly what the Huichols are like today. Are they still participating in the annual peyote pilgrimages? How has the drug trade affected them? Is modernity a tantalizing force attracting young Huichols away from their culture? In a short conclusion, I will bring this story up to the present.

IN THE LANDS OF FIRE AND SUN

1

From Native Neighbors to Spanish Conquerors

The Huichols and other indigenous peoples who lived beyond the valley of Mexico, in the mountains and deserts to the north of Tenochtitlán, remained just out of the Aztecs' reach. Yet the Aztecs knew about the various peoples, whom they termed "Chichimeca" (*Chichimecatl,* Nahuatl, sing.), a catchall phrase; through trade relationships that spread throughout Mesoamerica, the Chichimecs knew of the Aztecs. Shortly after the conquest of Mexico, Nahua scribes working with Bernardino de Sahagún explained some curious religious practices of the mountain and desert peoples. From their descriptions, Sahagún wrote:

> The real Chichimeca, that is to say, those who lived on the grassy plains, in the forests—these were the ones who lived far away; they lived in the forests, the grassy plains, the deserts, among the crags . . . where night came upon them, there they sought a cave, a craggy place, there they slept . . . they knew the qualities, the essence, of herbs, of roots, the so-called peyote was their discovery. These, when they ate peyote, esteemed it above wine or mushrooms. They assembled together somewhere in the desert; they came together; there they danced, they sang all night, all day. . . . And on the morrow, once more they assembled together. They wept, they wept exceedingly . . . thus they cleansed their eyes.[1]

While not using the word "Huichol," this passage depicted peyote ceremonies with startling accuracy. Indeed, this section of the Florentine Codex could describe a twenty-first century peyote ceremony, so little having changed in the past centuries.

The Nahuas' description illustrates a few key points that emerge in this chapter. First, Mesoamerica was truly an interconnected space, within which many groups interacted, either directly or indirectly. Second, the Huichols were not isolated in their mountain redoubts, despite the inability of larger, stronger groups to conquer them. (The Aztecs never could and the Spanish, as we shall see, had a difficult time.) Finally, the peyote ceremony made enough of a cultural impact upon someone in the central Mexican world that the practice was recorded for posterity. Even deep in the Sierra Madre Occidental, seemingly removed from the larger problems of competing empires before and after the conquest, the Huichols both participated in and adapted to their changing environment.

For centuries the native peoples of the Sierra Madre Occidental, its foothills, and the plains to the south lived with the presence of powerful empires that frequently surrounded them. By the post-Classic period (900 BCE–1519 CE), the Huichols' ancestors were but one of many indigenous groups that the Aztecs would call Chichimecas. The Huichols likely knew about the Aztecs, their warlike neighbors to the south; indeed, it is almost certain that the Aztecs knew at least something of the Huichols and their curious religious practices.

During the last century and a half before the Spanish arrival, a loose confederation of indigenous communities known as the Chimalhuacán found themselves hemmed by two powerful groups on two fronts: the P'urhépecha to the east-southeast (located in modern-day Michoacán) and the Aztecs to the south. This group of affiliated indigenous villages had existed since the late Classic period and covered a vast geographical area, including parts of modern-day Nayarit, Jalisco, Colima, Aguascalientes, and Zacatecas.[2] The Aztecs did not affect the Huichols to any large degree, in part because the P'urhépecha empire was located between the Sierra and the Valley of Mexico. Also, groups like the Huichols, who lived in the mountains, had learned to make their homeland a bulwark and safe haven against enemy invaders. This region of refuge protected mountainous tribes from the imperial designs of their southern neighbors; there is no evidence that any groups in the Chimalhuacán ever became tributaries of the Aztecs or the P'urhépechas.[3] Huichol oral history confirms their independence throughout the last centuries before contact with the Spanish.

The 1521 conquest of the Aztecs sent reverberations into Greater Mesoamerica and indeed eventually throughout the world. From the new imperial capital of Mexico City, multiple conquistadors sought their own slice of fame and glory and rampaged north and south, looking for El Dorado (the famed City of Gold) and large population centers to conquer and exploit. Except for the P'urhépecha empire, there were few areas of large, settled populations north of the Valley of Mexico. Francisco Cortés, a kinsman of Hernán, launched an exploratory mission up the western part of Mesoamerica into what are now the states of Colima and Nayarit. This expedition reached as far as the Río Grande de Santiago, near the towns of Xalisco and Tepic, on the western edge of the Mesa del Nayar.[4] The Cortés expedition contacted a number of peoples, including Tecuales (possibly a group of Huichols), Naguatatos, and Otomís. Most feared the Spanish, who "had killed many people"; the destroyed houses and farms demonstrated a violent, destructive campaign led by Cortés.[5] This sliver of evidence is the first instance of Huichol contact with Spaniards in this early period. The violence of it provides a possible explanation for Huichol attitudes toward Spaniards thereafter.

Nine years after the victory over the Aztecs, Nuño Beltrán de Guzmán began his own brutal quest for a piece of New Spain. At the end of 1529 Guzmán, originally from Guadalajara, Spain, began his march north with an assortment of Spanish and Tlaxcalan allies and some indigenous slaves.[6] In early 1530 Guzmán headed northwest from the P'urhépecha capital of Tzintzuntzan hoping to defeat the warlike Caxcans and secure a route to the northwestern coast.[7] Guzmán and his army first fell upon the town of

Tonalá, defeating the native peoples there and launching a bloody conquest of the west from this indigenous village.[8]

As Guzmán moved from Tonalá northwest and into the Sierra, he marched on a small Indian village named Teúl, in search of the powerful Caxcans. The Caxcans, apparently ruled by a female warrior "queen," could count among their occasional allies most of the mountainous tribes of the Sierra; they were a formidable opponent that the Spaniards needed to subjugate.[9] Living near the modern-day Zacatecas towns of Teúl de González Ortega, Nochistlán, and Juchipila, the Caxcans were the lords of the Sierra at the time of the conquest. Guzmán likely miscalculated Caxcan power, because before invading the their lands, he had sent part of his army across the Sierra toward the Pacific coast.

The conquest of the Caxcans and their allies ended in 1530. But what did this mean for power dynamics in the Sierra? Though the Caxcans certainly seemed vanquished, in reality the powerful indigenous group had gone underground while other peoples in the area flooded into mountainous areas, seeking refuge. This had been a common practice of avoidance in times past; it likely created tensions with indigenous groups living in the area, but there are no records to verify this. However, with the area reasonably secure, the Spaniards founded the city of Guadalajara, paying homage to Guzmán's Iberian roots. The security did not last long, as Caxcans and their allies regrouped and rebelled the following year, expelling Spanish settlers and forcing the new town's initial removal in 1531.[10] Guzmán headed northwest toward the coast, leaving behind a legacy of brutality: his practices terrorized "the natives with often unprovoked killing, torture and enslavement . . . the army left a path of corpses and destroyed houses and crops, impressing surviving males into service and leaving women and children to starve."[11] In his place, conquistadors who had served under him either remained in the area or, as in the case of Pedro Almíndez Chirinos (or Cherinos), left to survey parts of the countryside before rejoining Guzmán. Chirinos "passed through and nominally subjugated the Sierras of Tepeque, Xora, Cora, Huianamota [*sic*], and perhaps Huazamota, on the periphery of Huichol-Tecual territory."[12] The Caxcans and other peoples in the area fled the violence by taking refuge among friendly groups in the mountains. From there, they took stock of their losses and waited, seething at their treatment at the hands of Guzmán.

For more than a decade indigenous peoples in the Sierra Madre region of Nueva Galicia plotted their revenge. The Caxcans, Tecuexes, Zacatecos, and Guachichiles, among others, launched raids on Spanish settlements that strayed too close to the mountains.[13] These native peoples did not see themselves as subject to Spanish authority and certainly did not believe they had been "conquered" in any meaningful sense. However, by 1540 the pressure upon Nueva Galicia's indigenous groups gave way to a rebellion known as the Mixtón War. It began with the murder of *encomendero* Juan de Arce by Guaynamotecos contracted to work for him.[14] (An *encomendero* is a Spaniard who is given a grant of indigenous labor.) The Guaynamotecos likely did not plan to launch a large-scale rebellion; rather, surviving Caxcans probably contacted allies throughout the Sierra and coordinated the attacks.[15] Land pressures prompted many to join the Caxcans and Guaynamotecos.[16] Centered around the highlands of the Sierra Madre Occidental, thousands of indigenous peoples took up arms against the Spanish. Led by the Caxcans and Zacatecos, other groups joined in the rebellion from Teúl and Nochistlán (in present-day Zacatecas) to Tepic (in present-day Nayarit). Records are unclear as to the participation of the Huichols, but the scope and location of the rebellion suggest they might have taken part, or at least offered some support to those who fought to restore lost lands.[17]

The Mixtón War ended in late 1541 in most areas, while lasting much longer in some farther-flung regions. Defensive forces moved north from Mexico City toward Guadalajara to end the revolts, which continued to rage among the "Chichimecas, the hunting tribes of the Sierras."[18] In the end, thousands of indigenous peoples died as a result of the violence and the virulent epidemics that often followed Spaniards' presence. The Spanish sold scores of surviving women and children into slavery on plantations and haciendas far from home, and untold others fled or were forced out of their homelands.[19] Farther west in the Sierra Madre Occidental, groups like the Huichols remained untamed by the Spanish, though there is evidence that some Huichols joined the Spanish as *flechero* soldiers, helping to pacify more distant regions of the Sierra.[20] This area served as a refugee zone for those fleeing the repressive measures that the Spanish used to control their indigenous subjects.[21] Thus, though the Huichols may not have physically participated in the uprisings, they most certainly dealt with the survivors and understood that the Spanish activities had serious consequences for their neighbors.

Once the violence subsided in Nueva Galicia, the Spanish began the process of colonization. This was easier in some places than in others, as tensions and conflict existed for decades after the end of the Mixtón War. Yet political leaders planned to pacify even the most hostile areas. Expeditions into the mountains around Zacatecas and further west brought Spaniards into conflict with local indigenous groups, such as in 1550 when Guachichiles fought intruding Spaniards.[22] Spanish administrators assured a steady supply of labor for colonists in the region by requiring indigenous peoples without regular employment to present themselves for work (meaning that nearly every Indian could be forced to labor for Spaniards). For some native populations that had been dominated by the Aztecs, labor tribute would not have been an alien concept. All subjugated towns and villages had paid tribute to the Aztec emperor in Tenochtitlán, through either goods or services (or both). However, the lack of Aztec hegemony or influence in the Sierra Madre Occidental during the precontact era assured that groups like the Caxcans and Zacatecos would resist any sort of coerced labor.

Not only did Nueva Galicia become a tinderbox of Indian resentment as a result of *encomienda* (grant of indigenous labor to a Spaniard) obligations, but Lebrón de Quiñones's attempts to implement the 1542 New Laws incensed Spanish colonists, who saw nothing to gain by paying indigenous peoples for their toil. In 1549 Quiñones proposed that:

> Indians illegally enslaved were to be freed, and encomiendas held without proper title to be nullified . . . penalties placed upon encomenderos who demanded illegal service; or overtaxed their Indians . . . . Idle Indians were to be set to work—the clergy using their powers of persuasion—and proper wages paid: 12 *maravedíses* a day to labourers, 24 to native officials. The mountain Indians were to be induced to settle in villages and till the land "like reasonable people;" Spanish stock farms were to be kept away from the cultivated land of the Indians.[23]

The Mixtón War remained firmly implanted in the minds of all Spaniards living in the region, and officials such as Quiñones knew that antagonizing native groups, many of whom had little to lose, would only spur more hostilities.

Throughout the seventeenth century, but especially in the 1620s and again in the 1640s, the Crown made more concerted attempts to reach out to native peoples living in the Sierra. In the wake of the 1617 Tepehuan rebellion, two Franciscan priests, Francisco Barrios and Pedro Gutiérrez, tried to promote peace by Christianizing the "Huisare" Indians of Huainamota (Guaynamota). Barrios and Gutiérrez were partly successful in convincing some Huisares, who lived in the rugged Sierra de Nayarit, to receive baptism and learn catechism. Though the Huisares burned down a newly built chapel, native peoples accepted a limited degree of religious instruction, at least around Guaynamota.[24]

As Spaniards made their way deeper into the Sierra Madre Occidental, they encountered various ethnic groups. Added to the mix of serrano tribes were native peoples from central Mexico, such as the Tlaxcalans, who served as bulwarks against frontier cultures like the Huichols and Tecuexes, who farmed scattered *rancherías* (small farms) and occasionally raided other indigenous peoples and Spanish settlers. The Huichols lived around Huejuquilla el Alto by 1649 "and had towns nearby in Nostic, Colotlán, Mamatla and Ostoc." Further west, however, the Chapalagana River valley, a treacherous part of the mountains, had not been surveyed or explored by Spaniards in any meaningful way.[25] Explorers began documenting the different languages in the area, providing clues to both the impacts of conquest and colonialism and also definitively locating the Huichols and their neighbors in time and space: languages spoken in the area were "Tepehuan at Chimaltitán, Tepecano in the surrounding villages, Huichol and Caxcan nearby."[26] Where few Spaniards had settled, peace came relatively easily. But in other places, where miners moved in and ranchers grazed cattle, violence erupted occasionally.[27] For a time, while many Huichols had been in contact with Spaniards, particularly in the aforementioned towns, still others remained just outside of the sustainable reach of the Crown.

Over the course of the seventeenth century missionaries filtered into the high Sierra. The Franciscans were the most numerous of the regular orders working in western Mexico, though Jesuits did practice here and there. The earliest of the convents established in Huichol territory was at San Juan Baptista de Mezquitic in 1616, with the function of administering twelve towns in the area. The friars had their work cut out for them, as according to the writings of at least one individual, the indigenous peoples there were "barbaric."[28] Like elsewhere in the Americas, missionaries faced initial difficulties as they struggled to understand the myriad indigenous languages, and natives certainly did not understand Spanish at first. In August 1653 Juan Ruíz de Colmenero, the bishop of Guadalajara, inquired as to the best language with which to instruct the indigenous peoples. Some native peoples could be taught catechism in Spanish, while others, like the Huichols and Coras, needed to receive their lessons in "Mexicano," a reference to Nahuatl. Though some Huichols may have spoken Spanish, as Colmenero noted, most did not, and those who could read Spanish may not have read it well.[29]

A few years later a traveling Franciscan friar named Padre Antonio Arias de Saavedra described the major indigenous areas according to the groups who lived there; he divided the Sierra into four provinces, one of which belonged to the "Xamuca" or "Hueitzolme." Xamuca and Hueitzolme were two other words for Huichols; Arias named the other groups living in the area as "Chora," "Tzaname," "Tepeguanes, "Caponetas," "Xamucas," and "Totorames."[30] It is no surprise that missionaries had trouble understanding various groups in the area, considering the nuances in languages between each different peoples and even towns.

Thus by the 1650s, the Huichols had been in somewhat regular contact with Spanish missionaries, who corrupted their name in church reports. For this reason, it is difficult to get a sense of exactly when it is that the word "Huichol" appeared in the documentary record. Hueitzolme is the closest distortion, and a priest recorded that in 1653; but earlier, in 1607, Fray Pedro Gutiérrez worked among the Vitzurita nation.[31] Vitzurita is another name for the Huichol, and is, in fact, a corruption of the word that the Huichols call themselves: Wixárika. Wixárika (or Vitzurita) does not translate directly into Spanish, and at some point the term was substituted for Huichol. Even into the eighteenth century, Franciscans and Jesuits used Huichol (and its myriad spellings) and Vitzurita interchangeably when attempting to minister to their reticent flock.

Regardless of the variations of language and labels, missionary efforts were well underway throughout the Sierra Madre Occidental by the middle of the seventeenth century. To facilitate conversion efforts, friars gathered willing indigenous peoples into villages in a process known as reduction, and the *comunidad* (community) system emerged among the Huichols, which helped to integrate them into the colonial system.[32] At the same time, this living arrangement allowed for careful observation of the native peoples. In the Huichol area the Franciscans used the existing socioreligious organization, based around a temple and its corresponding lands, to create the comunidades.[33] In areas immediately surrounding the *municipio* (municipality) of Colotlán, reduction occurred rather quickly (see map 2); the town, which had been established in 1591, served "to administer activities necessary for pacifying and colonizing the Tepecanos, Huichols and eventually, Coras."[34] The friars had rather lofty goals, because though the Huichols were relatively few in number (compared to groups in the Valley of Mexico), they remained steadfast in their religious beliefs.

The reports kept by Catholic missionaries help us understand Huichol religious beliefs, though from a particular perspective that viewed their practices as idolatry.[35] The Huichols proved to be difficult charges, in part because of geography, but also because of the centrality of peyote to their religious beliefs. The first concrete description of Huichol religiosity came in the report compiled in 1621 by Franciscan friar and traveler Domingo Lázaro de Arregui. He reported what he had learned about the consumption of peyote, which increasingly had become a vexing problem for ecclesiastical officials. The Huichols that Arregui spoke to explained that peyote not only helped alleviate physical stress in their high altitude homelands, but that it also helped them divine the future.[36] He reported that:

> Peyote is the plant that gives energy and strength for long periods to the one who takes it. Furthermore, Indians say that they are able to predict (the future) with it, and it is true that it gives one some kind of numbness and warmth that diminishes tiredness and other efforts. And when taking a lot, they lose all senses in such a way that they say they can see things, and then they say that they can predict or know what is hidden and what they want to discover.[37]

Arregui noted that if the Huichols took too much, they lost their senses and saw visions that enabled them to predict the future. This presented a problem for the church. Others throughout New Spain used peyote for similar purposes, both mundane and supernatural, so much so that in 1620 (just one year prior to Arregui's report) Spanish officials issued an Edict of Faith against peyote in an attempt to curtail the use of all hallucinogens that allowed for such occult visions.[38]

Peyote use was not the only ritual practice that concerned Catholic officials in their earliest work with Huichols. During his travels in the Sierra in the seventeenth century, Fray Miguel Díaz discovered the peoples living around Huejuquilla to be worshipping a cadaver in what he described as a circular, thatched-roof temple used for Huichol religious ceremonies, most likely a *caligüey*.[39] Padre Arias de Saavedra had reported similar ancestor worship among the mountain peoples of the Sierra del Nayar.[40] Mummy and ancestor worship was part of Huichol spirituality, as important ancestors were often consulted before participation in other rituals. The reports compiled by Arias de Saavedra and Díaz depicted the temples in great detail; Díaz called it the domicile of the devil.[41] The practice of worshipping important ancestors presented a significant problem for Catholic authorities. However, the isolated nature of indigenous communities in the mountains required more than solitary Franciscan travelers; the Huichols had proven to be resistant to change, reticent toward outsiders, and only begrudgingly willing to accept influence from Spaniards.

As the seventeenth century drew to a close, many indigenous groups in the west had become more familiar with Spanish authority and either chose to live with it or fled. The Nayarita zone increasingly served as a getaway location for indigenous peoples who, for whatever reason, preferred not to live too close to Spanish colonists.[42] An example of both approaches to colonialism is evident in Atonalisco, deep in the mountains of modern-day Nayarit. In 1695 indigenous peoples who had previously lived in the area appealed to the Spanish authorities for the return of their rightful lands, since the inhabitants had fled to live with the "pagans" in the mountains. This illustrates three things in particular: first, that the native peoples who went to see don Alonso Ceballo Villa Gutiérrez had submitted to, or at least acknowledged, Spanish authorities and knew the appropriate channels to redress grievances; second, that the indigenous peoples had been pushed off lands (or left willingly) surrounding San Juan Baptista (Bautista) Tonalisco and felt a rightful claim to the land; and finally, that the individuals filing the claim were sufficiently Christianized—or at least claimed to be—so that they could distinguish themselves from non-Christian indigenous peoples, whom they called pagans.[43] Elements of Spanish society, in the form of laws and Catholicism, had crept into the Sierra Madre Occidental, but had yet to thoroughly penetrate it.

Violence ushered in the eighteenth century in the Sierra Madre Occidental when a multiethnic rebellion swept through a number of indigenous towns in the district of Colotlán. Among the rebellious towns were San Andrés, Santa Catarina, and San Sebastián, the three principal Huichol towns (see maps 3 and 4). The Huichols and their allies were aggrieved because increasing numbers of Spaniards moved onto and subsequently expropriated Indian lands; in response to the encroachment, the Huichols and some neighboring Tepecanos stole Spanish cattle. They presented their complaints to Capitán Mateo de Silva, but he apparently did little and, in fact, appeared to be the cause of some of their aggravation.[44] Indigenous peoples from Nostic (a smaller, satellite Huichol village) killed de Silva in a field not far from Colotlán, apparently within view of other Spaniards.[45] Though a short-lived revolt, lasting from July to October 1702, such activities deeply disturbed officials in Guadalajara and Mexico City in spite of indigenous claims that they were loyal to the king.[46] What this uprising illustrates is a disdain on the part of the Huichols and Tepehuans for their increasingly numerous Spanish neighbors, not necessarily because they were Spanish, but because they encroached on their territory and created competition for resources.

This brief rebellion demonstrated that the Huichols could present a vigorous resistance to the encroachment of their neighbors and that they possessed keen awareness of Spanish threats to their homelands. The hostilities ended once the Huichols and Tepehuans promised not to rebel again, bringing flowers, fruits, and sweets to the Conde de Santa Rosa; nevertheless, Spaniards could not help but acknowledge the simmering anger of the mountain peoples.[47] The Sierra continued to be a dangerous tinderbox, and authorities in Colotlán, Guadalajara, and farther afield realized that pacification had to occur with fervor and haste.

To Spanish clergymen idolatry—as they saw it—ran as rampant throughout the Sierra as arroyos and canyons that cut the rugged landscape, making subjugation much harder to achieve. Huichol cosmology emphasized the relationship between humans, land, and the plants and animals living there; as a result, Catholicism as a whole was not appealing. Jesuit missionaries who had begun work among the Coras, for instance, realized that to make any headway with them, they needed to erase their sacred, spiritual geography.[48] An equivalent effort would be necessary to achieve any success with the Huichols. However, it appears that conversion to Christianity did not present any advantage for the Huichols, either spiritually or materially, and so most declined to participate in missionary activities.

In a joint effort conducted by friars and military forces and ordered by King Philip V, Fray Antonio Margil de Jesús, a Franciscan missionary with considerable evangelization experience, trekked into the Sierra to try and pacify the Huichols and Coras.[49] Letters written by Margil illustrate his plans for pacifying the reticent "Nayarits"; the conquest would be peaceful, because the indigenous peoples in the area were "not numerous, nor unmanageable, but unarmed and not hostile."[50] Margil hoped to pardon crimes committed by the indigenous groups in the region as well as "to offer pardon to those who may have sought refuge among them, be they men or women of whatever rank . . . if they are slaves, they should be given their freedom . . . because they have lived as free men for so long a time."[51] That the Sierra del Nayar was a region of refuge was not lost on Fray Margil, but he underestimated the hostility that the Nayarits harbored toward Spaniards and Christianity.

On May 9, 1711, Fray Margil and his colleague, Father Luis Delgado Cervantes, approached the Sierra del Nayar. Margil sent a letter ahead with messengers, assuring the regional leaders that no Spaniards would harm them.[52] Fray Margil informed Hueitacat, the Nayarit leader, that he and Delgado Cervantes would come alone, without soldiers, to meet with them; if they chose to become Christians, they would be "the masters and lords of their lands; and that Gueytacat [*sic*] shall be their lord in perpetuity."[53] The indigenous leader refused to read the letter and would not receive Margil or his traveling companions.[54]

Fray Margil moved on undeterred, setting out for the frontier region, where he was met by "hostile," unnamed indigenous peoples. They too rejected Margil's overtures and attempts to meet with them. Margil admitted defeat and prepared to return to his work at the Colegio of Zacatecas.

Before doing so, he wrote to his superiors in Guadalajara, explaining the situation in the Sierra.[55] He told the president of the *audiencia* (high court), Toribio Rodríguez de Solís, that he had sent two interpreters, don Juan Marcos and don Pablo Felipe, with a copy of the royal decree to speak with the Nayarit leaders.[56] Don Pablo Felipe reported that the chiefs refused to comply after consulting "three times" with "their king . . . the first Nayarit, a skeleton, whom they venerate as their first idol, and through whom the devil speaks to them as he does through their priests." The chiefs declared, "'If they want to kill us, let them know that they can kill us, but we will not become Christians.'"[57]

Margil continued describing the conditions they experienced as the group trekked back to Guazamota. Once more they encountered Nayarits who warned them away from the area with various threats. Some indigenous people from the town of "Nostique" and a "scribe of Guajumiqui (Huajimic)" provided some assistance. However, the group received a warning that if they proceeded, "some will drink peyote and get drunk and fall upon us and kill us all, and the sacrifice of our life will not cause them to become Christians."[58] While Margil never actually specified any of the indigenous groups he met with, instead referring to all of them as "Nayarits," it is highly likely that, based on geographic and cultural descriptions, the most reticent among these groups—those who drank peyote and would kill the priests—were Huichols.

Though Fray Margil's work in the Sierra appeared fruitless, some Nayarits had been either moved by his message or converted previously and simply feared to come forward due to the hostility of their neighbors. One man in particular, the scribe of Guazamota, explained the behavior of the others, and said: "'Tell the fathers to hold us excused and not to come and see us, because it is inconvenient for us to leave when they arrive at our ranches, nor should we talk to them, for if the elders and chiefs from the interior find this out, they will kill us for being traitors; we wish them well but cannot do anything because of these reasons.'"[59] Guilt by association threatened any indigenous people who even talked to the Franciscans. The failure of Margil's efforts virtually assured that all indigenous groups in the area would feel the wrath of the Spanish Crown. By the early 1720s Spain prepared military expeditions to subjugate the last of the resistant mountain peoples. Based on the reports offered by Margil, particularly ones that related evidence of idolatry, the Spanish also expected to destroy indigenous idols and change the sacred landscape.[60]

In 1721, led by don Juan de la Torre and assisted by some "faithful Indians" from around Zacatecas, the Spanish began their violent crusade aimed at the subjugation of the idolatrous Coras.[61] Some Huichol flecheros served in the conquest of their neighbors; nevertheless, the conquest of the Huichols followed in 1722–23.[62] By 1725, after quashing some small skirmishes that resulted in several church conflagrations, the Sierra de Nayarit had been mostly pacified; indigenous peoples in Guazamota, a Cora town, had been assured that the church would protect them and that they could maintain their lands, as long as they obeyed the will of the Crown.[63] The identities of the "*indios fieles*" (faithful Indians) is unclear, but at least some appeared to be from the Huichol towns of Santa Catarina (under the command of someone named Phelipe) and San Andrés (led by a man named Melchor).[64] In this instance, Melchor's and Phelipe's peoples had much to lose and nothing to gain by allying with the Coras, and instead chose to mitigate disaster by working with Spanish authorities.

Despite the subjugation of the Coras and Huichols by the end of the 1720s, the process of land surveying had occurred and would continue throughout the century to establish boundaries and acculturate the Huichols to Spanish systems of governance. In 1703, a visit by the *oidor* (civil judge), don Juan de Somoza, began this process of demarcating boundaries. By the end of the eighteenth century, all of the principal Huichol towns had been measured and delimited. Somoza had, most likely, marked out the boundaries between Huichol towns and their Spanish *hacendado* neighbors and then let the situation rest.[65] It was only after the Spanish expeditions into Cora lands, which opened up the western mountains for settlers, that the Huichols realized their lands were still in danger.[66]

In a memo dated October 22, 1733, to an unknown Spanish authority, Antonio de Escobedo discussed a petition from Huichol leaders in Santa Catarina and San Sebastián. The towns of Santa Catarina (known as Cuescomatitán) and San Sebastián wanted legal title to their lands, just as their neighbors in the town of Nostic had received a few years earlier. Escobedo visited Santa Catarina and San Sebastián, located in an area of extremely rough terrain, and discovered that, while the two towns had been conquered some decades before, three years had passed since the Huichols had received any religious services.[67] It was clear to Escobedo that, since conquest, changes had begun to occur in the Huichol Sierra. First, the Huichols of both San Sebastián and Santa Catarina felt sufficiently threatened by some Spaniards' increasing presence that they hoped to commit their land boundaries to paper. They also may have become sufficiently comfortable with Spaniards, or the legal system, or possibly both. Second, both towns had remained loyal to the Crown since their conquest, some seventy or eighty years previous. (According to Escobedo, though we know that date is inaccurate.) Finally, despite having been conquered, the Huichols rarely had contact with religious authorities. While this petition did not solidify boundaries, owing to the difficult terrain that "only angels could traverse," Escobedo appeared to believe that keeping the two peaceful towns happy would preserve calm in the region.[68]

Five decades after Escobedo presented the two petitions, Huichol leaders in San Sebastián had not resolved their land issues. In a series of letters between authorities in Colotlán (which was the *cabecera* or head town of the region) and the audiencia in Guadalajara, a man named Miguel Maximiliano de Santiago tried to establish rights to a certain portion of San Sebastián's lands. Santiago received about twenty-five parcels of pasturelands from the Huichol town, which provoked a heated response from indigenous authorities. Juan Sebastián, the Indian governor of San Sebastián, complained that Santiago had illegally grazed his livestock on lands belonging to the town, in addition to using lands from the Huichol village of Ratontita. Don

Sebastián acknowledged a lack of written title to the lands, but pleaded with the court that his ancestors, and those of the other villagers, had lived there since time immemorial: this meant that the lands belonged to the Huichol village by way of *título de justa prescripción*, a fair usage title.[69] The audiencia ruled in San Sebastián's favor, and don Santiago had to remove his cattle from the Huichol lands.

By the end of the colonial period Spanish incursions into the Sierra became problematic for the Huichols, and indigenous leaders quickly learned how to petition royal authorities. Towns such as Santa Catarina and San Sebastián remained mostly far-removed from the centers of Spanish civilization, in Guadalajara and Zacatecas, yet the Huichols increasingly felt the pressure of unscrupulous Spanish landholders. The experiences that native leaders gained over the course of the colonial era served both to frustrate and educate: increased contact with Spaniards eroded traditional social and cultural mores, while thrusting serrano populations into a convoluted Spanish legal system that, at least on some occasions, worked in their favor. By the time independence came to New Spain, the Huichols were well aware of their foreign neighbors' potential to ignore town borders and disobey royal authorities. The Huichols had watched as violence swirled and occasionally swept them up, threatening their existence. However, by the end of the colonial period, the Huichols gained experience with outsiders that would benefit them as New Spain transformed from a vaunted royal colony to a troubled new republic.

2

Facing the Young Nation-State

In 1822 a group of Huichols visiting Tepic to trade encountered a British traveler name Basil Hall. This was likely their first encounter with a foreigner who was not a Spaniard, a Mexican, a priest, or a soldier. Hall took a keen interest in the Huichols that he met; the Huichols demonstrated their typical indifference upon meeting the English-speaking stranger. The Huichols gradually warmed up to Hall, or at least tolerated his presence enough so that he could write about what he saw.

The meeting was remarkable, not only for what Hall was able to observe and experience, but also because of his reception by the Huichols. Since Hall was not an agent of the Mexican government and was not in an area considered their homeland, the Huichols did not seem to view him as a threat. Additionally, Hall's presence in Mexico represented the opening experienced after the country's independence, which the Huichols would have to contend with moving forward. Mexico's emergence as an independent nation had important implications for the Huichols. First, the Huichols had to adapt to a transformed political apparatus on the state and national level, which had different attitudes toward land use. Additionally, Mexico's new independence meant that foreigners had a stake in the new nation's growth, which would require the Huichols to acclimate to their presence.

In part because of the Huichols' concerns with local issues, the pains of independence were not immediately felt in the Sierra. However, as officials debated Mexico's political identity both in Mexico City and Guadalajara, the Huichols needed to become more attuned to national politics and the influence that these changes might have on their lives and futures. The end of the colonial *fundo legal* (an agreement between Spanish kings and indigenous villages that ostensibly protected villages' lands) and the expansion of the hacienda seriously threatened Huichol existence, and we can begin to understand how this affected them. Nevertheless, despite laws aimed at incorporating indigenous populations into the national fabric, and in the face of ever-growing haciendas, the Huichols refused to submit to these external threats. Between the end of independence and the beginning of the Reform Era, in which Mexico's native populations faced changing attitudes toward land tenure, the Huichols struggled to retain their cultural identity and their territories against pressure from mestizo neighbors.

As independence movements, sparked by Father Miguel Hidalgo in 1810, engulfed Nueva Galicia in often horrific displays of violence, native people throughout the region became involved. This is unsurprising given the history of the region, because since the earliest years of Spanish colonization, indigenous peoples living in Nueva Galicia rebelled for one particular reason: lost land. Earlier uprisings in the colonial period, like the Mixtón Rebellion (1540s) and the Chichimeca War (1560s–90s), had occurred because of indigenous hostility over their shrinking territories.[1]

Though land motivated some indigenous peoples and peasants to fight for independence, it conversely provides a possible explanation why the Huichols mostly sat out the war. Unlike native villages in central Jalisco or central Mexico, which had more contact with Spaniards, Huichol villages and ranchos had not experienced the same degree of contact and land loss over the course of the colonial period and into the nineteenth century.[2] Thus, though it is important to account for indigenous support for or against independence, it is equally important not to overstate the case.[3] What little evidence exists from the Sierra Madre Occidental in this period demonstrates Huichols' ambivalence toward the wars, a willingness to fight if necessary, and a strong adherence to their culture despite the violence lurking in the mountains.

During the independence struggle, a few audacious friars remained in the Sierra Madre Occidental, tending to their frightened parishioners, while others led militias and armies. From their writings we can get a sense of what the Huichols experienced. Few documents exist to explain how the Huichols experienced independence, though there are some that provide an overall sense of the period in the Sierra Madre Occidental.[4] A Spanish Franciscan named Rudesindo Angles, who served as the commissioner of the ten missions in the Sierra del Nayarit, recorded some general observations about the indigenous groups he encountered.[5] Angles's observations fail to identify specific indigenous peoples with whom he came in contact, but based upon his location it is likely that he spent time with the Huichols.

Angles traveled throughout the Sierra del Nayarit not only to save indigenous souls, but also to recruit them in defense of the Crown. He marched alongside don Francisco Minjares east from the Cora towns of Jesús María and Peyotán (now in Nayarit) and across the mountains and canyons to Huejuquilla el Alto in extreme northern Jalisco. The distance is not far, less than forty miles as the crow flies, but the terrain and the cultural differences made the journey difficult. Angles's and Minjares's goals were to reassure and organize the nervous indigenous leaders in some of the pueblos and ranchos scattered throughout the Sierra.[6]

By the time independence broke out in Mexico, some Huichols lived within the boundaries of the towns of Huejuquilla el Alto, Soledad, and Tenzompa, all of which belonged to the municipio of Mezquitic. Importantly, Padre Angles noted that in December 1811, when he traveled through the Sierra Madre, he and Minjares encountered and ministered to indigenous peoples living on (or near) Hacienda San Antonio and surrounding ranches.[7] To Angles, it seemed that the indigenous people who lived in and around Huejuquilla remained either relatively peaceful or marginally on the side of the Spanish during the first year of the war.

While some native peoples in the northwestern reaches of Jalisco maintained harmonious relations with the Spanish, the same cannot be said about inhabitants in other parts of the Sierra. According to chroniclers living near Colotlán, to the southeast of Huejuquilla, several insurgents operated with relative impunity, counting hundreds, or even thousands, of indigenous allies. No doubt some Huichols existed among these insurgent groups. For instance one rebel leader, a priest named José María Calvillo, led between eight and ten thousand Indian archers from the Colotlán's militias. Again, it is unclear whether these native bowmen were Huichols, but geography suggests that at least some were; Colotlán, both a *cantón* (a small district, almost like a county) and a municipio, is part of the extreme southeastern reaches of Huichol territory.[8] Regardless of their indigenous identity, Calvillo and his allies fought at Puente de Calderón, the momentous battle that sealed Father Hidalgo's fate, in January 1811. Other unnamed groups in the area had fought valiantly for Spain (but experienced defeat), and Angles noted that clashes had occurred in the Sierra Huichol in 1812.[9] Unfortunately, Angles was not more specific in describing the peoples that he met and the precise roles that they played in skirmishes in the areas.

A second report, written by José Norberto Pérez, a priest from Teúl, pointed more directly to Huichol participation with insurgent leaders during the first half of 1813. Teúl lies not far from the old Spanish mining town of Bolaños. During 1813 townspeople in and around Bolaños and nearby Totatiche survived skirmishes and general lawlessness at the hands of an insurgent named "Indio" Cañas.[10] Cañas's identity is unknown, and his role in the region's Independence Movement remains unclear. Whatever the case, initially some Huichols supported Cañas, but they did not do so for long. According to Pérez, the Huichols switched sides on account of Cañas's unpleasant demeanor. At this point the Huichols fought under the command of the Bolaños *comandante* (commander) in pursuit of Cañas, whom Pérez called a wicked ringleader.[11] Cañas soon died at the hands of the Huichols, who then returned to their pueblos and refused to fight for the insurgents. In fact, by 1815, the three principal Huichol villages—San Andrés, Santa Catarina, and San Sebastián—had all declared support for the Spanish.[12]

Unfortunately, in his account submitted to the bishop of Guadalajara, Juan Cruz Ruís de Cabañas, Pérez was somewhat vague in his description of Cañas and the Huichols who initially supported, then defied him.

Regardless whom the Huichols supported, two problems were evident by the middle of the independence wars: poverty and disease. The *cura* (priest covering a particular parish or region) of Bolaños, Antonio Norberto Sánchez Martínez, wrote a detailed account to Bishop Ruíz de Cabañas in 1814, chronicling the effects of the war on the Huichols. Sánchez Martínez was deeply concerned about an epidemic that plagued the Huichols; because there were so few priests in the area, the Huichols died without spiritual guidance.[13] He despaired that so many native peoples were ignorant of Catholicism and that drunkenness and lust were so common. Sánchez Martínez suspected that many Huichol marriages were illegitimate in the eyes of the church.[14] While epidemic disease was likely a real and concerning problem for church officials, overzealous priests often exaggerated the levels of what they considered depravity.

To rectify this abysmal situation, Sánchez Martínez implored the bishop to send priests and friars from Huejuquilla to assist the Huichols. The towns of Camotlán and Huajimic needed aid to rebuild, as the places had been destroyed and the churches there were in disrepair. With money raised throughout the previous year, Sánchez Martínez hoped to create new parishes, repair churches, and save Huichol souls.[15] Part of the problem, he admitted, was that distance compounded all expenses: curates, parishes, and villages located deep in the mountain were hard to reach and transportation was difficult, if not impossible, at times.[16] Because of the scarcity of priests in the region, the Huichols had maintained their cultural, social, and religious norms, which deeply concerned Sánchez Martínez.

One aspect of Huichol social life that bothered priests was the way Huichols conducted marriage ceremonies. Historically Huichol men could have more than one wife, as long as he could support her care. Some Huichols allowed for "sororal polygamy," a practice by which a man married one woman and all of her sisters. Huichol marriage pacts also included a sort of "bride price" by which a woman's family might be paid in the form of a cow or some other valuable object. No aspect of Huichol marriage required the services of a priest, though some Huichols would present themselves for an "official" service when priests passed through the Sierra.

Such behaviors troubled Sánchez Martínez, as they demonstrated a disdain for Catholic ceremonialism and solemnity, in addition to illustrating how little the Huichols cared for Catholicism. Men like Sánchez Martínez viewed such resistance to Catholic dogma as a direct cause for the Huichols' "degraded" state. While he did not directly blame the war, in his mind the independence uprisings in the region had disrupted the normal flow of daily life. In the fearful minds of priests, this disruption allowed the Huichols to return to lamentable practices such as the public sale of women, drunkenness, and lustful behavior.[17]

After the carnage of independence subsided, travelers trickled into western Mexico looking to explore the still relatively remote Sierra Madre Occidental. While friars and priests returned to the Sierra, by the 1820s new foreign explorers—mostly shut out of colonial Spanish territories—made their way through western Mexico, describing the cultural and social intricacies of the resident indigenous populations. Two men in particular had some contact with the Huichols during the early to mid-1820s, and their travel accounts provide historians with clues to the state of affairs in western Mexico while simultaneously reporting on the Huichols they encountered.

Unlike the Catholic clergymen that the Huichols typically encountered in the past, travelers such as Basil Hall and George Lyon were military men. Basil Hall traveled along the Pacific coast of South and Central America, as well as Mexico, during his time as a member of the British Royal Navy. Originally from Scotland, Hall kept meticulous notes on a variety of topics. While traveling through the Nayarit countryside, he discussed at length the process of beekeeping, in addition to the current fashions and dances of the elite in Tepic. Hall compared what he witnessed in Mexico to his experiences in Chile, where he had spent time during his travels up the Pacific coast of the Americas.[18] Most importantly, Hall had a chance encounter in the city of Tepic with "a party of native Mexican Indians, who had come from the interior to purchase maize and other articles."[19] Hall would not have known the name "Huichol," but his description of the "native Mexicans" provides clues to their true identity.

Hall's report paints a vivid picture of Huichol culture and customs during this early transitional period. While describing indigenous dress, Hall noted that "the most striking circumstance, however, was, that all these Indians wore feathers round their heads . . . some had tied round their straw hats a circle of red flowers, so much resembling feathers, that it was not easy to distinguish between the two."[20] The Huichols were famed for brightly colored hats and other adornments on their heads, typically part of ritual clothing. Additionally, Hall noted that the men carried "bows and arrows . . . suited to their strength, being more like those of school boys than arms of men who had their country to defend."[21] The bows and arrows that Hall saw were not used for defense, but were instead ceremonial tools that many Huichol men carried with them. These arrows served as religious implements to convey prayers and offerings to the gods; Huichols traveling away from home typically had them, and all mara'akate used them in curing rituals.[22] Hall also apparently met a Huichol town political leader who traveled with the party; from the Scotsman's account, the man carried a staff and wore a feathered bird skin. Hall suspected the man was "chief of the village," a civil-religious authority figure in indigenous towns.[23]

The April 1822 meeting between Hall and the "native Mexican Indians" highlighted some key Huichol cultural characteristics that had endured the harsh realities of previous decades. The native people that Hall met did not speak or understand Spanish, a fact that stymied his attempts to communicate with them; this had been a common complaint of religious authorities during the colonial era.[24] When an interpreter arrived to assist Hall, the Englishman noted that while the Huichols seemed to relax a bit, a female member of the party separated herself from the inquisitive outsiders and the rest were quite frightened at all of the attention. This is understandable for a people who tended to shun outsiders. When Hall attempted to obtain some of the Huichols' goods from them for his personal collection, they balked. Hall remarked that "the old man could not be prevailed upon to part with his rod of authority, nor his official bird; neither could we induce them to sell, at any price, that part of their dress to which the inventory of their goods and chattels was appended."[25] Hall and his companions settled for the Huichols' bows and arrows, plus the feathered head adornments, but only after some convincing. Finally, that the people Hall met in Tepic were Huichols is fairly obvious: the region around Tepic has long been a trade destination for the Huichols and is not far from Tatei Haramara, Our Mother Sea, the westernmost point of the Huichols' sacred lands.[26]

A few years after Hall's visit to Tepic, his countryman, George Francis Lyon, traveled throughout Mexico to assess some of the country's mines. Born in Chichester, England, in 1795, Lyon also served in the Royal British Navy; but where Hall was an amateur scientist of sorts, Lyon was an adventurer and a mine inspector. Lyon's expeditions brought him to Saharan Africa and the Arctic, in addition to his travels in Mexico and South America.[27] Lyon's trip to the Bajío region of central Mexico to examine the mines allowed him to travel widely and observe area inhabitants. Like Hall, Lyon met with indigenous peoples; fortunately, Lyon had much more experience with, and an aptitude for, working among native populations and reported the names of those he met. In the small mining town of Bolaños, Lyon encountered "Guichola Indians" and heard the stories of Hall's encounter four years earlier.[28] Whereas Hall made general observations about the "native Mexicans," Lyon provided a glimpse into early nineteenth-century Huichol life outside of the rancho but still within the confines of the Sierra Madre Occidental.

Lyon's observations of the Huichols in Bolaños provide a picture of Huichol material culture during the 1820s. The Huichols that he met "scarcely understood even a word of Spanish, but fully comprehended what I wanted and were very quiet and good-natured."[29] Lyon particularly wanted a pair of thongs that each member of the Huichol party wore attached to their clothing, which contained purchased items, food, or a "register of his cows, and bulls, and calves." Nobody wanted to part with their items, but Lyon did manage to buy one set.[30] The Huichols that Lyon met carried their obligatory offertory arrows (along with regular arrows used for hunting); their dress consisted of a woolen-type homespun fabric, colored blue or brown, and some wore deerskin short pants. A young girl that Lyon happened upon wore elaborate bead and shell jewelry, paired with a plain woolen cloak and skirt. Finally, the lack of shoes allowed Lyon to observe Huichol feet, and he remarked that "the great-toes of all these people were much more separated from the others than is the case with Europeans."[31] In addition to clothing, Lyon noted that Huichol men carried "several large woolen bags, woven into neat and very ornamental patterns."[32] Even today, most Huichol men who have left their villages and dress in western-style clothing still carry these bags.

Lyon was a curious observer, and while certainly not an anthropologist, he was genuinely interested in native cultures. Upon discovering young people who did not wear any adornments upon their heads, Lyon learned who could wear head coverings and who could not. He noted:

> All married men wore straw hats of a very peculiar form, with wide turned-up rims and high-pointed crowns, which near their tops are bound with a narrow garter-shaped band of prettily woven woollen, of various colours, and having long pendant tassels. . . . I was informed that no unmarried man or woman may wear a hat, or bind the fillet round the head; and as we saw some young people who had neither of these ornaments, it may, in all probability, be the case. There were two young married females of the party, each wearing a hat similar to those of the men.[33]

The difference in material styles between married and unmarried individuals allowed Lyon to identify marital practices typical for the era. Lyon discovered that the Huichols practiced trial marriage, in which a man and woman could live together as a married couple for a period of time; if the man was unhappy with the match, his wife returned to her parents' home.[34] Even if the woman became pregnant, she suffered no shame by returning to her parents and might marry again in the future if she chose. If the match was successful, "they are married by a priest or a friar, who once a year goes round to perform this ceremony, and to christen the offspring of newly married couples."[35] Some Huichol couples did not have their marriages sanctified by the church, but those who received church weddings typically did so in January or February, when it was dry and Huichol farming obligations were minimal.[36]

Most importantly, Lyon realized that the Huichols were different from other native peoples, at least within the realm of the Bolaños mining region. He attributed their distinctive nature to the fact that the mountains between the town of Bolaños and the Pacific Ocean were not well known by outsiders, and Spaniards or Mexicans had not traveled as widely in this region as they had in other areas of Mexico.[37] Lyon remarked that "the Guicholes are in fact the only neighbouring people who still live entirely distinct from those around them, cherishing their own language, and studiously resisting all endeavors to draw them over to the customs of their conquerors."[38] Though distinct in relation to their indigenous neighbors immediately surrounding them, some of whom spoke Spanish and readily accepted Catholicism, the Huichols were not immune to transformations that began occurring rapidly during the 1820s and beyond. They chose which elements of Spanish/Mexican culture and society to accept and which to reject. Such careful adaptations would prove beneficial in later decades.

During these difficult, early decades of the new republic, more troublesome than visiting priests or curious foreigners were the mestizos who increasingly encroached upon Huichol lands. Land laws in Jalisco and elsewhere began changing long before the Mexican Liberals passed the national reform laws in the 1850s. These early laws summarily ended corporate identity and in theory abolished corporate land ownership for indigenous peoples and the church. In Jalisco, "efforts to partition and individualize village lands" began in years immediately following independence.[39] The few land documents that do exist from this period in the early republic are mostly legal codes aimed at settling disputes between indigenous villagers and their mestizo neighbors.[40] Mestizo elites gained power in early republican Mexico, particularly in the provinces, as more international ports opened up and money could be made trading commodities on the open market. This frequently resulted in an influx of outsiders into regions that had been sparsely populated. This was especially true in western Jalisco, where the port of San Blas (northwest of Tepic) became an international trading hub during the nineteenth century. Regional capitals such as Guadalajara grew in population and prestige, and the city's expansion undoubtedly pressed indigenous peoples in the surrounding countryside.

Meanwhile, the political climate of the early republic was often hotly contentious, with ambitious people jockeying for position, occasionally at the expense of indigenous people.[41] During the mid-nineteenth century, power came from land ownership (which increasingly was valued as a commodity), the ability to control the population, and access to the political process; this was power that millions of poor Mexicans, including the Huichols, could not have.[42] As political tensions increased and land became a target for privatization, indigenous groups throughout Jalisco felt the pressures of living in a modernizing nation.

During the first years of the republic, local and provincial governments began to address Indian land concerns, but not in ways that ultimately would benefit indigenous people. Government officials in Jalisco passed scores of laws aimed at preventing conflict between Indian villagers and *vecinos*, which in the legal code of the day meant town inhabitants who were either nonindigenous or who viewed themselves as mestizos.[43] A decree dated June 28, 1822, just before the republic was established, addressed communal lands in the cantón of Colotlán: simply put, once the government had divided up lands and distributed them to indigenous villages for their own use, the rest of the lands could go to the vecinos if the indigenous peoples did not need the space. The difference was that native villages did not have to pay the annual rent, while mestizos did.[44] While this may not have affected the Huichols directly, it reversed centuries-old Crown laws and could potentially expose indigenous villagers to exploitation. In a reversal of the colonial fundo legal laws, indigenous peoples could now lease or rent out lands that they were not using.[45] Taken at face value, the June 1822 decree appeared to give indigenous peoples more control over their own lands and demonstrated government willingness to intervene in conflicts; however, in reality, this decree had the potential to deprive Jalisco's natives of their territorial possessions.

An official provincial circular and a follow-up decree passed by the Jalisco government were designed to prevent outsiders from disrupting or disturbing indigenous villagers on lands that belonged to them.[46] It made property owners, in a legal sense, of native villagers, with all the rights that came with land ownership (except, ostensibly, voting rights). Indigenous peoples could sell or divide their lands, provided they had title to them, which they could obtain for the price of a stamp and official seal. The motivations for the December decree remain ambiguous, because legal documents such as this are frequently quite vague and lack supporting documentation. It is evident that the government of Jalisco favored the privatization of lands and believed, at least theoretically, that indigenous villagers should have rights to their lands.[47]

Privatizing lands was a double-edged sword. On the one hand, native villages with lands recognized by title now had concrete proof of their territory. On the other hand, lands were no longer protected by the fundo legal and could be divided and/or sold, allowing for unscrupulous mestizos to swindle indigenous people. Hoping to stave off indigenous protests, quick-thinking authorities in Guadalajara soon passed Decree 79, which declared that anyone who obtained Indian lands (by any means) without express indigenous consent could no longer retain title to those lands.[48]

Decrees 2 and 79 illustrated interesting transformations toward Indian land policy in Jalisco during the 1820s and early 1830s. The two laws were broad in scope, meaning that they addressed Indian land concerns that existed throughout the state of Jalisco and not simply issues in the Sierra Madre Occidental. Collectively they suggest that indigenous peoples around the city of Guadalajara and its mountainous countryside experienced increasing pressures as Mexican states struggled to define their laws and politics. Evidence suggests that indigenous villages needed protection from land-hungry Jalisciences during the 1820s. While there is more evidence for land loss in central Jalisco, the potential existed for large haciendas or even small farms to cut away at Huichols' lands.[49] The Constitutional Convention of Jalisco created the decrees to protect indigenous peoples, even though many individuals still managed to frustrate and circumvent the spirit of the law.[50] Yet while republican state governments designed legal codes to assist Indian villages, the long-term goal was to break up community ejidos. This would force indigenous peoples to privatize communal lands and become small farmers assimilated into the fabric of Mexico; and while never stated, nonindigenous Mexicans would be able to purchase lands that might have been held communally for centuries.

By the beginning of the 1830s the government of Jalisco realized that Decree 2, at least in its original form, no longer offered indigenous villagers the limited protection that the government (or at least some benevolent individuals in the government) had intended.[51] While allowing native Mexicans to divide and sell their communal holdings, it became clear that Decree 2 contained too many loopholes for fraudulent behavior on the part of mestizos. Conflicts between indigenous communities and haciendas emerged, a fact that required a rethinking of land laws. In February 1830 the government revised the decree by adding Laws 151 and 381. These two laws stated that products of community lands leased by the municipalities would be given to indigenous families and that the provisions of Law 151 existed upon any lands that were purchased through fair, legal means.[52] Laws 151 and 381 were somewhat vague and open to varying interpretations, not unlike most legal codes governing Indian lands. Law 151 provided some economic protection to Indian families on a municipal level, but it is unclear why this occurred. At any rate, as mestizos continued to flood into Jalisco, and as the demand for land increased, indigenous communities sometimes felt compelled to part with some or all of their holdings. To prevent strife and violence, politicians in Jalisco attempted to head off problems through legal means. It is obvious that their attempts were unsuccessful across the board, including in the Huichol Sierra.

By the mid-1830s town officials throughout the Sierra felt pressed by mestizos unwilling to acknowledge indigenous land rights and native villagers who were weary of unscrupulous outsiders. The governments of the municipalities of Mezquitic and Totatiche found themselves at odds with one another in a feud over lands that had little to do with the Huichols or other indigenous groups per se. However, the arguments by the two towns concerned *terrenos baldíos* (vacant lands), and the implications for indigenous towns were troubling. Mestizos in the area, technically residents of the municipio of Mezquitic, had moved onto "vacant lands" that Totatiche claimed. Mezquitic's political leaders contested this claim, yet it is unclear how officials rectified the situation.[53] But this small piece of seemingly insignificant legal news illustrated that mestizos were willing to occupy lands not belonging to them and refuse orders of town magistrates, to the point where politicians in both towns became involved.

Throughout the 1830s it became increasingly clear that indigenous communities needed to have clear legal title to their lands, lest someone deem the properties vacant. In November 1833 the district chief of Colotlán discovered that many indigenous peoples living around Huejuquilla had made land claims; instead of charging mestizos with stealing their land, these unnamed indigenous villagers (possibly Huichols or perhaps neighboring Tepehuanes or Coras) complained that properties they should have received via Decree 2 and Law 151 had never been distributed. The anonymous complainant, likely a legal advisor or lawyer for the Indian community, needed to seek the advice of the council charged with partitioning and distributing territories. While this case too lacks a clear resolution, it appears as though some political leaders in the eighth cantón tried to keep peace within Indian communities and between indigenous peoples and non-Indian Mexicans. By midcentury this became a far more difficult task.

By the early 1840s the Huichols had emerged from independence and the first two decades of the early republic relatively intact in a religious and cultural sense. While indigenous villages in the more populous central region of Jalisco lost their lands, the Huichols had only just begun to experience the pressures of land attrition. The state government kept a close eye on land affairs, periodically ruling in favor of native communities; they also issued legal orders (such as Decrees 2 and 79) that ostensibly would protect indigenous landholdings. Unfortunately, as the population in Jalisco increased over time, the "Indian problem" became more apparent and the state government found less incentive to ensure harmonious relations between their indigenous and nonindigenous residents.

While a complete picture of Huichol history between 1800 and 1830 is probably impossible, a few observations are evident. First, some Huichols undoubtedly participated in the independence movements that swept Jalisco between 1810 and 1821. Because the Huichols need to be viewed in local terms, one can surmise that unity behind an insurgent leader or Spanish commander never occurred. Though all Huichols shared language and cultural traits, no clear sense of ethnic identity (in a modern sense) existed among the nineteenth-century Huichols.[54] Thus it is unlikely that disparate villages would unite together against a common foe.

A second component of the story during this period concerns evolving relationships with the outside world. Though the Huichols were geographically distant from the centers of population to the south and west, the first decade and a half after independence forced the Huichols to make small adjustments to the changing political, cultural, and social environments. They learned to expect outsiders, though the frequency was nothing compared to what was to come. Although the Huichols did not lose much land during the period between independence and 1848, they gained some experience with encroaching Mexicans, unscrupulous attorneys, and the tortuous Mexican legal system. And finally, most Huichols realized that Catholic clergy would not leave them in peace for long and generally begrudgingly accepted the occasional visit. Yet the small changes that the Huichols made did little to transform their overarching culture, language, or religion. The Huichols simply absorbed elements of Catholicism if they chose, such as church marriages, baptisms, Holy Week celebrations, and the veneration of the Virgin of Guadalupe. However, they did not adopt Catholicism entirely. They learned to seek assistance from Mexican officials when outsiders impinged on their lands. These small changes, which Huichols made on their own terms, served them well through the first decades of the Mexican republic.

By the mid-1830s lessons learned from two decades of dealing with Mexicans and seventy years of continuous Spanish rule before that hardened Huichol leaders. As haciendas expanded throughout Mexico, and especially in northern Jalisco, the Huichols had to fight to protect their lands. Initially this fight was less about weapons and more about words and petitions. But the end of independence allowed for a return of Catholic clergy that would challenge the Huichols in a new way. Between the early 1840s and the late 1850s, the Huichols experienced a threat to their spiritual well-being that, combined with concerns about land, threatened their very existence.

3

Between Tolerance and Rejection of the Church

In an 1839 letter to the bishop of Guadalajara, Fray Vicente Buenaventura-Cárdenas lamented the conditions he found in the Sierra Huichola. Buenaventura had experience evangelizing with other indigenous groups in the area, such as the Coras, who had more or less accepted evangelization since their subjugation in the eighteenth century, but he could not make headway with the Huichols.[1] To Bishop don Diego Aranda, Buenaventura complained that the Huichols did not know how to pray and that they did not marry according to Catholic tradition. Customary marital practices disgusted him: if a man got tired of his wife, who might be old or ugly, he would simply trade her in for a new, younger woman. Men frequently traded wine and cows for women, more or less as a bride price; Buenaventura viewed such behavior as depraved.[2]

The end of the Wars for Independence in Mexico allowed for a return of Franciscans to the Sierra in the 1840s, though secular clergy had normalized operations by the 1820s. Most religious authorities had abandoned their posts with the outbreak of revolutionary hostilities around 1810. The friars who ministered to the Huichols of San Sebastián, for example, left the area in 1811.[3] The Huichols had shown little interest in conversion to Catholicism during the colonial period, only incorporating bits and pieces of catechism where it suited them. Would renewed efforts on the part of the Catholic Church force the Huichols to give up their ways, or would they continue to absorb only the elements of Catholicism that would not change fundamentally their own indigenous faiths?

Missionary records from the middle decades of the nineteenth century demonstrate a spiritual conflict between the evangelizing Franciscans and Huichols who had no interest in conversion. Franciscans lamented the Huichols' overwhelming—though far from uniform—dismissal of conversion efforts in these early years. From these sources, the Huichols' physical, cultural, and religious world emerges, though unfortunately through the lenses of men who rarely understood what they witnessed, or for whom indigenous peoples were little more than timid and capricious, with barbarous customs and ideas.[4] These sources also provide glimpses of the disunity that existed between Huichol villages; a lack of overarching political hierarchy meant that Huichols accepted or rejected Catholicism as desired, a fact evident in the Franciscans' writings and mission reports.

The church redoubled its efforts in the Sierra at the end of the 1840s and during the first few years of the 1850s, attempting to shepherd Huichol souls toward salvation. Though some Huichols tolerated their presence, it was far easier for the Franciscans to write about Huichol religious and cultural practices than to actually make changes. The friars walked a fine line with their presence in the Sierra, as the political culture gradually shifted toward anticlericalism by midcentury. For the most part, Franciscan missionaries were unsuccessful in their conversion attempts; nevertheless, they remained intolerant and ignorant of Huichol religious beliefs. The Franciscans faced numerous challenges: hostile environmental conditions; indifferent, unwelcoming, and occasionally even aggressive Huichols; and an increasingly anticlerical state.

Missionaries faced innumerable trials in the western Sierra Madre, including a difficult natural environment. The same regions of refuge that had allowed the Huichols to evade marauding nomadic groups and conquering Spaniards also helped them avoid Catholic missionaries. Huichol territory was difficult to navigate, a fact to which countless visitors in the past could attest. According to the unnamed Franciscan author of the "Informe sobre San Sebastián y sus pueblos de visita," which was written sometime after 1852, surveying land was rather challenging owing to the roughness and unevenness of the terrain. As a result, mission and town borders in the area were irregular, and traversing this region on foot or mule proved challenging for Franciscans.[5] The report is a valuable portrait of Huichol life in mid-nineteenth century Mexico.

The author of this report provided officials at the Colegio in Zapopan a glimpse into the lives of the Huichols. The friar noted differences in vegetation, agriculture, and local fauna. In his report, this particularly observant friar documented the variety of the trees in the Huichol Sierra and what one might do with the wood from such trees. The 1853 mission report explained that the Huichols were blessed with many fruit trees and countless wild plants, all of which they knew and used for various mundane and spiritual purposes.[6] The Franciscan clergyman commented that farming techniques were poor and "backward" in his estimation, but the Huichols managed to grow a variety of crops including chilies, corn, and squash. Huichols consumed a fairly standard indigenous diet of tortillas, beans, and the occasional piece of meat; corn was a staple of both physical and spiritual sustenance.[7]

Villages ranged across many hundreds of square miles, from hot lowlands between mountain passes to the remote redoubts on high mountains.[8] Some villages, such as San Andrés, had significant fluctuation in temperature within the town itself, from very cold in the upper reaches of mountains to extreme heat in the bottomlands.[9] Such geographic distribution of Huichol villages produced slightly varied linguistic dialects and minor differences in the veneration or importance of some deities over others. Yet all Huichols could understand one another and ascribed to the same core religious beliefs. The friars complained that they could not learn the language because there appeared to be a lack of rules, the aforementioned linguistic variations, and difficult pronunciation.[10] Perhaps these particular Franciscans simply made excuses; since the period immediately after the conquest of Mexico, the regular orders had worked diligently to learn indigenous languages. Was Huichol really so difficult and/or distinctive? Thus, as had been the case during the previous two centuries, language proved an often insurmountable barrier to Franciscan progress among the Huichols.

Linguistic, geographical, and climatological barriers notwithstanding, secular and religious authorities voiced concerns about the lack of religious instruction over the course of the previous decades. In a letter to the provincial priest of Jalisco, José María Castillo Portugal, a member of the "first Constituent Congress of Jalisco," inquired as to the state of the Nayarit missions.[11] Castillo Portugal wanted to ensure that someone would administer the sacraments to the inhabitants of San Andrés, San Sebastián, and Santa María de la frontera de Colotlán.[12] In this early national period, before the anticlerical attitudes of the 1850s took hold, it was not unusual for political authorities to be concerned for the salvation of indigenous villages. In November 1824 the vice-governor of Jalisco, working through ecclesiastical authorities, authorized an annual salary of four hundred pesos for two priests to travel to San Andrés, San Sebastián, and Santa Catarina to administer sacraments to Huichol villagers.[13] This was one of many such financial dispensations made by state or bishopric authorities aimed at bolstering evangelization in the Sierra del Nayar and the Huichol Sierra.

Political and religious authorities realized the difficulty of the missionaries' endeavors. Mountainous terrain and distance from the main convents in Guadalajara made travel to, and maintenance in, the Huichol Sierra rather complicated. Some of the smaller missions were so far from the curates that regular visits simply could not occur; the town of San Sebastián was one such place, though it had been a *doctrina* (a branch of a mission) during the colonial period.[14] Living too distant from the curate in Bolaños, Huichols who desired religious instruction and church-sanctioned marriages went without. The priest from Bolaños worked with both the bishop in Guadalajara and religious authorities in other areas to ensure that Huichol souls would not be forsaken.[15]

Religious authorities who neglected the Huichols blamed the geographical distance and terrain for their inability (or unwillingness) to do their jobs. Huichol communities, but particularly San Sebastián, were abandoned by Franciscans by the second half of the 1820s and throughout much of the 1830s, despite the efforts of state officials such as Castillo Portugal.[16] San Sebastián, which had been an important missionary town during the colonial period, found itself under the control of the curate in Bolaños; then, the commissioner of Jesús María, a Cora town, took over. Neither curate provided San Sebastián's inhabitants with sufficient religious instruction and evangelization.[17] Such abandonment may not have mattered to the Huichols; we cannot know how they felt about this, but there is no evidence that they sought the missionaries' teachings. Nevertheless, ecclesiastical authorities in Guadalajara tried to rectify the situation by the end of the 1830s.

Friars who returned to the Huichol Sierra wrote about the religious culture of San Andrés with a sense of dismay; however, from these ethnocentric reports, the beauty and complicated nature of Huichol religion emerge. Church attitudes toward Huichol spirituality remained consistent throughout the period. For instance, Catholic clergy failed to see any redeeming qualities in Huichol practices, deeming their religion barbaric, idolatrous, and depraved; their actions drunken and illicit; and their lives miserable.[18] The Huichols responded to the increased presence of Catholic clergy with a mix of suspicion and welcoming, depending on the circumstances.

Fray Buenaventura-Cárdenas visited San Andrés in 1839, at which point he wrote his aforementioned letter. There, he discovered that the Huichols had abandoned any elements of Catholicism that they might have adopted during the previous century of contact with the clerical authorities. In his June 1839 report to the bishop of Guadalajara, Buenaventura lamented that Huichols living in San Andrés "violated" the church by practicing their traditional religion within the sacred walls. The church building itself was in no condition for the celebration of mass. He noted that the Huichols did not hide their household idols, nor did they bother to practice their religious dances (the *mitote*) in secret.[19] In Buenaventura's mind, it was as if Catholicism had evaporated in San Andrés.

Fray Buenaventura traveled through the region between Jesús María and San Andrés, searching for and rooting out practices that he deemed "idolatry." Very likely using the writings of previous friars, Buenaventura knew where to find Huichol religious artifacts, searching in caves and crevices throughout the mountainous terrain to uncover the stone and wood idols sacred to the people. Once located, he smashed or burned them, enraging the Huichols.[20] The placing of little deities throughout the countryside was a way for the Huichols to mark sacred spaces.[21] Alongside their own gods and goddesses, Buenaventura noted that the Huichols also worshipped images of Jesus, but they did not believe in him.[22] Perhaps this was one of the more frustrating elements for missionaries. Some Huichols incorporated elements of Catholicism, including the veneration of Jesus and the Virgin Mary, yet they had failed to exchange one set of beliefs for the "correct" one.

Buenaventura attempted to explain why the Huichols refused to convert to Catholicism. He felt that the "Guicholes" simply did not believe in God because the devil had tricked them and led them astray.[23] As mentioned previously, Buenaventura complained that the Huichols did not know how to pray, nor did they respect the sanctity of the church. In decrying their supposed heresy, the friar listed a number of gods that the Huichols continued to worship: in addition to the Sun and the Moon, peyote, and snakes, the Huichols venerated two deities of obscure origins and meaning called Séautara and Juana Móa.[24] The absence of Catholic clergy in the Sierra was detrimental to the Huichols' religious education, but previous exposure to Catholicism had not reduced the importance of their indigenous beliefs.

Buenaventura's writings on the Huichols were some of the earliest missionary accounts after independence, but they were far from the only ones or the richest. With the return of the Franciscans in the 1840s, evangelization occurred with greater fervor, leading to a number of reports by friars such as Rafael de Jesús Soria, José María de Sánchez Alvarez, or Guadalupe de Jesús Vázquez.[25] The "Informe de San Sebastián," written in 1843, provided details on the state of the mission at San Sebastián. This report depicted unhappy Huichols who had—in the minds of friars—neglected or ignored their Catholic teachings. Friars found the Huichols to be passive and timid, but also capricious and tenacious at times. According to the friar who had written the report, they had not shed their "barbarous" practices and ideas; however, he also noted that some of their festivals demonstrated a mix of "religion and idolatry," though he fails to elaborate what these fiestas actually looked like.[26]

Multiple accounts of Huichol religious culture note the regular occurrence of festivals. For instance, while traveling and providing a brief history of the three principal Huichols towns, an anonymous author of the "Informe de Nayarit" reported several festivals that occurred throughout the year during each full moon. Though he noted that it was difficult to give an exact account of Huichol "idolatries," given the amount of them and the short amount of time he had to witness them, among the troubling ceremonies he counted fiestas to the cow, the deer, calabazas (pumpkins), *elotes* (ears of corn), *esquites* (corn kernels), and many others. All of these festivals marked important points in the Huichol ceremonial calendar relating to the harvest. This author also noted that the Huichols worshipped peyote, but did not elaborate on it.[27]

The veneration of peyote had captured the attention of Catholic officials since the colonial era. Indeed, the Spanish Crown had cracked down on nonindigenous use of the cactus and maintained a suspicious attitude toward native consumption of it.[28] Church fathers knew that peyote had curative properties, but were more aggrieved at the divining potential that the Huichols claimed it had. By the mid-nineteenth century Franciscans consistently noted peyote worship in their reports, but generally, the cactus only warranted a brief mention. However, one missionary provided a detailed account of the festivities related to procuring peyote. In the "Informe de San Sebastián," the anonymous friar commented on preparations for the peyote pilgrimage, which in his time began in September or October. He noted that pilgrims who planned to make the journey to San

Luis Potosí began abstaining from certain foods, such as salt; those who were taking the trip for the first time were blindfolded before leaving and remained that way until reaching San Luis Potosí. The pilgrims left little offerings along the way in various places, and when they arrived in San Luis Potosí, they dug for peyote. Upon returning, the pilgrims reconvened at a cave—likely one near Teakata, in Santa Catarina—and afterward the towns held large festivals, complete with deer meat that had been hunted the day before the festivities.[29]

This description is remarkable and the first of its kind. It demonstrates a significant shift in attitude toward Catholic authorities. There is no evidence in this report that the Huichols allowed a Franciscan, or any other outsider, to witness the peyote pilgrimage or accompanying fiesta. Yet the report is uncanny in its similarity to later reports from turn-of-the-century ethnographers and twentieth-century anthropologists. The abstention from certain foods, particularly salt, is noteworthy, and a common avoidance in modern peyote pilgrims. Upon returning to their homes from San Luis Potosí, pilgrims are welcomed by their families with much celebration and large fiestas, complete with dancing, music, and the sacrifice of deer. Much of the symbolism was lost on the Franciscans, but is evident in their writings, demonstrating that *someone* shared with them details of this sacred, annual rite of passage that Huichols undertook at the time of the report and which still occurs in the twenty-first century.

At first glance the Huichols often appeared placid and indifferent to the presence of the friars, though such characterizations belied their independence and desire to maintain their cultural identity, separate from their Mexican neighbors. According to missionary reports, many Huichols spent their days in states of drunkenness; they stole and lived in a generally obscene and apathetic state. Huichol couples refused to marry in Catholic ceremonies and occasionally even fornicated in the church. They lacked land to farm their crops, resulting in extreme poverty.[30] Instead of peaceful, timid Huichols, the Franciscans found murder and suicide, the stubborn refusal to stop worshipping idols in the many hidden caves and canyons throughout the region, and the failure to believe in God. They desperately needed the light of Catholicism, and the author implored his superiors to help provide resources and to foster cultural and social change within the Huichol towns.[31]

The Franciscan reports compiled between 1843 and 1855 point to some interesting developments among Huichol communities. In 1845 Franciscans raised sufficient funding to begin restoring a chapel at Santa Catarina, as the old one was in ruins. This was received enthusiastically by the residents of the town, who invited their neighbors in San Andrés and San Sebastián for the dedication festivities the following year.[32] Apparently, friars had been baptizing significant numbers of people in the two years leading up to the construction of the church, justifying the restoration of the new one.

This demonstrates a few important trends in Santa Catarina, long viewed as the most reticent of the three towns. First, the Huichols in Santa Catarina Cuescomatitán came to understand baptism as less problematic in the grand scheme of things as it pertained to their own indigenous beliefs; being baptized did not diminish one's own relationship with one's indigenous deities. Second, the Huichols living in Santa Catarina gradually warmed up to the Franciscans in the two years that they spent in the area. This was a monumental accomplishment, one noted by the friars in their report.[33] Finally, that Santa Catarina invited its neighbors from the adjoining Huichol towns demonstrates community solidarity, something not always present in the Sierra (which will become more evident in later decades). Nevertheless, over the course of the next decade, Santa Catarina remained the town most removed from the reach of the church.

While the exact population of each town frequently remains unclear, by the mid-1840s the region certainly had enough demand for priests to warrant the creation of a new mission in San Andrés.[34] It is not certain where this request came from, but if the circumstances in Santa Catarina are any indication, San Andrés also witnessed increased interest in baptisms and marriage. Whereas San Sebastián initially commanded much of the attention of the church as the main village in the region, San Andrés surpassed its neighbor in terms of need. Between 1843 and 1853 San Sebastián suffered a marked reduction in inhabitants seeking the church sacraments of baptism, marriage, and Christian burial. Priests working in the area occasionally experienced an increase in adults seeking marriage or baptism for children, but for the most part, residents of San Sebastián and Santa Catarina rejected the presence of the Catholic Church. On the other hand, the inhabitants of San Andrés, when compared to their counterparts in other areas, overwhelmingly married under the auspices of the church and baptized their babies. In 1853 demand for church services was so great in San Andrés that Catholic leaders created a new mission to serve that town and its satellite, Guadalupe Ocotán; this mission became known as Nueva Señora de Guadalupe Ocotán.[35] Unfortunately it is unclear why some Huichols sought catechism while others refused it. This should come as no surprise. Though the inhabitants of San Andrés and Guadalupe Ocotán indicated a willingness at least to tolerate the presence of friars and the ceremonialism of the Catholic Church, those in Santa Catarina were lukewarm.

Though many indigenous peoples might blend some aspects of native religion with acceptable Catholic beliefs and ceremonies, Huichol religion continued to be a vexing problem for mid-nineteenth century officials like Padre Miguel de Jesús María Guzmán and Padre Guadalupe de Jesús Vázquez.[36] Every festival, even those with secular purposes, contained elements of what these men considered idolatry. Upon witnessing the political festival known as "*cambia de varas*" (literally the change of staffs) in San Sebastián, in which secular officials are elected for new terms in office, the friars noted that the Huichols had not rid themselves of "bad" customs and behaviors. The tolerance for Huichol idolatry, in its various forms, had gone on long enough.

The Franciscan response was harsh. Guzmán insisted that the Huichols cease their evil ways and proceeded to burn their sacred caligüey.[37] When the friars destroyed sacred objects, including a stone idol displayed prominently in the temple, the Huichols demanded to know who sent the priests, why they were there, and what their ultimate motives were. The Huichols were understandably enraged. The friars managed to avoid a catastrophe at the hands of angry indigenous peoples, but Huichol aggravation with the intruders continued to fester.[38] This event fractured relations between Franciscans and Huichols in Santa Catarina for some time.

During their travels throughout the Sierra, Franciscans frequently discovered that, despite the fact that some Huichols might attend church, their religious conversion was not remotely complete. The Huichols maintained their religious traditions, mixed with Catholic ceremonialism, as earlier friars had attested to. Priests found troves of idols and other objects, such as sacred arrows and offerings of chocolate and feathers to strange statues.[39] To Guzmán and Vazquez, their goal of extirpating superstition seemed as far away as ever.

By the mid-1850s, though some Huichols appeared interested in baptisms, marriages, and increased contact with Franciscans, that did not mean they planned to give up their indigenous spirituality. The account written by Guzmán demonstrates how difficult rooting out Huichol religion would be. While the Huichols practiced their religion in a temple, it also existed out in nature; idols lived in Huichol homes, in caves, in ponds, and in the sky. Huichol religion surrounded them. Significantly, by the end of the 1850s, while some Huichols still chose to maintain their distance from the Catholic missionaries, others showed indifference or even moderate interest. Interest in Catholicism depended entirely on the town and even the individual.

Diego de Aranda, the bishop of Guadalajara between 1836 and 1853, made a point toward the end of his life to ensure that indigenous peoples of his bishopric received proper spiritual care. To this end, he lobbied on behalf of area friars to obtain money for ministerial works. From December 1849 to January 1850, Aranda y Carpinteiro managed to gather small sums of money from the Finance Ministry (*Secretaría de Hacienda*) to ameliorate the Huichols' "misery and ignorance."[40] The Catholic Church had failed in the past to maintain a presence in the Sierra, partly because of the Huichols' reticence, their frequent refusal to pay for the friars' upkeep, and finally because the main church body rarely supplied the funds.[41] But in 1850 the ministers of finance and justice offered three hundred pesos for the establishment and upkeep of a mission in Nayarit. Officials noted that the church should match those funds and were grateful for their work among the native peoples.[42] In fact, the president of Mexico himself—José Joaquín de Herrera—authorized the expenditure because it was important to the church's mission.[43]

The church plunged into their work and, by 1852, it was obvious to Franciscan leaders that the Huichols needed much spiritual improvement in their lives. The absence of Franciscans during the previous decades had led to "backsliding" among the Huichols, a situation that Aranda y Carpinteiro hoped to remedy through renewed evangelical efforts. Though the primary motivation was to teach Catholicism to the "ignorant" Huichols, this was difficult and potentially dangerous. The Huichols would not give up their "idolatry," which included the consumption of peyote, and so they generally paid little attention to the Franciscans. The reports that the friars compiled helped to justify the continued presence of the church in places like the Sierra del Nayar, while simultaneously providing detailed information to others on everything from the type of climate a town had, to what language a group spoke, to the history of missionization in the area. The friars remained there, traveling to outlying pueblos like San Sebastián and its satellites, Santa Catarina and San Andrés, when the need arose.[44]

What we unfortunately lack from these reports are Huichol voices. We may never know what they thought of the influx of Franciscans in their midst during the middle decades of the nineteenth century. Close reading of these sources reveals that there was, in some instances, syncretism; that is to say, some Huichols had begun incorporating some elements of Catholicism into their cosmology. Franciscan reports point out that some Huichol festivals demonstrated a blending of "religion and idolatry," that is, Catholic and indigenous beliefs. But why the Huichols did this or what purpose Catholicism served is not clear. The Franciscans' tenure in the Sierra Huichola was not long enough to make a significant impact; perhaps longevity would not have mattered. Even if the Huichols had expressed their desires, would the Franciscans have listened or even cared to record them?

The anticlerical attitudes that swept Mexico in the 1850s forced missionaries out of the highlands for more than two decades. During this period political transformations dramatically affected indigenous groups nationwide, and the Huichols were not immune to such changes. Land privatization led to shrinking territorial bases, forcing peasants and indigenous peoples out of the countryside and into the cities. Those who stayed frequently suffered. Rebellion and unrest swept parts of Mexico, including Jalisco and Nayarit, leading to desperate times for the Huichols and other indigenous groups in the region. By the 1880s, the era of Porfirio Díaz, the situation was grim for indigenous Mexicans.

The Mexican Catholic Church took an interest in the well-being of native peoples during this period of spiritual and physical turmoil. The dismal outlook for indigenous peoples in Nayarit and northern Jalisco bothered the clergy in the early years of the 1880s and, no doubt, national political and intellectual discourse about the Indian condition alarmed the Church as well. The archbishop of Guadalajara at that time, Pedro José de Jesús Loza y Pardavé, wanted to establish scholarships to train young teachers to educate indigenous children. Such programs died a predictable death, but the fact that Archbishop Loza y Pardavé tried to initiate Catholic education in western Jalisco illustrated the mood of the Church toward indigenous youths.[45] Decades of warfare and little to no care from secular or religious authorities had taken their toll, according to priests.

4

In Defense of Lands

Evidence of the tensions generated by land encroachment came in the form of periodic episodes of violence. In 1854 unknown assailants murdered don Benito del Hoyo, proprietor of the Hacienda San Antonio de Padua, and three of his sons.[1] Del Hoyo had been a thorn in the sides of area indigenous peoples, particularly the Huichols, because his workers continually strayed across the hacienda boundary and onto native properties.[2] The ruthless hacendado treated the local native population as best suited to serve as his personal workforce.[3] Tensions between del Hoyo and Huichols living near the towns of Huejuquilla and Tenzompa had boiled over as early as 1848. In one particularly aggravating episode, cattle from the hacienda trampled Huichol milpas. Another time some Huichols in Tenzompa faced a harsh jail sentence because they had built houses on properties that had been theirs without question for as long as anyone could remember. Del Hoyo's ranch hands burned the houses down and accused the Huichols of illegally squatting.[4]

It is unclear who actually murdered the del Hoyo family, but in October 1854, supporters influenced by rebel leader Manuel Lozada were becoming active in the western Sierra. Lieutenant Colonel Félix Llera captured a Huichol man who likely supported Lozada. Llera ordered his execution, but to save himself, the Huichol volunteered to guide Llera and his men through the Sierra to where some Lozada supporters had camped out. Upon leading the army to Rancho Carrizales, the Huichol scout and Llera's men encountered four men, ostensibly supporters of Lozada, whom Llera then accused of spying.[5]

Between the 1850s and 1890s land grievances pushed the Huichols to their limit, and this helped attract some Huichol supporters to the Lozada movement. Unfortunately, this story involving Lieutenant Colonel Llera and one or two other anecdotes are the only evidence historians have of Huichol support for the Lozada Rebellion or any armed action in defense of their territory.[6] The so-called "pax porfiriana" (Porifian peace) that spanned the regime of Porfirio Díaz more or less prevented armed insurrection. In light of political transformations that emerged in the 1850s, and which lasted until the revolution in 1910, this chapter will explore how the Huichols reacted to the political and ideological threats that aimed to unleash modernization upon the Huichols' Sierra. This political pressure forced them to come to terms with the encroaching outside world.

The Liberal political movement, which began with the ouster of Antonio López de Santa Anna in 1854, charged ahead from the mid-1850s to the end of the century and was directed by Benito Juárez and Porfirio Díaz.[7] Staunch nineteenth-century Liberals had little use for what they considered the trappings and superstitions of the Catholic Church, and they coveted the land and finances that the Church controlled. While many adherents to Liberal ideology no doubt considered themselves practicing Catholics, modernization meant stripping the Church of its economic and political power. Liberals also believed that individual ownership of small plots of land would improve Mexico's productivity and modernize the struggling nation.[8] The reform laws enacted by Juárez and other Liberals—such as ley Juárez and ley Lerdo—and enforced during the Porfiriato consequently outlawed corporate ownership of lands while simultaneously stripping the Church's economic power.[9] How did the people respond?

For the Huichols, this period required adaptation and accommodation. As a result of Liberal reforms, the Franciscans and other missionaries no longer worked in the Sierra.[10] This meant that Huichols who were uninterested in conversion or Catholic influence gained a reprieve. On the other hand, however, the reforms threatened the comunidad system that had been in place since the earliest years of the eighteenth century.[11] This system offered Huichols the protection of town living without necessarily affecting their overall cultural and social norms, mostly because the comunidad was based on a precontact social structure. In effect, the reforms ended the protections that the Franciscans offered and potentially opened up Huichol lands to acquisitive settlers and ranchers.[12] Though the Lerdo law did not immediately strip indigenous pueblos of communal landholdings, the threat of such action sparked unrest in the Sierra Madre Occidental.

Land attrition in the 1850s and 1860s was not a new problem for Jalisco's indigenous population, as legal documents from earlier decades attest.[13] Occasionally, local governments would find in favor of Indian communities that contested territorial boundaries, particularly if the land in question had been occupied for a long time without incident. At that point a magistrate would typically call on a surveyor to demarcate land boundaries.[14] Land distribution and the setting of firm boundaries may have seemed like a good idea to the government, and indeed, to some indigenous people. However, these good intentions often had unintended and confusing consequences for Jalisco's native populations. Land became privatized, with all the rights and privileges that private property engendered. Meanwhile, aggressive and acquisitive ranchers cared little for Jalisco's laws and did everything possible to take advantage of Mexico's deepening changes.[15]

Officials attempted to address the rumblings of discontent throughout much of the mountainous areas in Jalisco. Various *jefes políticos* (local political leaders or bosses) received word from Guadalajara that the violence in the region needed to be addressed quickly.[16] Indigenous peoples, incensed at the overreach of area hacendados, began squatting on territories that they believed they rightfully owned. These actions spurred hacendados to action: they began arming themselves and their employees in defense of the disputed territories. The emerging cycle of violence in the highlands of Jalisco frightened citizens and government alike.[17]

To stem the violence, the state government in Guadalajara issued a proclamation to the jefes políticos of various municipalities. The decree asserted that anyone in possession of disputed lands for a year and a day could retain them until the courts could determine rightful ownership; that if there was a dispute over property rights, the parties involved had to go through the appropriate channels; and that political authorities could *not* proceed without consulting judges in such cases. The point of the circular was to make political authorities proactive in preventing violence. Authorities in Colotlán, which was one of the municipios in which many Huichols lived, vowed to abide by the governor's request and circulated it among the jefes políticos in the area.[18] Not long after the creation of such legal stipulations, Ignacio Herrera y Cairo and Miguel Contreras Medellín appointed an attorney to help protect indigenous peoples in civil cases and help prevent their mistreatment.[19]

By the mid-1850s peasants and some indigenous people in western Mexico, furious over the expansion of haciendas, grew tired of ineffective or nonexistent government help. In this increasingly tense atmosphere, Manuel Lozada experienced the same frustrations. He was a mestizo of humble origins who followed relatives to the Hacienda San José de Mojarras, whereupon he became a peon laborer.[20] Lozada resented the ever-expanding, unchecked power of the estates in western Mexico. He despised the growth of haciendas because of his peonage and because of their impact on local peasant and indigenous villages.[21] Lozada and other men of mixed descent who identified closely with their indigenous heritage—such as José María Leyva of Sonora and José María Barrera in Yucatán—realized that the government provided no redress against the avarice of encroaching mestizos. In some ways these mestizo leaders understood the problems of both worlds and worked to address them effectively.[22]

Huichol participation in Lozada's movement, which began in 1857, was minimal, owing in part to their disjointed political culture. As had occurred previously, many Huichols rejected outside interference in their affairs, and taking up arms in a concerted, coordinated effort against intrusion felt alien to them.[23] But some Huichols evidently lent some support: in 1861 Carlos Rivas, a trusted Lozadista general, "influential landowner in Tepic," and ally who acted on behalf of indigenous peoples in Guadalajara, attacked and seized Colotlán, the municipio that contained several Huichol towns.[24] His forces comprised indigenous individuals from Bolaños, Jesús María, San Lucas, and Chimaltitán; Rivas noted that his indigenous soldiers, poorly armed with lances and garrotes, include Huichols with their arrows. The indigenous peoples under Rivas's command successfully overran the small town on the Jalisco-Zacatecas border.[25] Riots broke out near Mezquitic, where rebels either associated with Lozada or had occupied the town under his direct command; once the occupation occurred, townsfolk rose against the local authorities.[26] In an attempt to quell the violence, Benito Juárez and Pedro Ogazón, the governor of Jalisco, placed bounties upon the heads of Lozada and Rivas.[27]

Lozada's men launched all-out assaults against large landholders at the end of 1869 and during the first months of 1870. According to reports, his indigenous supporters were "boisterous" and blinded by "the communistic principles taught by . . . Lozada."[28] Lozada even went so far as to declare Tepic independent on January 1, 1870, though the proclamation was retroactive to Lozada's visit to San Luis on November 22 of the previous year. Lozada's priorities were to establish schools for children on haciendas and in pueblos, protect and support orphans, and guarantee security through the proper administration of justice. Lozada's goal was to ensure that indigenous (and perhaps mestizo) people could "live as one great family of true friends and loyal companions."[29] To reach his goals he sought out the help of an equally ostracized rebel, General Porfirio Díaz, whom Lozada apparently met in 1871. The details of their meeting are mostly obscure, but Lozada did provide Díaz with money and supplies as the rebel general fled north.[30]

Lozada's indigenous rebellion came to an end in 1873. By eight o'clock in the morning of January 28, General Ramón Corona and his force of more than twenty-two hundred arrived at Rancho Mohonera, and scouts advised them of an enemy presence nearby.[31] Lozada and his Cora and Huichol allies attacked from the west and at the outset sustained heavy losses from artillery and rifle fire; by noon, Lozada had regrouped and tried again. He lost all of his artillery, along with scores of men, in his attempts to dislodge Corona from his fortified position. By the next day, Corona turned his forces away from Lozada's decimated troops and back to Guadalajara. Lozada had to retire to his stronghold in the Sierra de Alica and watched bitterly as Tepic—his capital—fell.[32] With roughly four hundred allies left, and most of his indigenous supporters having fled back to the mountains, Lozada was captured by the military on June 17, 1873.[33] He was summarily executed on June 19 at 6:45 a.m.[34] Defiant until the end, his last words were that he had never committed a crime and that everything he did was for the happiness of the people.[35]

Porfirio Díaz took the presidency of Mexico in November 1876 with the promise of returning lands to peasant communities, but it quickly became apparent that he had little intention of upholding that pact.[36] An ardent Liberal on economic matters, Díaz believed that outdated ideas like communal landownership held back both indigenous villages and the nation as a whole.[37] His overtures toward peasants were smokescreens.

A mere seven years into Díaz's regime, the Mexican government passed the 1883 Land Surveying Law, which accomplished several things.[38] First, it authorized *deslindadoras* (surveyors) to examine lands and determine which lands were being used and which were vacant (terrenos baldíos); then, the government partitioned the land into thirds, with the surveying company receiving a portion.[39] This resulted in the removal of indigenous communal lands on a vast scale, doing exponentially more damage than the ley Lerdo had ever accomplished. In nine years companies "surveyed" 38,249,373 hectares.[40] These developments boded ill for community land rights. Note, though, that not all lands were treated or viewed equally: not all lands had access to water, or had good timber resources, or were flat, even spaces that proved to be better for cultivation.[41] Instead of giving up, native groups used their centuries of experiences with outsiders to ensure their survival, working within the confines of Mexican law, not against it, to secure their land. As a result of the national land law, indigenous villagers throughout the Sierra Madre and elsewhere began to feel pressure on a greater scale from outsiders who tried to benefit from "vacant lands."

Between 1887 and 1888 Huichols in the town of Guadalupe Ocotán, part of the municipality of San Andrés, confronted members of the Navarrete family because of their consistent abuse of land boundaries. In August 1887 officials from Guadalupe Ocotán and Tepic met with principal members of the pueblo.[42] Vecinos from the town of Huajimic, in the seventh cantón (Tepic), constantly encroached on Huichol land. Over the next year there were a series of meetings and correspondence between the jefes políticos of Tepic and Colotlán—the state government in Jalisco—and representatives of the indigenous government of San Andrés Cohamiata, which served as the "head town" for Guadalupe Ocotán. Huichols in Guadalupe Ocotán sought land documents for their town, which they hoped would lay out exactly which space belonged to them and what territory around them was open or unclaimed.[43] Guadalupe Ocotán's representative, Catalino Arriaga Albáñez, knew that resolving the matter could be difficult because the Huichol town was near the district of Tepic; resolution would require the cooperation of both state and territorial officials.[44]

The experiences faced by the Huichol leaders in Guadalupe Ocotán illustrated the many problems that the Huichols had, not only with their non-Indian neighbors, but also with Mexican officials. Arriaga Albáñez argued that Guadalupe Ocotán had belonged to Colotlán, not Tepic, and he implored someone to save the Huichols from the predatory behavior of the Navarrete family. By February 1888 the offending members of the Navarrete family—Candelario, Luis Esteban, Longinos, and Anselmo—learned that they would be punished by authorities if they continued to antagonize Guadalupe Ocotán's citizens.[45] Though the final outcome of this case remains obscure, what it suggests is that the Huichols successfully negotiated the realm of regional governments to defend their own territory.

A few months later another land dispute came to the attention of Jalisciense officials, partly because of the Porfirian land policies. Don Vicente Medrano, from the small municipio of Mezquitic, coveted what he believed were vacant lands surrounding the Huichol pueblo of Nostic. The jefe político in Mezquitic, Enrique Pérez Rubio, sent the case to his superiors in the capital, arguing that such matters needed to be handled by federal authorities.[46] The political boss suggested that he had no jurisdiction to supervise the case, particularly because it called attention to recent federal legislation. Officials in Guadalajara, however, felt that the aggrieved parties could work through the legal system and come to an agreeable conclusion. So, instead of further delaying the matter, authorities determined that Medrano might receive some of the territory in question. Whether Medrano ever resolved his case against the pueblo of Nostic is unknown, nor is it possible to determine how much land, if any, he received. What is certain is that lawsuits such as these drew the attention of jefes políticos on a somewhat regular basis, illustrating the heated atmosphere that enveloped the Sierra in the late 1880s.

Not every instance of disputed lands in the Huichol Sierra pitted indigenous villagers against mestizo outsiders. Intertown rivalries often boiled over as a result of land encroachment or conflicts over resources. Tensions like these erupted periodically during the mid-1870s as, for example, when an individual named Zenón Hernández, assisted by men from Soledad Tenzompa and San Nicolás, murdered five Huichols and stole thirteen mules.[47] Without definitive ethnic identities for the men involved, it appeared as though Huichols killed other Huichols in this instance, as Soledad Tenzompa had traditionally been considered a Huichol town. Such pressures from without had the ability to either unite or divide; in this case, a divide-and-conquer strategy appeared to be the motive of Hernández.

The lack of political solidarity became even more apparent, however, during the Díaz regime when land pressures began to affect intertown relationships.[48] Porfirio Guevara, a trader from the Huichol pueblo of San Sebastián, complained to government officials that other Huichols living in

San Andrés and Santa Catarina constantly invaded San Sebastián's lands, causing unrest among the three towns.[49] The jefe político of Colotlán called in the leaders of each town so that they could find a solution. The town borders had to be addressed satisfactorily because attacks resulting from intracommunity disagreements were proving too disruptive.[50] Unfortunately, it was unlikely that any one government official would be able to stop the cycles of violence. The Huichols of Santa Catarina allegedly had been committing abuses against those of San Sebastián for some time, including stealing lands in the previous year. In response, by the end of May 1888, the Mezquitic's jefe político pacified the Huichols in the aforementioned towns by agreeing to determine town boundaries.[51] Additionally, San Sebastián would receive a school that Guevara would run as thanks for his service.

What peace had been established between the three principal Huichol towns seldom lasted, in part because of tensions between the towns themselves and between the towns and their longstanding enemy, the hacienda San Antonio de Padua.[52] Serious friction typically flared and then died down in a matter of days or weeks. In October 1888 some forty-five men from Tenzompa signed a petition imploring the government to delineate firm boundaries between the Huichol towns and nearby haciendas. They claimed that they had respected the boundaries between their town and the hacienda San Antonio de Padua, but time and again the hacendado, don Benigno Soto, extended his property over the boundaries.[53] Land grabs such as these had triggered the Lozada Rebellion and the poverty that resulted from land attrition. They knew how to use the memory of the Lozada Rebellion to their own benefit. When haciendas expanded onto Indian lands, Huichol towns in turn frequently usurped the lands of their neighbors. This subsequently created strife between San Andrés and Santa Catarina.

Though the situation between the Huichols and hacienda San Antonio de Padua would not be handled to the Huichols' satisfaction, their interpueblo hostilities drew the attention of at least one person responsible for land measurement. In November 1888 the governor of Jalisco, General Ramón Corona, sent his brother Rosendo Corona from Mezquitic to the Huichol Sierra to survey their lands.[54] The state engineer did not intend to demarcate the San Andrés-Santa Catarina boundaries in order to auction the lands; instead, both Coronas hoped to settle the discord.[55] Rosendo Corona also wanted to ensure that Huichol lands would be respected and not simply be declared vacant.

The Corona brothers oversaw a state in turmoil, not only because indigenous groups fought among themselves and with outsiders, but also because the state of Jalisco experienced much growth over the course of the early Porfirian period. What Rosendo Corona saw after about a month in the Sierra led him to believe that serious change needed to be implemented. Corona had some sympathy for native communities, and there were those in local and state office who, while perhaps not sharing his sensitivities, certainly did not want a state of war erupting in Jalisco between jealous Indian villagers. The surveyors' presence generated considerable anxiety since indigenous towns now knew they needed the legal protection of a title to safeguard their territory.[56] Possessing titles would also help the pueblos guarantee protection against encroaching haciendas, though Corona was decidedly less concerned about this, so long as the hacienda property was in Jalisco and not Zacatecas.[57] Nostic, Tenzompa, and unnamed pueblos that fell under the jurisdiction of Mezquitic did, in fact, have land titles on record, and this helped in two ways. First, it assisted Corona in setting boundary limitations; second, a local Land Commission that had been set up in the early 1870s to protect indigenous resources near Huejucar could finally exert some authority in the region. The Land Commission ensured that timber and firewood would be defended from theft by nonindigenous parties, and officials could determine where the timber existed based upon extant documentation.[58] The jefe político of the eighth cantón named several men to the position of *guardamonte* (warden or ranger), assigning them to protect the mountain and grasslands and only allowing firewood to be cut by authorized individuals. This helped maintain some civility between the Huichol towns, though relations with haciendas remained testy and suspicious at best.

Regardless of finite boundaries established by state authorities, the Huichols still faced problems with neighboring haciendas, which expanded with impunity throughout the Porfiriato. The owners of haciendas San Antonio de Padua, Hipazote, and San Juan Capistrano periodically antagonized Huichol villagers by establishing ranchos on Indian lands, stealing supplies, and generally harassing people with no regard for established town boundaries.[59] Time and again, Huichol *principales* (indigenous town leaders) begged the state to send out someone on their behalf, but those authorities had little incentive to side with indigenous demands. Rather than physically fight battles, which Huichols knew from their own and others' experiences would not serve them well, they now sought legal means to resolve their troubles. In 1889 Huichol leaders from San Andrés asked F. Castillo Ramos and Salvador Correa y Chacon to intercede with state officials because don Soto, proprietor of San Antonio de Padua in Zacatecas, built a rancho within the boundaries of their town.[60] It is unlikely that don Soto or any other hacendado was ever seriously reproached or punished by the state for encroaching upon Indian lands. This was particularly true of haciendas that fell completely within the boundaries of Jalisco; Soto's hacienda required negotiations with Zacatecas that nobody seemed willing to address.

By the end of the 1880s the three principal Huichol towns fought among themselves and with their Mexican neighbors on bordering haciendas. Oddly enough, however, they rarely experienced troubles with other indigenous groups, despite the fact that the Coras lived quite close to their western limits. The Huichols and Coras occasionally banded together against perceived mutual threats, as was the case when some Huichol fighters joined with the Cora Lozada; at other times, the elusive and divided Huichols could not be counted on. As land pressures threatened indigenous livelihoods throughout northern and western Jalisco, even former allies could end up enemies, and such enmity could last decades. A Cora elder remarked that the Huichols brought their problems upon themselves because "the Huichol is like a guacamayo, a parrot with brilliant plumage who makes a loud squawk and attracts the attention of all," while the Cora "is like a little sparrow hawk, with dull feathers and little sound and is seldom noticed."[61] This particular man's comment is interesting; in general, the Huichols' "squawks" seemed to help protect their lands.

In December 1889 a tenuous peace between Huichols in San Andrés and Coras in San Juan Peyotán broke down, at which point the jefe político of Tepic and the justice of the peace of San Juan Peyotán petitioned Jalisco's governor to intervene on their behalf. Rather than working with the Huichols directly, the governor of Jalisco implored the jefe político of Colotlán to bring San Andrés in line.[62] Both towns asserted their rights to the property, and each claimed to have older titles to the land (though neither actually produced anything of worth). The jefes políticos of both Tepic and Colotlán feared violence. The presence of increasing numbers of outsiders began to put pressure on indigenous villages and their residents throughout the Sierra. Díaz had sent soldiers to the region, which only heightened tensions.[63] Ultimately, the jefes políticos of both Colotlán and Tepic reached an agreement that fixed the boundaries between San Andrés and San Juan Peyotán, but unfortunately, the Coras ended up as losers in the deal. However, such rumblings in the Sierra caught the attention not only of state officials in Guadalajara yet again, but also of President Díaz in Mexico City.

Normally, by the time Díaz learned of problems in the rural areas of Mexico, the situation had escalated out of control, and such was the case of the Huichols in November 1889. In general, Díaz paid little attention to the plight of indigenous peoples because it was his land law that caused most of the strife. Additionally, politicians and administrators only reported bad news to the president when things became unmanageable at the local level. Occasionally, though, Díaz would intervene on behalf of peasant villages or indigenous towns when land issues had the potential to become explosive. In November 1889 he urged the director of Mezquitic, Antonio de la Cruz, to listen to the aggrieved parties and bring the troubles to a happy conclusion. The government of Mezquitic had the full support of the federal government, according to the memo; each Huichol town should have its lands measured, and originals were to be forwarded to the national magistrate in Mexico

City. This, Díaz hoped, would quell the troubles with the aggravated native population and bring the matter to a close.[64]

Díaz was inconsistent in his treatment of native peoples. This is because he believed they were a negligible factor politically, socially, and economically; positivist ideology, so prevalent in late-nineteenth-century thought, instructed that native peoples blocked national progress.[65] Just as Díaz demanded that authorities in Colotlán and Mezquitic settle disputes between native villages, he ignored the plight of the Indian town versus the hacienda, a much more common problem in northern Jalisco. Though the 1880s had ended on a more hopeful note for them, the Huichols of San Andrés faced troubles with the San Juan Capistrano hacienda as the new decade dawned. Máximo Villa, the commander of public safety in San Andrés, complained that his townsfolk could not plant their fields without being harassed by both the administrators and workers of San Juan Capistrano. The political director of Mezquitic hoped that Señor Castillo Ramos, the jefe político of Colotlán, could provide him with some advice; little was forthcoming.[66]

Two years later, in 1892, a new jefe político in Mezquitic took matters into his own hands. Tired of the constant fighting in his own district and in neighboring Colotlán, Sóstenes Rodríguez sought the support of the governor of Tuxpan in quelling the violence. Rodríguez believed that the indigenous leaders of Santa Catarina, San Andrés, San Sebastián, Tuxpan, and Guadalupe Ocotán needed to take responsibility for the public safety in their respective towns. Any crimes committed in their domains should be the responsibility of the governor, and he must apprehend the suspects and submit the perpetrator for further justice.[67] Native leaders could count on the full support of the state in pursuing criminals to keep the peace. For much time the newfound powers of the Huichol village authorities did appear to cut down on violence, strife, and intercommunity tension. By the early 1890s, then, Rodríguez's solution to local problems pacified the eighth cantón.

Liberal ideologies that emerged in the 1850s had done so as part of a philosophical and logistical debate about Mexico's native populations. Along with physical battles that indigenous peoples fought, they faced an ideological war in Mexico that linked land, modernization, and civilized life together. Elites in Mexico City and Guadalajara decried the misery of the lower classes and their supposedly negative impacts on the larger Mexican society. In *La voz de alianza*, the official newspaper of the Liberal party in Mexico, an editorial suggested that efforts among the rich to aid the poor would prove fruitless if indigenous peoples (and nonindigenous peasants) "chose" to remain "ignorant."[68] Like *La voz de alianza*, other newspapers asserted that a so-called cultural backwardness, in addition to communal lands, helped the native peoples resist civilization.[69]

A decade later "Mexican philologist Francisco Pimentel called Indians an 'enemy' of the other inhabitants of Mexico and suggested European immigration and racial mixing as an answer to the problem of the indigenous peoples."[70] While Pimentel held an extreme view of Mexico's indigenous populations during the 1860s, he influenced a cadre of like-minded men in later decades.[71] The so-called "Indian problem" necessitated influence from the government and, in some instances, indigenous peoples reacted to that increased ideological and physical presence of the state.[72]

An editorial written in 1865 in *El Imperio* suggested that Tepic's "uncivilized past" caused its problems. Yet at the same time, elites in the area and elsewhere glorified the ancient societies being dug up through archaeological efforts. Mexican scholars and politicians believed that this long-dead past had a firm grasp on indigenous peoples in the nineteenth century, preventing their advancement toward civilization.[73] The Mexican nation in general, and Tepic in particular, would be unable to shake its myriad problems until its citizens accepted modernization.[74]

Observers watching developments in Nayarit after the violence had died down placed much of the blame for the issues in Tepic squarely on the shoulders of indigenous villagers. Twenty-seven years of intermittent warfare, in addition to rough terrain and Tepic's distance from Guadalajara and Mexico City, created problems in governance. Newspaper reports and editorials held the Huichols, Coras, and Tepehuans in the area responsible for the strife.[75] While most reporters did not necessarily suggest that Indians were the sole cause of the destruction, critics argued that because indigenous people were essentially unable (or unwilling) to think for themselves, they were more likely to be swept up by the likes of Lozada or to rebel, as in the case of Yaquis and Mayas. One writer offered history as a reason for the continued violence: Nayarit had been a place of chaos since the time of colonial rule. In his telling, Nayarit was too distinct geographically and too distant to be successfully ruled by Jalisco (or Mexico City for that matter), and decades of military violence among the state, indigenous groups, and glory-seeking individuals proved this viewpoint.[76]

Some editorials offered solutions to the "Indian problem," suggesting that the gaze be turned north toward the United States. One anonymous author believed that religion might help with the "*diablos colorados*" (red devils) of the seventh cantón, because missionary programs in the United States had met with some success.[77] It was a common belief in Mexico that without the guiding principles of priests, Indians would quickly revert to savagery.[78] This had been a concern of officials in the 1850s, as noted in correspondence between the governor of Jalisco and the archbishop of Guadalajara. The two lamented the lack of missionaries willing and able to help "forgotten" groups like the Huichols.[79] In reality, however, the anonymous author of the editorial "*La cuestión de Tepic*" (the Tepic Question) did not have the interests of Tepic's indigenous populations in mind. Instead, he believed peaceful relations with Indians were a means to soothe tensions between Mexican citizens in the seventh cantón and the state government based in Jalisco.

The issue of Mexico's indigenous peoples deserved some careful scrutiny, considering that more than 3.7 million Mexicans—or about 38 percent of the population at the time— considered themselves, or more likely were assumed to be, Indian.[80] Increasingly, some Mexicans argued that their nation failed to progress because of the indigenous population; they thought they should simply be wiped out, a policy implemented in Sonora against the Yaquis.[81] Still others took a more "benevolent" approach, believing that by giving indigenous villagers land and tutoring, they might be encouraged to abandon their traditions and customs. Fortunately, of all these policies, education won out, and throughout Mexico schools opened on haciendas for adults and in towns and cities for children.[82] During his tenure as governor of Jalisco, Ramón Corona and his successor, Miguel Ahumada, designed a predictably stillborn program to bring indigenous youths in, educate them, and send them back to teach their people Spanish. The desired effects would be threefold: first, indigenous people would learn Spanish; second, some would receive beneficial jobs; and finally, having indigenous people speaking Spanish would cut down on abuses by translators.[83] Still, the Porfirian education system met with limited success among indigenous peoples because of underfunding, poor administration and teaching, and ultimately racism toward native pupils.

Reformers made other attempts to "improve" the lives of Mexican Indians, and the Huichols did not escape such efforts. For instance, in Colotlán in 1888, a town law required the Huichols to dress "properly." Not wearing appropriate clothing could result in arrest and fines until the person rectified the situation by finding the proper pants.[84] There is no evidence, however, of some sartorial revolution, or that any Huichols received fines for not wearing the proper attire (and in fact, the Huichols still dress in a distinctive, wholly indigenous manner). All indigenous people, regardless of how they felt about their neighbors, had to abide by new laws created by the ruling mestizos if they wanted to trade in town. Huichol men typically *did* wear pants, but occasionally their outfits consisted only of a long tunic with a belt at the waist. Forcing Huichols to dress like mestizos was an attempt to eliminate traditional forms of clothing linked intrinsically to Huichol culture. Reformers argued that these were necessary measures to preserve sanitation, something not lost on nonindigenous Mexicans, particularly in the wake of a typhus outbreak in 1892. Four years later it became a fundamental part of national Indian policy to "*empantalonar*" (colloquial: to clothe) indigenous peoples throughout Mexico. Nonindigenous Mexicans became almost frenzied in their obsession about Indian clothing; others, however, felt that it was improper to fine such poverty-stricken people for simply wearing their traditional clothing.[85]

The dawn of the twentieth century did not bring new hope for the Huichols; rather, it only highlighted problems that had not gone away. Once again, leaders of San Andrés desperately sought land titles to protect their land from marauding vecinos and unscrupulous surveying companies. The bishop of Zacatecas, however, disagreed with reports about the misery of the Sierra. During a visit he observed that the economic system of the frontier zone between Zacatecas and Jalisco was continually improving and that the indigenous villagers should begin to see benefits from the assistance of teachers, money, and improved farming techniques.[86] Yet it is doubtful that despite schools and cash, San Andrés's Huichols wished to accept surveyors stealing their lands. The leadership in San Andrés wrote to officials in Guadalajara, asking for a copy of their land title, which they knew (or at least believed) could be located in the National Archives.[87] The Huichols in San Andrés and elsewhere feared that left unchecked, surveying companies and haciendas would turn their towns into private property, in much the same way that they had with Santa Catarina. A school for children was only beneficial if the children could return home to sacred lands that were *not* part of a hacienda.[88]

The last quarter of the nineteenth century also brought misfortune in other ways. Disease and economic ebbs and flows affected indigenous and mestizo alike. Disease killed many Huichols in Guadalupe Ocotán in the aforementioned typhoid epidemic of 1892; those who survived the epidemic were frequently too ill to farm or support their families. Thus starvation also took its toll on Indian survivors. Corn, not available in Guadalupe Ocotán, could be purchased in Tepic, but at prohibitive prices; survivors were often too weak to make what is normally considered to be a mundane journey for the Huichols. To make matters worse, a temple burned down, and many thought that the suffering they experienced came directly from God.[89] Fewer than ten years later, soil exhaustion also brought about starvation; claiming that the Huichols did not make necessary land improvements, mestizo town leaders blamed the local native population for the agricultural misfortunes.[90] Despite periodic epidemics and episodes of starvation, the late-nineteenth century saw a marked improvement in the economy, which benefited all of Jalisco's residents, Indian and mestizo alike.

The Porfiriato was an unsettling period for the Huichols. They lived their lives in conflict and at peace with their Huichol neighbors, practicing their syncretic religion, speaking their native language, and avoiding mestizos unless it was necessary to seek them out. The Porfiriato changed this, but not in such a way that the Huichols themselves became "Hispanicized." Land issues fragmented intercommunity ties but created new ones at the same time. The Huichols learned how to function within the confines of the Mexican justice system when demanding titles to their land to protect them from deslindadoras. They adapted, adjusted, and yet, as we will see, maintained a deep connection with their cultural beliefs that had not been erased by shifting boundaries.

5

Foreign Scholars as Tools of Resistance

By 1900 Huichols living in Santa Catarina had grown weary of outsiders over the previous decades. Land speculators, priests, and even fellow Huichols created problems for them, and they seemed to grow increasingly insular. This was their defense mechanism, to build a figurative wall between themselves and others, shutting out what threatened their existence. When Carl Lumholtz traveled through the Sierra, rumors swirled about him, his motives, and the dangers he faced. Huichol leaders in Santa Catarina tried to ward off the Norwegian botanist; Lumholtz said that he was "warned that the alcalde of Santa Catarina, the capital, threatened to take my life should I venture into his presence."[1] The Huichols in Santa Catarina eventually relented and welcomed him, once they realized that Lumholtz posed little danger.

The increased presence of mestizos, land speculators, and priests over the previous half-century forced the Huichols' hands. Previously reticent toward foreigners, Huichols (especially those living in San Andrés and to some extent in Santa Catarina) eventually appreciated the purposes that outsiders could serve. Mexican lawyers appointed to help indigenous villagers might prove useful in protecting lands in the legal arena, for instance. However, in the last decade of the nineteenth century, the search for "wild" native peoples in Mexico drew academic explorers to western Mexico to study "tribal peoples." These inquisitive scholars forced Huichols to adapt to outsiders living among them, asking countless probing questions about their life, society, and culture. Why were some Huichols willing to accept such prolonged intrusions into their lives? Why did the Huichols share such intimate details about their religious culture? What purpose did it serve to adapt to the presence of these foreigners?

Three European researchers traveled to the Huichol Sierra in the 1890s and early 1900s. Carl Lumholtz (b. 1851) visited the Huichols on two separate occasions, in 1895–96, and then again in 1898. His observations and collections provide modern-day scholars with unique insights into many aspects of Huichol life, culture, and history. Lumholtz's contemporary, Léon Diguet (b. 1859), traveled extensively in western and northwestern Mexico; Diguet published his observations in 1898, while Lumholtz was still in Huichol country. Diguet's work emphasized the importance of peyote to Huichol religious life. Influenced by Diguet and Lumholtz, Prussian scholar Konrad Theodor Preuss (b. 1869) studied and recorded Huichol religious songs and customs in 1905. As a result of the work carried out by Lumholtz, Diguet, and Preuss, we now know that the Huichols had created complex and intricate societies that had existed for centuries and that had survived nearly two decades of Porfirian modernization that swept Mexico.[2]

As we have seen previously, some Huichols accepted foreigners when it served a purpose for them, thus demonstrating a nuanced adaptation to the world that threatened to envelop them. For the Huichols, Lumholtz, Diguet, and Preuss were not agents of the state or the church; they brought with them no land surveying equipment, no crosses for conversion. In short, it appears as though the Huichols did not feel threatened by these ethnographers and perhaps concluded that the foreign scholars' presence could be beneficial in some way. Thus this chapter will show an emerging tension among the Huichols between their typical aloofness toward outsiders and a growing curiosity about the outside world. At the same time, looking at the Huichols' interactions with ethnographers will offer a deeper understanding of Huichol cultural practices.

Huichol attitudes toward traveling European scholars were curious and presented some challenges for both indigenous and European alike. In spring 1895 Lumholtz arrived in the Sierra Madre Occidental mountains and first encountered the Coras, who were—like the Huichols—fearful of strangers.[3] The Coras also had grievances with their neighbors, complaining "that the Huichol tried to keep clouds from reaching the Cora country by placing small back shields on the roads . . . to frighten clouds back and prevent them from leaving the Huichol territory."[4] Understandably, the Coras detested Huichol manipulation of the weather, which stood to prevent the life-giving rains from soaking Cora lands. However, despite a fear of outsiders and anger at their neighbors, some Coras served as porters into Huichol country.

Meanwhile, the Huichols had heard rumors about a traveling party of strangers heading their way and reacted in a historically typical way: they attempted to avoid contact with Lumholtz. Apparently, locals had spread rumors that the European was dangerous, and "three civilized Indians had even been planning to kill" Lumholtz, as well as his Mexican guides and Cora porter.[5] A Mexican worker traveling with Lumholtz declared that "the Huichols were bad; they were assassins and would kill us [the traveling party] all."[6] Near the town of Santa Catarina, some Huichol leaders encountered the Lumholtz party; those he met were immediately suspicious of his intentions and, as the party approached the town, the Huichols abandoned their homes and fled into the nearby woods.[7]

The Huichols initially feared Lumholtz as terrifying stories spread throughout the area that a strange man traveled in the area, eating women and children, whom he had "killed by the camera."[8] The Huichols also heard a frightening story, told to them by a "stupid and superstitious Mexican trader," that Lumholtz "was fattening people in order to kill and eat them" and that he "used the blood for dying [*sic*] cotton cloth."[9] It was fairly common for stories such as these to spread, and the originators might have been local merchants who feared any threats to their bottom line. Bearing in mind the terrifying stories that swirled around Lumholtz and the Huichols' tendency to distrust outsiders in general, it is no wonder that they ran away when he approached. Eventually, the Huichols in Santa Catarina sufficiently warmed up to the group and begrudgingly allowed the Lumholtz party to approach, though with caution. This shift is notable, as it demonstrates behavior that had become more common within some Huichol communities over the late nineteenth century: adaptation to external threats. They would not, however, accommodate Lumholtz in all manner of his scientific ventures.

The Huichols humored the scientific work of their new visitors except when the studies included disturbing the dead. Museum curators in the United States implored the Lumholtz party to "get into as many caves as possible and dig thoroughly" for skulls and skeletons.[10] The Huichols strongly discouraged such digging expeditions, as they still worshipped their ancestors, whom they placed in sacred caves.[11] This behavior had carried over at least from colonial times (and was likely much older), as Spanish priests like Padre Arglegui noted in the eighteenth century and Fray Buenaventura described in the nineteenth.[12] Lumholtz's patrons at the Museum of Natural History wanted skeletons to improve their scientific collections that in theory would contribute to the understanding of racial difference.[13] But he risked alienating his indigenous subjects. Digging among the dead would have been highly taboo. In fact, Huichols near Mezquitic had warned Lumholtz "not to have anything to do with their dead."[14] Lumholtz ignored their counsel: while digging, he found a "decayed skeleton . . . with it, many gold objects."[15] At any rate, instead of crates full of skeletons, Lumholtz took extensive photographs and collected cultural artifacts to satisfy his bosses in New York.

The Huichols grudgingly accepted Catholic priests in their environs, as ethnographers and Franciscan friars had noted. Two priests lived in the region at the beginning of the twentieth century, "one in San Andrés and one in San Sebastián," and according to Preuss, the Catholic missionaries had little effect on their Huichol charges.[16] The priests frequently complained that they treated churches like they did their caligüeys, a common grievance levied against the Huichols in centuries and decades past. The Huichols "devote a truly incredible part of their lives to them and . . . are proud of this."[17] The focal point of Huichol life was their religion, the sacred inextricably interwoven into the mundane activities of daily life, which Preuss witnessed through ceremony.

Huichol religion blurred the lines between the spiritual and secular. Songs that lasted hours implored the gods to continue the seasonal rains.[18] Even by the 1890s Catholicism played little part in the Huichols' lives; instead, they believed that humans lived in a precarious world, at the mercy of mercurial Huichol deities who must be appeased.[19] Western religious thought had not influenced the Huichols much at all; they did not know what Protestants were, and even by the late 1890s and early 1900s, it remained uncommon for priests to visit the area.[20] What church buildings existed had fallen into ruin and "the impress made on their religion [by Catholicism] was exceedingly slight."[21] The Huichols did observe certain Catholic feasts, such as Holy Week and Christmas, but by and large their traditional religious practices were much more common and important to them.

Huichols living in Santa Catarina appeared to be the most unchanged in terms of their religious culture. In fact, in this village, inhabitants demonstrated a "devotion to their gods" that seemed most fervent to outside observers; indeed, Lumholtz noted that the Huichols' religious dedication was a lifelong vocation.[22] Santa Catarina is home to the Huichol god of fire, Teakata; the largest and most important temple dedicated to him is there. From this location peyoteros paid homage before beginning their annual pilgrimage. Santa Catarina, or more specifically the temple of the god of fire, "is in the middle of the Huichol country, or from the Huichol point of view, in the middle of the world."[23] Parents bathed their newborn infants in springs near caves in Santa Catarina, and the temple nearby contained a small volcanic-rock idol dedicated to the gods of fire. While visiting Santa Catarina, and specifically Teakata, a Huichol informed Lumholtz that many gods of fire existed, "just as with the saints" and all other Huichol deities.[24]

A central part of Huichol spirituality was the ritual cycle, which provided order for the year. The consumption of peyote, and its relation to deer and corn, gave the Huichols a framework for harvest time, the hunt, and the peyote pilgrimage.[25] The Huichols treated corn and peyote similarly because corn nourished the body as peyote sustained the soul.[26] The peyote hunt commenced once the October corn festival ended. This festival marked the termination of the dry season and roughly coincided with the harvest. As harvesting activities occurred, those undertaking the pilgrimage began to prepare for their arduous trek.[27]

The Huichols explained the basis for peyote in their religion and the importance of the pilgrimage to their annual cycle. To obtain the small cactus, a strenuous pilgrimage first took place that recreated an important event that occurred in the distant past.[28] According to Huichol oral history, long ago Kauyaumari, the first mara'akame and one of the principal Huichol ancestors, led his followers on a trek in the wilderness. During their expedition they came under the attack of neighboring, warlike peoples.[29] While fighting, these neighboring enemies destroyed all of the goods used to prepare food and store water. Kauyaumari prayed, and because he had faith, the gods took pity on him and his people, providing them with peyote, which would alleviate hunger and thirst. In reverence, modern Huichols reenact the sacred journey to Wirikuta, where Kauyaumari obtained peyote for the first time.[30] His religious convictions determined the behaviors to which all subsequent mara'akate adhered when making pilgrimages. Diguet's observations helped to contextualize the importance of the hunt at the time he recorded them. His subjects made it clear that the Huichols must make the pilgrimage, as opposed to obtaining peyote from a third party. Instead, as Diguet's subjects pointed out, Huichol men lovingly carried out the pilgrimage as part of sacred obligations to their deities, which included maize and deer gods.

In the 1890s the Huichols did not permit outsiders to take the peyote pilgrimage to Wirikuta. As a result, visitors had only been able to document the predeparture preparations. Lumholtz noted that the trip lasted roughly forty-three days and began in October or November. "Delegations are sent from each of the main temples," he wrote, and one "singer" who represented Grandfather Fire, led the peyoteros. "Grandfather Fire" was the only person permitted to light fires along the trail, as it was he who carried with him the sacred flame from the temple in Santa Catarina. Tobacco pouches and squirrel tails were important parts of the ritual dress. While in camp, Huichol leaders who had not traveled with the peyoteros kept a record of the journey on pieces of knotted fiber; in this way, the rest of the villagers would be able to know when to begin preparations to mark the returning party. Finally, women whose husbands sought peyote had to observe similar restrictive behavior: "until the feast of *hikuli* (Hu: peyote) is given, which may be four months [from the time of initial departure], neither party washes except on certain occasions and then only with water from hikuli country [i.e., Real de Catorce]. They also fast much and eat no salt and are bound to observe strict continence [abstinence]."[31] Once the peyote seekers returned—and they were easily spotted "by the happy smile on their faces and the peculiar glare in their eyes"—a welcoming festival commenced in which the villagers treated the peyoteros like gods and sang and danced throughout the night.[32]

The Huichols also elaborated on the importance of the pilgrimage to the landscape of their homelands. They explained to Diguet that Tamatsi Maxa Kwaxi, a powerful deer deity, gave detailed instructions to Kauyaumari as to how to carry out the annual pilgrimage, including locations in the Huichol sacred landscape that pilgrims must visit.[33] Diguet listed the towns that the devotees passed through and their relevance to Huichol mytho-history. The journey to Real de Catorce took between ten and twelve days at the turn of the century, and the Huichol shamans typically led the rest of the group, singing songs and praying along the way. In each town or rancho, the peyoteros stopped and offered prayers because all of these places were (and still are) either significant stops on the original peyote trail or hold some importance to the Huichol sacred landscape.[34] About halfway through the trip, within five days from reaching the sacred mountain Re'unar (or El Quemado in San Luis Potosí), all participants began a rigorous fast. The peyoteros dedicated these five days to Kauyaumari, to commemorate his suffering in the ancient past and to prepare themselves for the consumption of their sacred deity.

This story helps explain the symbolism that required the Huichols to adhere strictly to the ancient guidelines. The cycle of deer, corn, and peyote was an ancient tradition that the Huichols believed had been passed down by Tamatsi Maxa Kwaxi and Kauyaumari. It was not a cult or even a trinity, as Lumholtz had called it, though he too acknowledged the connections between the three parts; this trio of entities was a core component of Huichol cosmology.[35] Taken together, this cycle illustrated two critical aspects of Huichol spirituality: first, that everything in the natural, physical world had a sacred function for the Huichols, and mundane items possessed supernatural purposes; and second, that peyote as a deity held deep religious meaning for the Huichols that helped keep them intrinsically tied to their ancient ways and their ancestral homelands. A strong sense of patriotism of sorts has motivated the Huichols to maintain this pilgrimage to the "original ceremonial house."[36]

The deer-corn-peyote cycle made up an important part of the Huichol religious songs that Preuss recorded at the beginning of the twentieth century. Though Preuss wrote about the importance of corn in its ritual and mundane senses separately (as Lumholtz also had done), he understood that all three aspects were integral parts of Huichol symbolism. For instance, while observing the prepilgrimage rituals, Preuss recorded a song that elaborated on this idea:

> It is the sacred deer hunt of the gods that is here reenacted on the peyote hunt, and this deer hunt in the land of peyote, the place where the sun comes up [Wirikuta], is repeated again in different forms during the ritual of the toasting of the maize in March, and again in June during the Haxári kuáixa ritual, the eating of the coarse maize. People representing deer are chased into noose traps . . . or the Sun god Tayáu, Our Father, and a variation of the fire god Tatusí Maxa Kwaxí, Great-Grandfather Deer Tail, track the deer impersonator to Paríyakutsiyé, the place of the rising Sun. [37]

This ceremony and others like it intrigued Preuss and led him to the conclusion that little had changed within the Huichol religious mythology, despite contact with Spaniards since the 1720s.[38] While his belief is an overstatement, Huichol religious practices were strong and reasonably consistent, considering Lumholtz's and Diguet's fieldwork verified different components of the same stories.

Preuss discovered that Huichol religious songs, which often involved incantations to various deities, could be quite lengthy; Huichol chants continued "all through the night, and another the whole following day, if the ceremony lasts that long . . . to understand the meaning always requires the complete text. In this way the chants become truly monstrous in length."[39] He discovered that certain gods or divine beings figured prominently in Huichol songs, including the fire god Tatewarí and Kauyaumari.[40] Preuss realized that the Huichols placed religion squarely at the center of their lives: their songs explained the religious significance of mundane objects, the natural world, and the importance of the spiritual universe that surrounded all Huichols living in the Sierra. This verified what Lumholtz and Diguet had observed and what long-dead Franciscans had noted but failed to understand. This characteristic of Huichols' society might explain why they showed such a long-lasting resistance to outside forces, but accepted relatively quickly, if cautiously, the ethnographers' presence.

Huichol society exhibited considerable complexity in terms of the judicial system, community hierarchy, and social norms and relations among the towns themselves. At the turn of the twentieth century four towns dominated the Huichol zone: Santa Catarina, San Andrés, San Sebastián, and Guadalupe Ocotán, though many Huichols lived in countless tiny pueblos in the immediate environs (see map 5). Huichol political culture mixed religion and secular rule, though theoretically "this condition of affairs" was "contrary to the laws of the republic" at the time. Each Huichol town had an alcalde, a *gobernador* (governor), a captain, and messengers in addition to *alguaciles* (bailiffs) and *mayordomos* (administrators, but in this case, religious officeholders in charge of caring for the saints).[41] At some point in the past women held prestigious political offices; the only community jobs that women could hold at the end of the nineteenth century were as *tenanches*, or women who cleaned and kept up the churches.[42] The Mexican courts handled serious crimes, such as murder, while Huichol judges adjudicated minor community issues, mostly nonviolent. If land troubles became serious, such problems required the mediation of jefe político in Colotlán or Mezquitic.[43] In the nearly two centuries since their conquest by the Spanish, the Huichols had adapted to a western legal and civil system of governance, yet one that served their communities well.

Civil-religious authorities, who were the only people to wield authority before the arrival of the Spanish, worked to maintain order.[44] A village hierarchy apparently existed, split between the nobility and the people, though this appeared less rigid than in more highly stratified cultures. As with every other aspect of Huichol life, oral history explained the dichotomy: according to Diguet, Tamatsi Maxa Kwaxi determined that there should be a nobility who received the names of certain gods and who were then responsible for electing civil-religious authorities every five years. Once chosen, elders then chose the new authorities.[45]

Though Huichol towns had more or less the same political structure, in addition to autonomy, they tended toward localism. Rivalries emerged as a result of political disunity. Men who might have held some sway over affairs in San Sebastián, for instance, "had no influence in San Andrés," as was the case with a man named Maximino whom Lumholtz had hired.[46] This identity, which made one simultaneously Huichol but also primarily a member of a particular town, led to the "clannish" behavior that Lumholtz had commented on. Like Yucatec Maya speakers who rejected overarching ethnic labels, the Huichols that the ethnographers met exhibited distinct political and personal attitudes, only banding together with other Huichols when it suited them.[47]

Such a fierce sense of local identity often caused boundary disputes, particularly between the towns of San Andrés and Santa Catarina. Lumholtz attributed these problems to village personalities that prevented ethnic unity on a daily basis. In fact, intercommunity animosity could become so hostile that Lumholtz remarked "it is not too much to say that no one district would much care if the 'neighbours' [nonindigenous Mexicans] were to gobble up all the rest of the tribe's domain so long as its own particular district remained intact."[48] However, at other times, as documentary evidence illustrates, Lumholtz did not always experience the times of ethnic harmony that did exist among the Huichols.

Diguet offered a possible explanation of the disunity and even disharmony that occurred among the Huichols. He suggested that many Huichols might relate with their neighbors only during certain times of the year to practice their religion. Over time, this created slight differences in customs and dialects between the districts. Additionally, prolonged contact between Huichols and Spaniards/Mexicans created degrees of changes, depending upon one's location. For instance, the inhabitants of San Andrés were more open to the Spanish and to missionizing by Christians.[49] On the other hand, residents of Santa Catarina developed a reputation for reticence to any sort of outside interference or influence, according to both Lumholtz and Diguet (as well as modern-day observers).[50] Diguet suggested that Huichols from Santa Catarina were quite proud that they retained many of their ancient customs, and even though they would adopt some new ideas, Santa Catarina did not embrace outsiders in the same way that San Andrés did.[51]

The daily life of the Huichols was a remarkable adaptation to the social realities of the late-nineteenth century and again illustrates a blend of the sacred and the mundane. Customs such as polygamy, for example, had been a common practice in the past, something Franciscans occasionally mentioned upon their initial encounters with Huichols. Some men could support multiple wives, but this became less and less widespread as community disharmony and disunity occurred as a result of local and regional conflicts and economic problems.[52] Women and men worked side-by-side with their children in the fields and in the home, and women often accompanied men on business away from the community. Additionally, women cooked, made clothing, raised children, and frequently tended to small household gardens.[53]

Allowing a foreigner to witness intimate parts of their lives marked a significant shift in the Huichols' attitudes. While Catholic priests and friars had learned pieces of Huichol religious practices in the past, and mostly in the context of conversion attempts, there is no evidence of average Mexicans witnessing ceremonies or acquiring knowledge about Huichol religion. Yet the Huichols shared some intimate details with the three European ethnographers; however, the ethnographers evidently did not learn everything there was to know. Perhaps this is why the Huichols allowed them to witness their rituals: they showed them only what they wanted them to see.

By the beginning of the twentieth century the Huichols were featured in American newspapers, based on the research completed by Lumholtz. Reports of his expeditions made the *Dallas Morning News*, the *Los Angeles Times*, and the *Biloxi Daily Herald*. Readers learned about the beautiful artwork created by the Huichols and discovered certain elements of their religion. However, some of what people read was fundamentally flawed, either because of early twentieth-century racism or because Lumholtz simply made errors. For instance, while Lumholtz correctly asserted that Huichol art was a representation of their prayers, he incorrectly suggested that somehow Arabian influences had infiltrated their styles.[54] The author of a *Los Angeles Times* report on the Huichol primordial deluge story sarcastically commented that the biblical story of Noah "is all a fake . . . Noah wasn't a Jew . . . and the flood was not merely a forty-days' go-as-you-please. It lasted five years. They do things thoroughly, these savages."[55] This particular author deemed it impossible that native peoples could challenge Western religious thought and ridiculed the Huichol primordial flood myth that provided the basis for their pilgrimages to Lake Chapala (about 145 miles southeast of their homelands). Finally, historical facts in newspapers were often simply incorrect, as evidenced by the *Dallas Morning News*. A reporter asserted that the Spanish conquered the Huichols some time before 1722, at which point the Coras finally succumbed to the invaders. The reporter declared this to be true because the Huichols "are such cowards."[56] In the waning days of Victorian sensibilities, reports like these served to prop up white American racial superiority over native peoples in Mexico and the United States. But in the long run such commentaries were losing ground to the important work that Lumholtz, Diguet, and Preuss accomplished.

Besides training the academic mind toward the importance of Mexico's lesser-known indigenous peoples, men like Lumholtz, Diguet, and Preuss paved the way for future generations of scholars. In the 1930s Robert M. Zingg, an American anthropologist, worked extensively among the Huichols and Tarahumaras. His important work, *Huichol Mythology,* focused upon the Huichols, but forty years later. Important comparisons can be made to trace how quickly modern society enveloped the Huichols in the immediate aftermaths of the Mexican Revolution and Cristero Rebellions, in which the Huichols played minor roles. As Mexico continued to improve its infrastructure, particularly in relation to rural areas, Zingg's work was important in illustrating how drastically this affected the Huichols.

6

A Revolution Comes to the Huichols

Huichol ceremonies are colorful, vibrant affairs, from the fiestas celebrating the return of peyoteros to marriages. "Woven bands, kerchiefs, and clothing are taken to the girl's parents. The groom makes his own house before the wedding occurs. At the wedding, he receives a bead collar from his wife and gives one in return. These collars are buried with them at death. The wedding fiesta lasts one night (five nights in Santa Catarina)."[1] In other ceremonies men danced, almost in a ranchero style, with one another to lively violin music.[2] In the 1930s American anthropologists traveled and lived among the Huichols, following the paths of their European predecessors. They found villages that had weathered the storm of revolution and that carried on in spite of the horrific violence and upheavals of the previous decades.

In the 180 years since Spaniards claimed to have conquered the Huichols, the Huichols had come a long way in terms of adjusting to a modernizing world. By the turn of the twentieth century Mexico had become a much more open society and, as a result, Mexico's indigenous peoples could no longer escape the scrutiny of foreign scholars, who had taken a keen interest in them and their intriguing ways. The Huichols were not immune from this foreign gaze; though Carl Lumholtz believed that Mexico would ultimately subsume the Huichols (and other indigenous peoples) by undermining their culture, his personal opinion was that this would not have a negative impact on their lives. This was not an uncommon opinion. In similar vein to *indigenista* thinkers of the post-revolutionary era, Lumholtz surmised that such melding together of Mexican and Indian would be beneficial on the whole, because indigenous peoples would be treated "well by those in power" and would reap the benefits of citizenship.[3] He may have anticipated the future, but Lumholtz was no keen observer of the political sentiments of the time. Positivist thinkers and nonindigenous Mexicans mostly had little desire to include their indigenous brethren in the larger Mexican nation; in general, the beliefs of the nineteenth century—namely that indigenous people were barriers to progress—carried over to the revolutionary era, and there was no reason to believe that the new century would usher in any kind of ethnic tolerance on the part of Porfirio Díaz.[4]

Until the dawn of the new century, President Porfirio Díaz brushed off grievances from faraway Indian groups, but the early 1900s brought challenges not so easily dismissed. Nineteenth-century land policies had concerned the Huichols, but they managed to meet the challenges head on; such experiences echoed others from Sonora to the Yucatán, where indigenous peoples reacted in different ways. Additionally, nonindigenous mestizos also suffered land loss and labor injustices carried out by an oligarchy that ruled with profound insensitivity. Thus, whether or not they were aware, the Huichols had partners in their struggles against the Díaz regime.

In the period immediately leading up to the outbreak of war, the Huichols continued their legal battles to protect their lands in the Sierra del Nayar. Some met with success, while others experienced the indignity of seeing their territory slip away to neighboring haciendas. Turmoil brewed in rural areas, adding to the general sense of unrest that pervaded Mexico as a whole. By 1910 even Díaz could not contain the frustrations of his fellow citizens, though such grievances tended to emerge unevenly throughout the nation.[5] Land hunger, coupled with severe economic downturn and a growing class of ambitious but politically excluded elites, plunged Mexico into a revolution that is now the stuff of legend and scrutiny.

How do the Huichols fit into this picture of national struggle? As with other local, regional, and colonial uprisings, the Huichols did not present a united front, and many wanted to resist bringing any increased and unwanted attention to themselves.[6] Additionally, evidence is often scant or contradictory regarding loyalties during the revolution itself.[7] What is evident is that throughout the revolutionary era, the Huichols maintained their tradition of attempting to protect their lands, typically through legal channels, but occasionally by use of force. That violence swirled around them between 1910 and 1920 and provided a good opportunity to vent frustrations at a system that was deaf to peaceful solutions. So although the picture of the Huichol Sierra during the revolutionary era was clouded frequently by the fog of war, snapshots of a modern indigenous people emerge. Those images depict a shift in Huichol mentality that becomes rather apparent by midcentury.

The earliest years of the twentieth century presented little more than a maintenance of the status quo in the Sierra Madre Occidental, at least as far as the Huichols were concerned. The first years of the twentieth century were a continuation of Porfirian policies that aimed to privatize land throughout Mexico. The Huichols experienced and reacted to Díaz's policies unevenly, as was typical for them. With the presence of Lumholtz and Diguet, we see a willingness—on the part of at least some Huichols—to incorporate outsiders when necessary. As demonstrated previously Lumholtz in particular served as a useful tool: to arbitrate on behalf of the Huichols in land disputes, which he did on at least one occasion.[8] Yet these disputes did not end with the new century and, in some ways, took on a new urgency.

Between 1900 and 1910 Huichol gobernadores submitted repeated requests to obtain copies of land titles. Their previous experiences with hacendados, vecinos, jefes políticos, or even other indigenous towns had taught them that titles could help safeguard village lands.[9] In a series of requests from Huichol governor Juan Ignacio de la Cruz, which spanned 1901–4, he claimed that dividing the land of the four principal towns of San Andrés Cohamiata, Guadalupe Ocotán, San Sebastián, and Santa Catarina was destroying them. Curiously, the governor's plea included a remark that demonstrated Huichol knowledge of national events: he stated that the Huichols were peaceful, unlike the Yaquis, who had been fighting a prolonged campaign against the

Mexican government. Finally, de la Cruz remarked that the four Huichol towns were united, a notable feat indeed, and that they had seen the light of life. They just needed a copy of their title, which they believed to be in the archives in Guadalajara. The leaders of San Andrés received a response shortly thereafter: their title could not be located.[10] While this appeal to authorities in Mezquitic and beyond likely fell on deaf ears, it did not stop the Huichols from continuing their campaign to protect themselves.

The biggest issue for the Huichols remained unscrupulous hacendados. Countless Huichol leaders wrote on behalf of their citizenry, typically complaining of cattle permitted to roam on Huichol territory or resources stolen from villages. In one case in December 1901, Huichol leaders from Santa Catarina accused their old enemy, don Benigno Soto, of letting his cattle trample Huichol lands and of taking advantage of them. Other vecinos in the region did the same. The complaints levied against Soto and his ilk mattered little; in this particular instance, Huichols living in Santa Catarina faced the indignity of having a portion of their lands stripped from them *before* their leader had issued his letter to authorities in Guadalajara.[11] This effectively allowed the hacienda to exist with impunity, forcing Santa Catarina residents to pay rents on territory that they had claimed for centuries.[12] By the early years of the twentieth century, the inhabitants of Santa Catarina were suffering. In a 1902 request to government officials in Mezquitic, leaders in the town pleaded to be released from tax obligations and rent payments. Unfortunately, as instances such as this demonstrate—both in the Huichol Sierra and elsewhere—vecinos simply refused to acknowledge indigenous land holdings.[13] As a result the back and forth between indigenous leaders and Mexican authorities created complicated legal scenarios in Mezquitic and Guadalajara and heartache in the Sierra.

Border disputes between towns and haciendas (the "legal" means through which vecinos obtained Huichol land) and conflicts between Huichols and their neighbors led to an increasingly hostile yet almost dejected attitude in the Huichol Sierra. As surveying companies continued their work, mostly helping greedy individuals despoil indigenous lands while making a nice

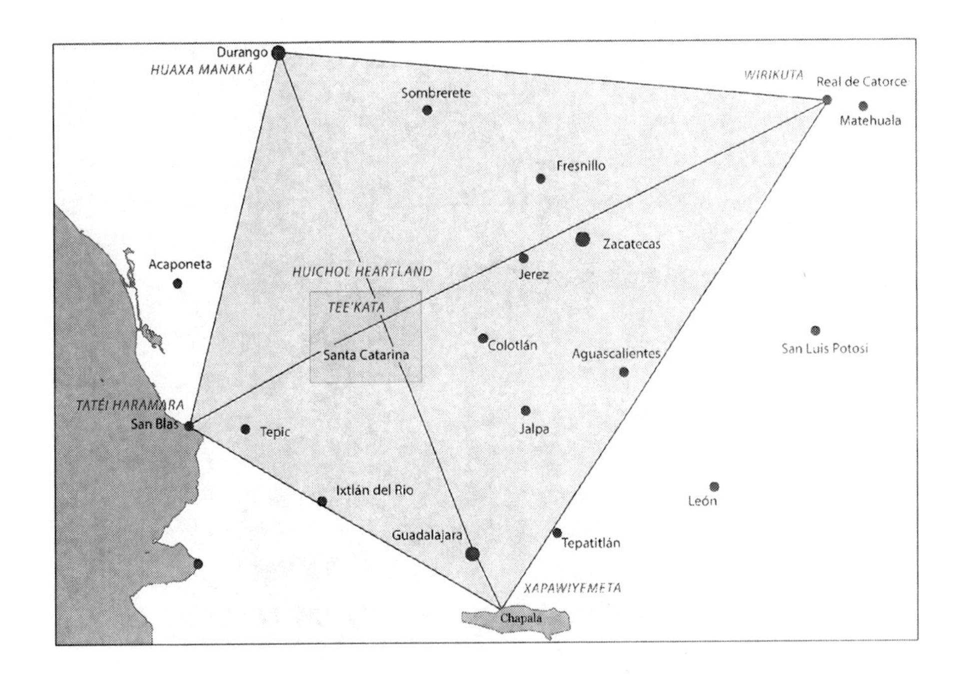

MAP 1. Location of the Huichol homeland (the center of their spiritual world, located in the square) in relation to Wirikuta (in the east) and other pilgrimage sites. Map by Thomson Gross, 2016.

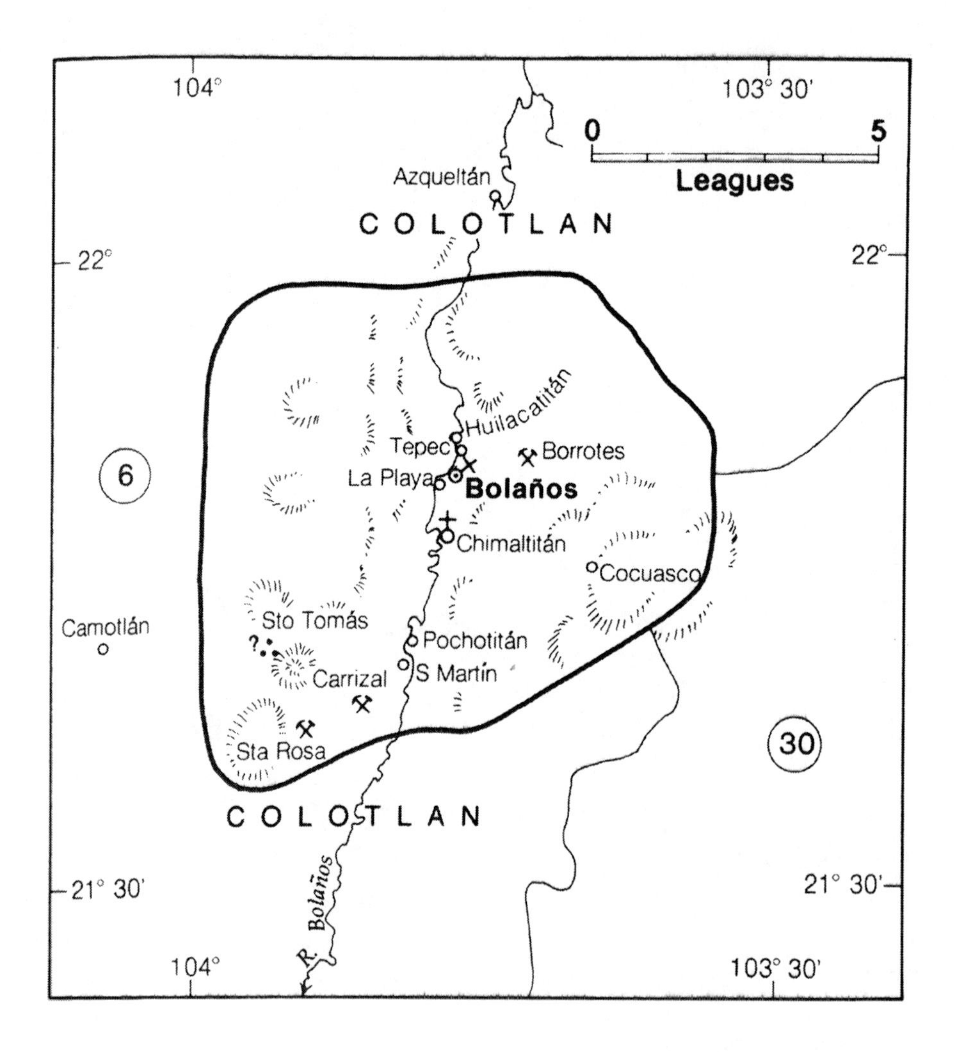

MAP 2. The municipality of Colotlán. Bolaños, in the center, was a mining hub during the colonial period and was home to a number of Huichols. Map originally published in *The North Frontier of New Spain* by Peter Gerhard.

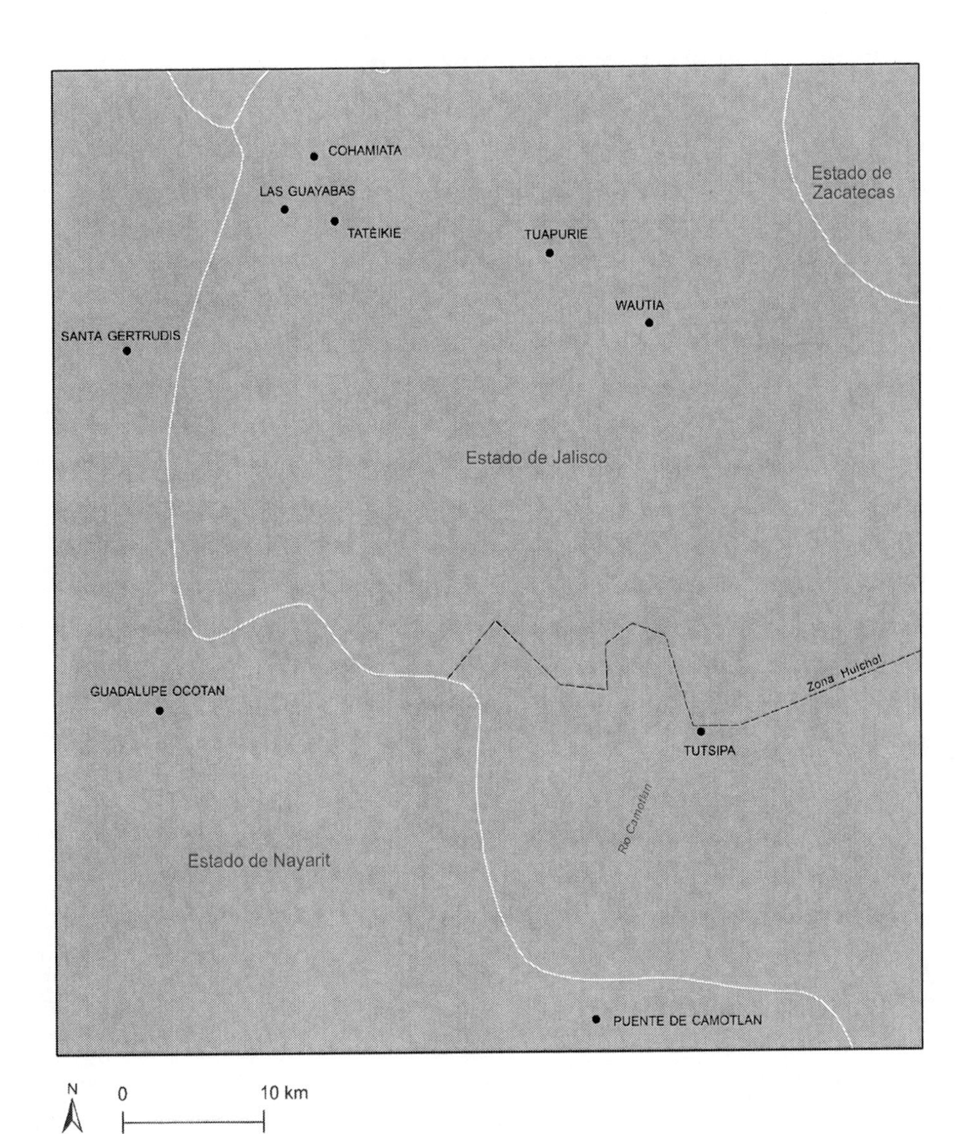

MAP 3. The three principal towns, known here by the Huichol names, appear in the top-center of the map. The towns are Wautia (San Sebastián), Tuapurie (Santa Catarina), and Cohamiata (San Andrés). Map by Thomson Gross, 2016.

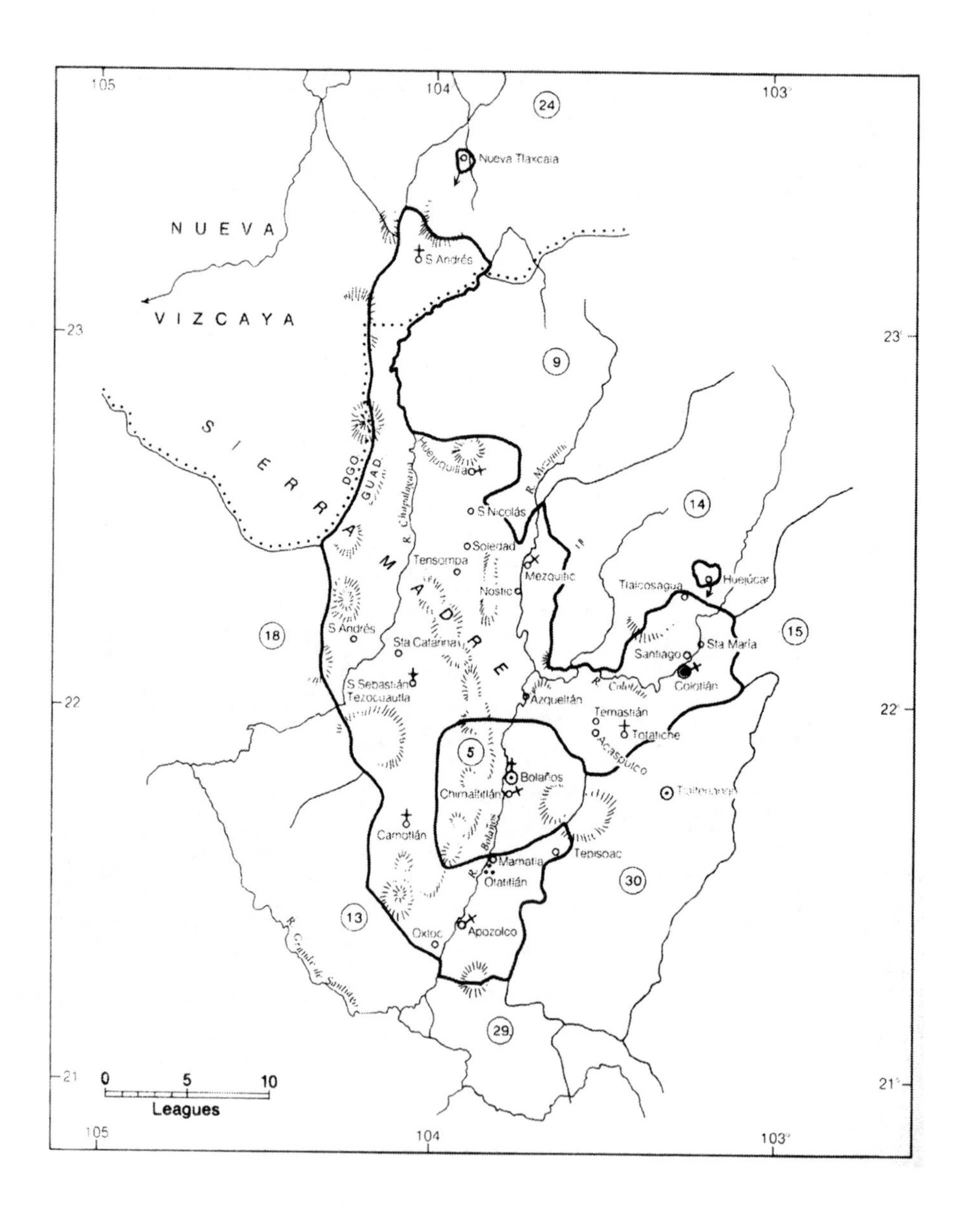

MAP 4. Location of principal Huichol towns, in the center of the image. Map originally published in *The North Frontier of New Spain* by Peter Gerhard. Copyright © 1993 by the University of Oklahoma Press, Norman. Reprinted by permission of the publisher. All rights reserved.

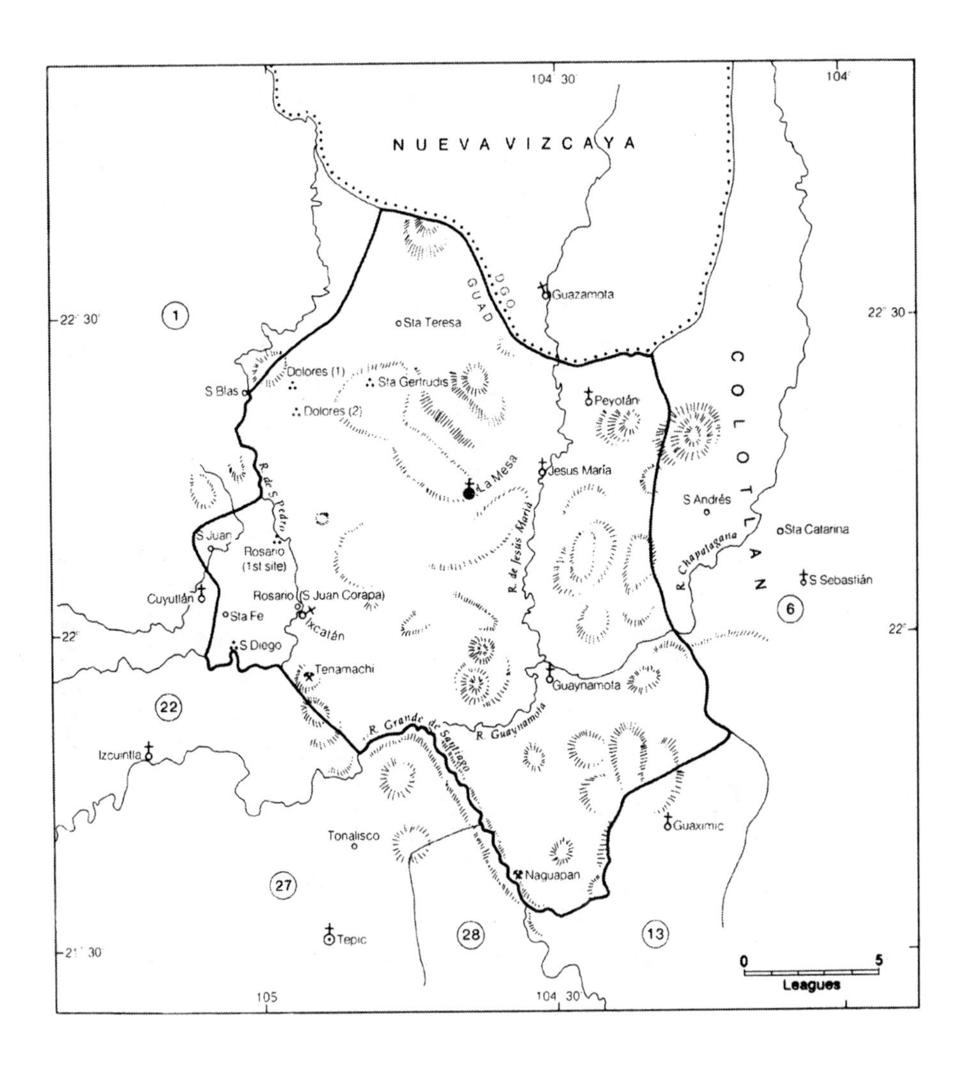

MAP 5. Proximity of the three principal Huichol towns, to the right, and the primary Cora towns. Map originally published in *The North Frontier of New Spain* by Peter Gerhard.

FIG. 1. Yarn painting depicting Kauyumarie and peyote. Created by Reymundo de la Rosas (Wixárika), circa 1965. Catalogue # 26/2625, National Museum of the American Indian, Smithsonian Institution.

FIG. 2. Shaman's straw hat, with feathers. Photo taken by Edwin Forgan Myers, 1938. Catalogue # NAA 00802400, Department of Anthropology, Smithsonian Institution.

FIG. 3. Huichol peyoteros. Photo taken by Carl Lumholtz, 1896. Image # 412449. American Museum of Natural History Library.

FIG. 4. Huichol Indians at Teakata, birthplace of the god of fire, near Santa Catarina, Jalisco. Photo taken by Carl Lumholtz, 1895. Image # CL2260. American Museum of Natural History Library.

FIG. 5. Huichol Indians at Teakata, birthplace of the god of fire, near Santa Catarina, Jalisco. Photo taken by Carl Lumholtz, 1895. Image # CL2261. American Museum of Natural History Library.

FIG. 6. Lithograph created by Ángel Bracho, titled "La Familia Huichola." © 2016 Artists Rights Society (ARS), New York / SOMAAP, Mexico City.

FIG. 7. Lithograph created by Ángel Bracho, titled "Congress of Huichol Indians."

FIG. 8. Lithograph created by Ángel Bracho, titled "Salute to the Sun." © 2016 Artists Rights Society (ARS), New York / SOMAAP, Mexico City.

FIG. 9. Huichol Indians: man of Los Juntos, Nayarit, with painted face dressed for the peyote ceremony, 1940–41. Photo taken by Donald Bush Cordry. Cooper Hewitt, Smithsonian Design Museum/Art Resource, New York.

profit, indigenous leaders continued their struggles. Little could be done unless villages had their titles, which most did not. Some, like Santos Sebastián de la Cruz, argued forcefully that their towns were old and that this should help preserve their holdings.[14] Ultimately, however, nonindigenous local leaders felt that the presence of "whites" would bring civilization to the indigenous peoples, and indigenous land claims were therefore generally ignored or denied.[15]

The suffering of the Huichols during this prerevolutionary period emerges in the writings of Josephine missionaries, who established contacts with the Huichols. Beginning in 1885 Padre José María Vilaseca began corresponding with the bishop of Zacatecas to establish a mission to convert the "*indios bárbaros*" (barbarous Indians, or barbarians) in the Sierra del Nayar. In 1901 Bishop José Guadalupe de Jesús Alva authorized missionaries to work with the Huichols, and by November of that year, they reached Santa Catarina.[16] They moved on to San Sebastián and created a mission there as the new year dawned, describing the poor conditions they encountered among the Huichols living there.

The poverty that the priests witnessed was stark and reflected decades of shrinking land bases, which made subsistence farming difficult. In a letter one of the young missionaries, Juan Antonio Martínez, wrote to Vilaseca, he noted that the sad situation of the unhappy, unlucky Huichols; they had little food, and a few would surround the friars as they took their meals, hoping for something to eat. Martínez noted that the parents ate very little, giving what food they had to their children. The situation was grave enough that Martínez ordered double rations of beans and tortillas to alleviate some of the hunger. He also suggested that the Huichols were in as bad a state as what he had witnessed among the Tarahumaras.[17]

In November 1902 two Josephine friars and a brother established a mission at San Andrés, affording them the opportunity to try to convert their new charges. While exploring the area Padre Macario Ramírez described the natural landscape as well as the living conditions and rituals of area Huichols.

Curiously, Ramírez wrote that he witnessed indigenous families living in the caves that dotted the deep canyons and ravines, something others had reflected on in the past. They chose to live in caves during the rainy season to take care of their cornfields.[18] Ramírez expressed disdain for the Huichol ceremonies he either witnessed or heard about, as it became evident to him that Catholicism was not a deeply engrained belief among the Huichols, at least at San Andrés. Writing that they sacrificed bulls to their gods before the harvest, he lamented at these feasts of great sinfulness, drunkenness, and disorder. He also quipped that the Huichols could be suffering from starvation, yet they would not complete their harvest until the bull could be sacrificed.[19] Taken together, the reports of the missionaries from San Sebastián and San Andres demonstrate that land issues had curtailed the Huichols' ability to sustain themselves with farming, leading to desperation in the Sierra Huichola. However, to the dismay of the Josephines, Huichol spirituality did not appear to be affected by such deep poverty, as evidenced by the harvest festival and the sad state of the church in the area.[20]

One of the ways that the Josephine missionaries tried to alleviate some of the problems they perceived among the Huichols was through education. Because the Huichols did not allow their children to mix with "whites," it made educating them at the mission school quite difficult.[21] One of the missionaries' strategies was to establish a school for orphaned Huichol children, which occurred during 1903–4; here they would be trained as missionaries, undoubtedly to convert their brethren to the faith.[22] While education might not alleviate the poverty that the missionaries witnessed, it would—in their minds—fix the spiritual "problems" that the Huichols faced. The missionary efforts in the Sierra were aided by an auxiliary society, established in Mexico City, whose goal was to provide assistance to the friars in their quest to bring the word of God to the Huichols.[23] Finally, a Huichol-Spanish catechism missal demonstrated the efforts that the Josephines were willing to make to educate and Christianize the Huichols.[24]

The Josephines' missionary strategy began to change after the election of Miguel María de la Mora to the bishopric of Zacatecas in 1911. He felt that the

Huichol missions were too geographically distant (and increasingly dangerous) and the friars too ignorant in their knowledge of Huichol cultural and religious practices to have the desired effect. Instead, he proposed that the missionaries focus on San Andrés, likely the most needy of spiritual help.[25] De la Mora's 1912 report contains some important insights into the situation in the Sierra, as he instructs the Josephines about their roles. He declared that missionaries should never use violence in stamping out what the Church viewed as idolatry. They must be patient and act with charity; the missionaries must not help or support nonindigenous Mexicans if they exploit the Huichols in Nayarit. Finally, he stressed that the missionaries were there for the Huichols, though they could of course help "whites" living legitimately in the area.[26] So, while the missionary plan on a grand scale came to a close, the bishop emphasized that Huichols remaining under their care needed to be treated with respect. De la Mora's report demonstrates a broad understanding for the Huichols' desperate situation, as well as the willingness of mestizos to flout local laws and ignore indigenous land holdings, which of course created a tense atmosphere in the Sierra as the revolution loomed and erupted.

When the Mexican Revolution began in 1910, it did not immediately affect the Huichols. Furthermore, as events progressed, and as the Sierra became a theater in the violent fight among various factions, whatever Huichol "unity" had existed—in reality, or for the benefit of maintaining lands—fragmented once more.[27] As revolutionary bands picked their way across the Sierra Madre Occidental, Huichol leaders faced difficult choices: unite politically, which occurred occasionally; flee their homes for the coast, which would offer sanctuary and had been customary in times of extreme duress; or follow different factions.[28] Each option presented different challenges as the revolution progressed.

Revolutionary fervor heated up in the Sierra Huichola in 1912. Admittedly, the history of revolutionary action in the region is a bit muddled, but a few clear events emerge.[29] The first rumblings of discontent among the Huichols, in relation to the government, occurred in San Andrés Cohamiata. In August 1912 Francisco Martínez, a political commissary appointed to San

Andrés, complained to the governor that the Huichols would not obey his authority and spread dissent and false accusations. All of this undermined his authority in the area and created problems with the governors of the other Huichol towns in the area with respect to Martínez's authority.[30] Additionally, the leaders in San Andrés rejected the government-appointed schoolteacher, who apparently cheated and extorted the villagers.[31] While these events may seem small in the grand scheme of things, they represent symptoms of a greater sickness: a system of abusive outsiders, dissatisfied Mexican authorities who complained about their indigenous charges, and unhappy Huichols who wanted to be left alone.

Huichols began to choose sides by 1912 in response to discontent over land, political officials, and the fact that mestizos generally lined up behind Pancho Villa.[32] According to Beatriz Rojas, some Huichols living in the southern part of the Sierra Huichol (near Huajimic) joined up under the command of Camilo Rentería, about whom little is known.[33] Other units similar to those patrolled further north and west and were led by chieftains or cooperated with better-known military leaders in the area, such as Cándido Aguilar. Such small, armed, almost militia-type groups appeared to be common throughout the revolutionary era.[34] Unfortunately, they left behind little evidence of their activities, much less their existence, besides acts of violence that generally terrorized the region.

Some Huichols had an eye toward events outside the Sierra Madre Occidental. In spring 1912 Guadalupe Hernández, a leader from Santa Catarina, wrote to the governor of Jalisco, Alberto Robles Gil, asking his opinion about one of the revolutionary factions. It seems, according to the letter, that some residents of Santa Catarina wanted to follow the Zapatistas, a group that was unknown to Hernández and other authorities in Santa Catarina. Hernández and two other authority figures in the town, José María González and Francisco Hernández, sought the advice of state officials. They were curious as to the political affiliation and character of the Zapatistas and whether they should prevent their residents from joining up with them. The response from the governor's secretary was swift and brief, stating that the Zapatistas had no political allegiance and were interested in little more than robbery and plunder.[35] What would make Huichols from Santa Catarina interested in joining the Zapatistas, whose movement was localized to central Mexico? Their message of *tierra y libertad* (land and liberty) was one that certainly would have resonated with all Huichols and was similar to the cry of Manuel Lozada during his rebellion in the nineteenth century. Perhaps it was as simple as that message, which likely had traversed the countryside by 1912, sweeping up indigenous peoples who, while unable to travel south to Morelos, at least supported the Zapatista cause.

Nevertheless Villismo dominated much of the area, with many Huichols (and some Coras) supporting the revolutionary cause under the command of Sinaloan General Rafael Buelna.[36] Buelna understood the "social and economic woes that led people to take up arms" in western Mexico, and drew much support from Tepic.[37] Though pockets of support for Pascual Orozco emerged early on, this seemed to evaporate—or was at least not particularly evident—with the collapse of the Madero government and Francisco Madero's execution by the regime of Victoriano Huerta in 1913.[38] Huerta, a noted "Indian fighter" who saw action in campaigns against both the Yaquis and Mayas, was part Huichol and born on the outskirts of Colotlán. Some Huichols who did not support Villismo lined up behind the government, though it is not clear (and probably doubtful) that Huichol loyalty to Huerta created such affinities.[39]

Amid these shifting alliances, generalized violence, political turmoil, and land issues remained a significant source of frustration for the Huichols and local Mexican authorities. Francisco Martínez, the old political nemesis of San Andrés, remained the commissary and relayed his complaints to the governor of Jalisco. In November 1912 he asked for a transfer to San Sebastián and the establishment of a new commissary for Santa Catarina, whose inhabitants did not want to have to come into San Andrés.[40] For their part, by January of the following year, Huichols in San Andrés had simply refused to acknowledge any political authority held by Martínez, instead asserting that they would only follow an individual by the name of Jesús Carrillo, a man that they chose; they also would not hold any elections.

Martínez also protested that his hands were tied figuratively in all matters: supporters of Camilo Rentería prevented the administration of justice, particularly in criminal matters, if his followers were in any way involved.[41] The aforementioned elections, which should have been held in November 1913, had been postponed as a result of rebels and revolts in San Andrés. Again writing to government officials in April 1914, Martínez hoped that new elections would occur later in the year, and he proposed provisional officials to take over in the meantime.[42] The complaints that Martínez conveyed demonstrate instability in the area, the Huichols' reticence to work within the system, and a general breakdown of political norms in San Andrés by the middle of 1914, if not before.

Loyalties shifted throughout the revolutionary period, as had been typical to this point. Some Huichols used this period as a pretext to take out their frustration on local mestizos or other indigenous peoples of the area; others used the violence of the revolution to attempt to remove invading Mexican settlers from their territory.[43] To that end, a popular war chief named Patricio González had a reputation of being one of the more violent and bloodthirsty rebel leaders in a period of untold violence and bloodshed. González, a Huichol, earned the nickname Patricio Mesquite because he was a particularly cruel, hard, unyielding man, characteristics reminiscent of the mesquite tree. In an account recorded by an anthropologist some years later, Mesquite and his followers sold cows to some Mexican merchants; later, they killed the men in the mountains and brought the cows back. It is unclear to whom he lent his support, as the Sierra was a complicated patchwork of shifting allegiances.[44]

By the mid-1910s, as Pancho Villa's armies faced one defeat after another, the revolutionary fidelities and agreements collapsed, and the Sierra became a much more chaotic place. Villa's soldiers committed acts of banditry as they carried out their frustrations, and this is evident in parts of Huichol country.[45] Though some of Villa's supporters remained entrenched in the Sierra de Huichol, factions supporting the constitutional government emerged with fervor.[46] A pocket of constitutionalist support existed in San Andrés, where Huichols "remained loyal to the government" as the revolution wore on, lining up behind the Carrancistas.[47] On the other hand, Huichols living in San Sebastián had reportedly committed numerous violent crimes in support of rebel chiefs, figuratively setting the Sierra on fire.[48]

Indigenous peoples and mestizos in the region often fled the violence and either never returned, or did so only after peace had been restored to the Sierra Madre. In accounts retold to him during his fieldwork in 1934, Robert Zingg noted that Huichols from San Sebastián had a reputation among Mexicans and other Huichols for being "violent and bloodthirsty."[49] Neighboring Huichols in Tuxpan were so fearful of San Sebastián that they took up residence near Bolaños, a predominantly mestizo settlement, to escape the violence. Other Huichols further west fled for the coast of Nayarit, long viewed as a safe haven in times of upheaval and violence.[50] San Sebastián supported the revolutionary cause and provided cover for those that sought to do violence against other peoples, indigenous or not, who did not support the revolution. The result was a period of intertown hostilities that caused many Huichols to leave their homeland for more stable, peaceful environs; it also resulted in the near destruction of the town of San Andrés.[51]

By the close of the revolution San Andrés had borne the brunt of revolutionary fury in the region. It appears as though past problems with local hacienda owners reinvigorated efforts among Huichol leaders to secure titles to their lands. A Huichol leader named Ignacio de la Cruz pleaded with his superiors (at either the local or state level) to help his people against the encroachment of Hacienda San Juan Capistrano. De la Cruz claimed that officials in San Andrés only had "*copias simples*" (simple copies) of their original title, with surveys from 1703; the hacienda in question repeatedly extended their land possessions onto lands claimed by the pueblo.[52] Several weeks later de la Cruz's letter was followed by another, this time from the governor of San Andrés. In this instance Clemente Villa argued for assistance with much more force, now claiming that in addition to the hacienda owners, Huichols from Santa Catarina encroached on their land as well.[53] Leaders in San Andrés feared being fully engulfed by outsiders who had little regard for their property or the law and by the continued violence of the revolution.

It is unfortunate that so few archival sources exist to inform us more concretely about the revolution in Huichol country and its effects on the people living there. Whispers of the upheaval are all that remain to instruct us about the war's impacts. Clemente Villa, the governor of San Andrés, lamented the situation in his village, which helps to capture a moment in time. He wrote that his village had been destroyed by Luis de la Torre, Felipe de la Cruz, and José Chalote, who murdered twenty-three people (including women and children) while robbing and destroying at their leisure. These men used the revolution as a pretext for their violent ways.[54] Yet from what fragmentary evidence exists, important conclusions emerge.

The revolutionary dynamics that played out between 1900 and 1920 in Gran Nayar thus kept faith with several important trends in Huichol history. First, Huichols continued to react to internal or external stressors without any clear sense of ethnic and political unity, occasionally battling against each other over land or during war. Although Huichols may speak the same language, albeit with regional variations, it is not possible to write a singular history of the revolution in Huichol country. Each town had its own agenda and, even within those towns, Huichols did not act unanimously. This makes discerning loyalties a complicated endeavor. Years of abuse by local mestizos and political officials created an atmosphere of tension before the outbreak of hostilities. Santa Catarina's leaders had attempted to address land grievances through legal channels. By the time hostilities erupted, Huichols in Santa Catarina, ignored and abandoned by the government, used mestizos' fear of violence to attempt to regain lands. On the other hand, and for reasons that remain obscure, San Andrés chose to support a government that mostly scorned the idea of indigenous rights.[55] And San Sebastián, which had long been an outpost for Franciscan missionaries, became virulently antigovernment over the course of the early twentieth century.[56] Such variation among Huichol towns during the revolution undoubtedly created intertown conflicts, particularly as pressures and tensions mounted. Rather than stay and risk their lives and livelihoods, many Huichols simply left the area. Their specific reasons for doing so are lost to us.

However, a second trend emerged in the wake of the revolution. Towns that had once been on opposing sides of an issue at times put their differences behind them to work for solutions that would benefit all Huichols. After the revolution ended, some Huichol towns that had lost lands fought to get them back. In 1921 the Huichols who lived in San Andrés received titles to their lands to protect them from future thefts at the hands of outsiders. Many Huichol towns received titles to their lands in the postrevolutionary period, securing their borders and providing inhabitants with a modicum of comfort against future encroachment; if they had troubles with their neighbors, Huichol leaders felt comfortable notifying authorities and seeking either title or land measurement.[57] Thus the Huichols, as keen observers of both local and regional issues, used the revolution to rectify some of the wrongs levied against them in the thirty-four years of Díaz's reign.

Though an uneasy peace descended over much of Mexico in the immediate aftermath of the revolution, such sentiments did not last long. Despite the positive gains achieved by many Huichols after 1920, periods of violence continued to disrupt indigenous families in the Sierra Madre Occidental. The Cristero Rebellion brought instability and unrest to western Mexico, forcing many to flee. For Huichols that had just returned to the Sierra, this was likely an unwelcome event. This war, which began in 1926, grew mostly from mestizo ranchers' resentment over the increasingly aggressive presence of the secular, anticlerical state.[58] But it affected Huichol communities because *cristeros* and *agraristas* killed indiscriminately.[59] The rebellion itself centered in Jalisco, though in the Los Altos region, which is some distance to the east of the Huichols' homelands. Nevertheless, the nature of the conflict forced people to choose sides. San Sebastián took up arms in support of the cristeros, seeing this as a way to strike out against an indifferent and hostile government.[60] Whether rebelling Huichols cared about the plight of Mexican Catholics is unknown. Santa Catarina officially maintained a policy of neutrality, while San Andrés continued its support of the government, as it had done during the revolution. The violence had scattered Huichols once more, and intercommunity cooperation failed to provide a groundswell of support for either position during the Cristero War.[61] By the time that Robert Zingg undertook his fieldwork in 1934, Huichols living in Tuxpan de Bolaños "had been exiled from the sierra" due to decades of revolution and rebellion.[62] Yet despite the dislocation in some parts of the Huichol Sierra, new communities sprung up elsewhere in the region.[63]

What were the results of two decades of war on Huichol territorial holdings and culture? In the years following the hostilities, American anthropologists like Zingg, Elsie Clews Parsons, and Ralph Leon Beals made their way into the Sierra. From their records, observations, and writings, we know that the Huichols maintained a significant degree of cultural autonomy, despite whatever acculturation plans intellectuals or the Mexican government had hoped for. Catholic practices that had influenced religious ceremonies did not transform them completely. "Huichol culture in general presents a strange combination of pre-Colombian and Catholic elements," evident in their religious beliefs.[64] Fiestas were social as much as religious events, which was true in the 1890s as well as today.[65] The peyote pilgrimage remained the most significant element in the Huichols' ceremonial calendar, and its accompanying festival required care and preparation. The Huichols' degree of religiosity was unmatched in the Sierra even as late as the beginning of the 1940s.[66]

Conclusion

In May 2011 Wixárika leaders acted on a serious situation that had plagued them for several years. The Regional Wixárika Council for the Defense of Wirikuta wrote to President Felipe Calderón and other presidents and peoples of the world to explain the significance of Wirikuta and the devastation that mining would cause if First Majestic Mining Corporation were permitted to operate in the region. Citing their pilgrimages to the area, the importance of the biodiversity for the planet, and Wirikuta's relevance as home to thousands of Wixárika ancestors, the letter demonstrates Wixárika unity, their continued defense of their homelands and culture, and a willingness to adapt to a changing world to protect their way of life.[1]

Over the two centuries since independence from Spain, the Huichols faced numerous external threats that they then internalized and responded to in various ways. Some of these experiences and exchanges with outsiders were peaceful; others created strife that exacerbated intertown rivalries or sparked tensions with Spaniards and nonindigenous Mexicans. Because the Huichols were culturally unified, but politically distinct, leadership in each Huichol town determined the best courses of action according to its unique circumstances. As a result, the history of the Huichols is a history of political and ethnic resistance and accommodation in patchwork form, as opposed to a story of unity against a common enemy.

The threats of Spanish colonialism, the burgeoning state, Catholic evangelization, Liberalism, foreign scholars, and revolution endangered Huichol cultural and physical survival in different ways. Liberalism, for instance, threatened the Huichols' land base, which presented a problem in terms of physical survival *and* the maintenance of religious customs. As Franciscan missionaries remarked—although they did not realize what they were witnessing—Huichols left religious figurines throughout the landscape, marking their territory in a spiritual sense.[2] The presence of Franciscans risked destroying ancient practices that had been passed down over the generations. To be sure, Huichol religious cultures changed as they absorbed some elements of Catholic traditions, but the core beliefs have remained remarkably stable in the face of such threats to their own indigenous traditions.[3]

Several larger conclusions emerge from the Huichols' centuries-long struggle to confront the challenges of colonialism, evangelization, and modernization. The first of these concerns political unity among Huichol towns, or in this case, a lack thereof. Despite an extensive spectrum of shared cultural attributes, each Huichol town governs itself and acts of its own accord. For example, during the Porfiriato, Huichol villages chose different strategies to protect their territories; in the end, such a multifaceted approach often produced desired effects.[4] Likewise, as revolution erupted throughout Mexico between 1910 and 1920, Huichol villages carefully weighed their options. It is safe to say, then, that in their political disunity they found strength, though this appeared most tenuous in the wake of the revolution. Such strength-through-discord may never have been Huichol leaders' intention, but in the end it worked for them and protected their interests. Measured responses to difficult circumstances—particularly during the Porfirian era—meant that the Huichols rarely experienced extreme retaliation on the part of the Mexican state.[5]

The Huichol case thus calls attention to a second point regarding the history of indigenous populations in the nineteenth and twentieth centuries; that is, the often vacillating and inconsistent state approaches. The state, either in its local or federal incarnation, hardly served as benefactor to the native peoples of the Gran Nayar. To his credit, though, Porfirio Díaz never adopted any strict "Indian policy" relative to the region during his thirty-five-year tenure, and this helped the Huichols weather the storm. Other groups certainly experienced worse treatment. Campaigns of outright genocide occurred among the Yaquis, whom the government forcibly removed to the henequen plantations of the Yucatán peninsula. That latter region also had a long history of violence, as agitated Mayas struggled against specific policies and practices during the decades-long Caste War.[6] Across the isthmus in the Mexican southwest, an area with a heavy concentration of indigenous peoples, the economy languished, and the government essentially turned its back on the population. Chiapas and its residents are among the poorest in the country. Like the Huichols, indigenous groups in Chiapas whom Mexican politicians largely ignored retained much of their cultural mores. The inconsistent way in which the government treated indigenous peoples in the nineteenth century is an intriguing subject that warrants more thorough investigation. Many factors contributed to state inconsistency toward indigenous peoples, chief among them being a given region's pressure for land commercialization. While a full picture of nineteenth-century state-indigenous relations has yet to be written, it is safe to say that Huichol and Cora experiences did not fall on the harsher end of the spectrum.

A third point concerns the extraordinary longevity of certain religious-material complexes found among preindustrial peoples. The question of what came first—the cold facts of existence or the cosmological meanings that came to be invested in places, goods, and animals—will probably never be resolved to universal satisfaction. But the Huichol case does illustrate how tenacious the interweaving of place, material culture, and religious belief can be. Any attempts to commercialize and privatize land usage in the Gran Nayar has constituted an assault on a carefully balanced human relationship with the triad of corn, deer, and peyote; for that reason it has met with stiff-necked resistance (armed or otherwise). Much like the Yucatec Mayas' organization around seasonal rain, milpa farming, and cyclical land usage, the Huichol method of doing and believing survived the assaults of mestizo-ranchero culture and continues to this day, albeit in modified form.

The late-nineteenth- and early-twentieth-century European ethnographers provided key pieces of evidence for increased study and long-range comparisons as a new generation of anthropologists emerged in the 1960s and 1970s. Emphasizing the importance of peyote as a focal point in Huichol religion, scholars like Robert Zingg, Barbara Myerhoff, and Peter T. Furst used the works of Diguet, Lumholtz, and Preuss to understand the arch of Huichol religion. Myerhoff finally explained what earlier scholars could not quite understand: the somewhat elusive "trinity" or symbolic complex of peyote, corn, and deer and its paramount importance to Huichol religion and sustenance. This complex ties the Huichols to their location in time and space, as Myerhoff pointed out in her studies. Thus it is religion, linked intimately with geography, that intricately binds the Huichols to their specific place in the Sierra Madre Occidental. Lumholtz, Diguet, Preuss, and later Zingg laid the foundation for modern scholars to understand this sacred geography. This is precisely why the Huichols refuse to give up their land and why their religion, while certainly infused with Catholicism, is still Huichol at its core.

Americans were not the only ones intrigued by the Huichols and their religious beliefs. The government of Lázaro Cárdenas, for example, began implementing educational reforms throughout Mexico that certainly affected the Huichols. While only a few schools for Huichol children had been established by the end of the 1930s, it was clear to political officials that there was a dire need for education in the Huichol Sierra. A report compiled by officials in 1936 pointed to the need for education to "de-fanaticize" and introduce better hygiene programs for the Huichol and Cora populations.[7] Children in this particular area needed a more rigorous education system; according to a newspaper report from Tepic in April 1936, hardly any Huichol children spoke Spanish.[8] This report, however, was not followed up immediately by the establishment of schools. Whether because of parental resistance, Huichol disinterest, or government underfunding, most schools in the Huichol area did not operate until after the 1940s.[9]

The Cárdenas administration and its predecessors spurred legions of reformers who wanted to improve the lives of native peoples by improving their economic and social conditions.[10] Scholars such as Alfonso Fábila, working under the auspices of the Instituto Nacional Indigenista (created in 1948 and also known as the INI), conducted research trips to the Huichol Sierra in the late 1950s to gather information about the reticent peoples. The Huichols probably harbored a certain distrust of the Mexican observers because the INI employees and academics had an agenda that American and European scholars and observers did not. The INI's goal was assimilation of indigenous peoples—that is, a shedding of language, culture, and adherence to communal land use—at least when Fábila worked in the Sierra Huichola. Fábila's account, titled "Situación de los Huicholes de Jalisco," chronicled the geographic features of the Huichol territory in Jalisco, lamented the poor quality of the available lands, and discussed such cultural aspects as marriage, dress, and vices.[11] During the period in which Fábila conducted his research, men typically married between fifteen and twenty years of age and women between thirteen and eighteen. Though at times mechanical, Fábila's work among the Huichols introduced this little-understood group to the Mexican bureaucracy, and INI subsequently published the report in 1959.

There also exists an undated, anonymous INI report that briefly describes the Coras, Huichols, and Tepehuans living in Jalisco, Nayarit, and Durango. Like Fábila's work, this account explores the geographical distribution of the three indigenous groups in western Mexico in addition to describing the climate, flora, and fauna.[12] The report, produced after 1974, explained that the population density in the region is quite low and that Huichol ranchos are normally located near water sources.[13] The similarities between the anonymous pamphlet and Fábila's account are numerous and point to the INI's continuing interest in relatively mundane and material facts about the Huichol Sierra and the people living in the region.

The work of INI may not have brought about the government's desired assimilation, but it did foster increased interest in the Huichols that translated to nonprofit support for Wixárika communities in more recent decades. In light of significant developments in the twentieth century, Juan Negrín wrote a small study of Wixárika history and culture and then moved on to establish a website dedicated to the preservation of Wixárika art, history, and culture.[14] Negrín's use of the Internet to illuminate the strife in the Sierra has helped American scholars better understand the reality of daily life in Jalisco, and his work among the Wixáritari has shed light on modern problems such as deforestation, mining in Wirikuta, and government projects in the region. In the future these recent developments in the Huichol Sierra will surely warrant more intensive examinations.

The dawn of the twenty-first century has introduced new dangers to the physical and spiritual homelands of the Wixárika. These include the building of modern highways, the advent of ecotourism projects, and the development of new mining contracts. The Wixáritari have roundly rejected these dangers, unanimously for the most part. But there are threats to their spiritual homelands that are more problematic. They have protested, not only presenting a united front, but also have garnered the support of many other indigenous groups in Mexico as well as the backing of thousands of average Mexicans.

Mining poses the most significant threat. Transnational mining corporations have begun to stake claims to mineral rights in the area, reopening the region to destructive mining practices that threaten the ecology and the spirituality of Wirikuta in ways that are hard to repair. Reactions to mining in Wirikuta have been swift and unifying. The Wixáritari have issued protests with the Mexican government and numerous nongovernmental organizations. It remains to be seen what impacts these recent developments will have on the Wixáritari, their livelihoods, and their religious culture. According to one journalist writing recently, "the context seems like a movie script, but it is deadly serious to the Wixárika, whose core cultural practice for more than a thousand years has consisted of regular pilgrimages to Wirikuta, the birthplace of the sun: a magical desert where the balance of life on Earth is maintained through a sacred cactus that carries the wisdom of a blue deer."[15]

More recently, at talks between the Wixáritari, the government, and mine owners, "Wixárika leaders have said the issue is not negotiable. Wirikuta is much more than the Cerro Quemado and the sacred springs, explained Humberto Fernandez Borja, founder of Conservación Humana, a conservation group that has worked with the World Wildlife Fund, UNESCO and others to defend the site for more than two decades. It comprises the entire range of the Catorce mountains and the desert that lies below, for a total of more than 140,000 hectares, all of which acts as a sacred, integral whole."[16]

Drug cartels pose another threat to the Wixáritari, particularly in the area of San Sebastián. Again, the terrain makes the area sort of a blessing: it is inhospitable to and fairly inaccessible by cartels; but the terrain is also a curse. The inaccessibility makes the area attractive for cartels' marijuana- and poppy-growing operations. The presence of cartels along the routes north into the United States of course attracts police. This has made the pilgrimage to Wirikuta more complicated in recent years, as in 2010, when three pilgrims were interrogated by police while gathering peyote in San Luis Potosí. Since the Wixáritari are permitted to gather peyote, the actions of police were roundly criticized. The government apologized and gave the pilgrims a police escort out of the state at the end of their ceremony.[17]

Thus there is only really one way to think about the Huichols as a unified ethnic group, and that is in relation to their spirituality, which links land and religion. The Huichols have come together over the centuries with a unified voice to proclaim that their lands and their religion in Jalisco or San Luis Potosí are sacred and not negotiable, despite the actions of Spanish priests in the eighteenth century; jefes políticos and hacendados in the nineteenth century; and government officials, corporate interests, and cartels in the twentieth and twenty-first centuries.

Despite all these changes occurring around them and despite the denigrating attitudes of nonindigenous Mexicans in centuries past, the Wixáritari and other indigenous peoples in Mexico have endured. Motivated by the protection of their lands and cultures, they were keen observers and participants in their daily existence. Rather than viewing history as having negatively affected the Wixáritari, a perspective that strips them of their ability to understand and interact with the larger world, we must acknowledge how the Wixáritari negotiated a system that has stacked the decks against them. Though with each passing decade the modern world inches closer, the Wixáritari still maintain a vibrant presence in their mountain homelands, paying homage to their gods and to peyote, whose celebrations ensure that life will continue in all Wixárika towns.[18]

NOTES

Prologue

1. There is a slight discrepancy in names. Nineteenth-century French ethnographer Léon Diguet called this ancestor Maxa Kwaxí (or as he heard it, Majakuagy); twentieth-century anthropologist Barbara Myerhoff makes two suggestions: that Kauyaumari was a semidivine figure and that the deity was called Tamatsi Maxa Kwaxí. See Myerhoff, *Peyote Hunt*, 85; Diguet, *Por tierras occidentales*, 122; de la Peña, *Culturas indígenas de Jalisco*, 85. Myerhoff acknowledged that this concept of Tamatsi Maxa Kwaxí and Kauyaumari is incredibly complicated to non-Huichols, which is probably why Diguet misinterpreted it. For the names of the sun, see the glossary in Schaefer and Furst, *People of the Peyote*, 529, 531. The name of the sun varies, as he is also known by the name Werikúa.
2. Diguet, *Por tierras occidentales*, 145.
3. Benítez, *Magic Land of Peyote*, 14.
4. Myerhoff, *Peyote Hunt*, 122. When Myerhoff undertook the hunt with Ramón Medina in the late 1960s, some acculturated Huichols who remained behind "could not be trusted with the sole responsibility for keeping the fire lit and observing the rituals necessary for the well-being of the pilgrims."
5. Benítez, *Magic Land of Peyote*, 17, 19; Myerhoff, *Peyote Hunt*, 132–36. Both Benítez and Myerhoff discuss the confession of sins of a sexual nature at length for their non-Huichol audience. The explanation is as follows: essentially, harboring jealousies or secrets about one's sexual partners can create "terrifying visions and even insanity in Wirikuta," according to Myerhoff, 133. These relationships are forgiven in the context of the ceremony, which Myerhoff acknowledges is not truly a "confession" in an English (or Christian) sense of the word.
6. Lumholtz, "Explorations in Mexico," 138–39.

7. Fresán Jiménez, *Nierika*, 40. See also Benítez, *Magic Land of Peyote*, 25.
8. Fresán Jiménez, *Nierika*, 39; Diguet, *Por tierras occidentales*, 144–46.
9. Diguet, *Por tierras occidentales*, 146.
10. Myerhoff, *Peyote Hunt*, 152–53.
11. Myerhoff, *Peyote Hunt*, 153; Lumholtz, *Unknown Mexico*, 2:153; de la Peña, *Culturas indígenas de Jalisco*, 65. Here, Myerhoff noted that the mara'akame's arrow pierced the flesh of the cactus in two spots, so that it could not escape. She wrote that this contradicted the reports of Carl Lumholtz, who said that the peyote must be taken alive, and therefore should not be wounded.
12. Myerhoff, *Peyote Hunt*, 155.
13. Benítez, *Magic Land of Peyote*, 51.
14. Myerhoff, *Peyote Hunt*, 161. Peyote use is important to the Coras, but they do not make the journey, and it is unclear whether a pilgrimage akin to that which the Huichols undertake was ever part of their cosmology. Myerhoff explains that the Huichols view peyote as something to be revered, whereas the Coras and the Tarahumaras (who also consume peyote) fear the power of the visions that peyote produces. For the other two indigenous groups, peyote has a negative power, whereas for the Huichols, peyote is benevolent. The pilgrimage, the act of obtaining the sacred cactus where it grows, is integral to Huichol religion, and indeed, to their existence.
15. Benítez writes that the Huichol peyote tradition has retained most of its basic components, unlike the Christianized Native American church in the United States. He suggests that the difference is that Native American peyotism in the United States is a reaction against white triumph and dominations, whereas "the worship of the deer-peyote-corn trinity has served to maintain a way of life in the face of expulsion, segregation and genocide that began with the Spanish conquest." See Benítez, *Magic Land of Peyote*, 150. My goal is not to compare the two, but it is an important distinction for some.
16. In a longer version of the peyote story, ethnographer Léon Diguet lists fourteen or fifteen towns that nineteenth-century Huichols passed through en route to Real de Catorce. In each town the Huichols made offerings to one deity or another who needed supplication. See Diguet, *Por tierras occidentales*, 156. For a brief article on the subject of sacred geography, see Corr, "Ritual Knowledge." Huichol views on sacred geography can be compared to Andean beliefs. For

example, in her work on Andean religion, Sabine MacCormack commented that "in Huamachuco, as everywhere in the Andes, the plains and the mountains, the sky and the waters were both the theatre and dramatis personae of divine action." See MacCormack, *Religion in the Andes*, 146.

17. Anthropologists debate from where the Huichols originated. Some suggest a northeastern deserts origination, which would make sense given the relationship to peyote. See Furst, *Rock Crystals*, 143; Fresán Jiménez, *Nierika*, 39. Others suggest that the Huichols evolved out of extant groups in the western Sierra. See Weigand and Fikes, "Sensacionalismo y etnografía," 52–53.
18. Benítez, *Magic Land of Peyote*, xxiii.

Introduction

1. Fresán Jiménez, *Nierika*, 27. Teakata is the location of a sacred cave where Tatewari (Grandfather Fire) was born.
2. Aguirre Beltran, *Regions of Refuge*, 24–25; see also Basauri, *La población indígena de México*, 3:67. Here he says, "*Son indios muy encerrados en sus costumbres y creencias religiosas, y extremadamente reservados.*" ("The Indians are very closed off in their customs and religious beliefs, and are very reserved.)"
3. Schaefer, "Culture Summary," 2.
4. Gutiérrez Pulido et al., "La población indígena de Jalisco," 111. http://docplayer.es/23341733-Desarrollo-humano-y-demografia-de-grupos-vulnerables-en-jalisco.html
5. A compilation of indigenous language speakers notes that more than twenty-five thousand inhabitants of Nayarit speak Huichol; more than one thousand speak the language in Zacatecas; and finally, in Durango, roughly two thousand. This, combined with Jalisco's numbers, would point to a significant increase in the Huichols since Weigand reported roughly seven thousand to eight thousand Huichols in the core communities in 1979. See Negrín, "The Huichol: Wixárika." For a summary of population figures, see Schaefer, "Culture Summary," 2.

   For census data, see the following: http://www.cuentame.inegi.org.mx/monografias/informacion/nay/poblacion/diversidad.aspx?tema=me&e=18; http://www.cuentame.inegi.org.mx/monografias/informacion/zac/poblacion/diversidad.aspx?tema=me&e=32; http://www.cuentame.inegi.org.mx/monografias/informacion/dur/poblacion/diversidad.aspx?tema=me&e=10.

6. For a description of gods and pilgrimage sites, see Fresán Jiménez, *Nierika*, 24–27.
7. Smithsonian Institution, National Anthropology Archives (NAA hereafter), Ralph Leon Beals Papers, Manuscript of Writings and Lectures, Unpublished Manuscript on the Huichols and Coras, box 86. Beals and Elsie Clews Parsons studied the Huichols in the 1930s and reported that there are a few Huichol ceremonies that are Catholic in origin, such as the Virgin of Guadalupe festival. See also Zingg Huichol Footage, 1933–34, Smithsonian Institution, Human Film Studies Archives, in which he shows a Virgin of Guadalupe festival.
8. Fresán Jiménez, *Nierika*, 17; Diguet, *Por tierras occidentales*, 138.
9. This idea will be discussed in greater detail throughout the book.
10. I would like to say a word about language in the following chapters. I use the common, more recognizable word "Huichol." As a historian, I feel this is appropriate, because this is the term that appears in nearly all historical records describing the people. The Huichols call themselves "Wixárika" and anthropologists tend to use both. Some strictly use Wixárika, while others switch back and forth. According to Arturo Gutiérrez, the Huichols use Wixáritari because it is their word and not pejorative: "*Por lo general ellos prefieren que se les domine así y no con el término huicholes, con el cual los conocen los mestizos, quienes en muchas ocasiones hacen uso de ese nombre de manera peyorativa.*" See Gutiérrez del Ángel, *La peregrinación a Wirikuta*, 17; Fresán Jiménez, *Nierika*, 17; Diguet, *Por tierras occidentales*, 138. However, I will usually use Huichol terms for things such as *mara'akame* (shaman), Wirikuta (Real de Catorce), and for the names of deities (although English translations do exist). Finally, I will use the English plural form of the word Huichol—that is, Huichols—as opposed to the Spanish Huicholes. This is simply a personal preference. In the conclusion, however, as I write about the modern issues facing the Huichols and draw heavily from media reports, I switch to Wixárika. Again, here I feel that my sources dictate my actions.
11. Negrín, *Acercamiento histórico*, 13–14. Negrín's comments here are somewhat contradictory.
12. Levi, "New Dawn," 8.
13. See recent studies such as Moksnes, *Maya Exodus*; Faudree, *Singing for the Dead*; Ruiz Medrano, *Mexico's Indigenous Communities*.

14. See Van Young, *Hacienda and Market*. Van Young considers hacienda expansion for central Jalisco during the eighteenth century, an area considerably south of the area under study here. However, it is not unreasonable to suggest, based on documentary evidence, that as the nineteenth century progressed, haciendas expanded, putting pressure on groups like the Huichols and mestizo peasants in the area.
15. Scott, *Seeing Like a State*, 39. Scott argues that when land becomes increasingly scarce, more value is placed on it. I will explore this in greater detail in chapter 4.
16. Craib, "Nationalist Metaphysics," 33–34.
17. Craib, "Nationalist Metaphysics," 52–54. For a lengthier discussion, see Craib, *Cartographic Mexico*. I must note here, taking a valuable cue from Emilio Kourí, that public land and indigenous community lands were not viewed as the same, though sometimes they were treated similarly. See Kourí, "Expropriation of Pueblo Lands," 72–73.
18. This last question is difficult to address regarding the Huichols in a historical sense—within the scope of this book, for example—but might be possible if the study were extended into the twenty-first century. See Eisenstadt, "Indigenous Attitudes."
19. Palka, *Unconquered Lacandon Maya*, 66, 122.
20. Palka, *Unconquered Lacandon Maya*, 20.
21. Palka, *Unconquered Lacandon Maya*, 26–27, 94.
22. Sissons, *First Peoples*, 13.
23. Campbell, *Zapotec Renaissance*, 71. Campbell's analysis of the Zapotecs demonstrates that purity of blood took a backseat to community identity.
24. Gabbert, *Becoming Maya*, xi–xii.
25. Gabbert, *Becoming Maya*, xiii.
26. Lutes, "Yaqui Indian Enclavement," 12. See also Erickson, *Yaqui Homeland*. Erickson's work examines the modern Yaqui after the disastrous Porfirian extirpation campaigns of the late-nineteenth and early-twentieth centuries.

1. Native Neighbors to Spanish Conquerors

1. Sahagún, *Florentine Codex*, 10:172–73. German anthropologist Eduard Seler made this argument in 1901, which I discovered while working in the archive at the *Ibero-Amerikanisches Institut* (IAI hereafter) in Berlin, July 2014. See Seler, *Die*

Huichol-indianer, 141. For the English translation see Seler, "Huichol Indians," 180–81. Here, Seler analyzes the Nahuatl:

> *yehoantin in tlaiximach yn mitoa peyotl (the so-called peyote is known to them) inique im ic quiqua peyotl octli ipan quipoa manoço nanacatl (those who eat the peyote use it in place of pulque or in place of poisonous mushrooms), mocentlalia cana ixtlavacan monechicoa, (they meet at a certain place in the desert) vncan mitotia cuica ce yoval cem ilvitl, (dance there the entire night, the entire day) Auh in imoztlayoc occeppa mocentlalia, choca cenca choca, (and on the next day they gather there again and weep, weep copiously) Quil mixpaca ic quichipava in imixtelolo, (they say they wash out their eyes [with tears], cleanse their eyes [recover their senses, see clearly again]).*

I proceed with the assumption that the group described in this passage was Huichol, or at least very closely related. As we shall see, Spaniards who traveled in the region in the late-sixteenth century placed the Huichols in the right area.

2. Trigger, *Cambridge History*, 142. The Chimalhuacán was a confederation that perhaps emerged in response to Toltec ascent. See also Van Young, *Hacienda and Market*, 17. He argues that "ethnically the region was hopelessly jumbled," though it also acted as a buffer between Aztecs and P'urhepechas. The P'urhépechas periodically raided the Etzatlán area, located in modern-day Jalisco, which was rich with obsidian. This area is about one hundred miles as the crow flies from the heart of the Huichols' homeland. Frequent raids likely caused some friction among various groups in the Sierra. See Evans and Webster, *Archaeology of Ancient Mexico*, 249.
3. Negrín, *Acercamiento histórico*, 14. Here, Negrín argues that Chimalhuacán rulers were never tributaries of the Aztecs.
4. Altman, *War for Mexico's West*, 10–11.
5. Altman, *War for Mexico's West*, 10–12, 16–17, 235n49; Gerhard, *North Frontier of New Spain*, 60. Gerhard argues that the Naguatatos were Caxcán speakers, while the "Otomies were Huicholes." Altman suggests Naguatatos were Nahuatl-speakers. See also n29, this chapter.
6. Gerhard, *North Frontier of New Spain*, 42. It is widely suggested that Tangáxuan II, the "king" of the P'urhépecha, immediately sought peace with the Spanish upon learning of the Aztec defeat and an approaching Spanish force; this occurred despite a massive P'urhépecha military. When Guzmán arrived in the area, en route to the West, he had Tangáxuan executed and enslaved hundreds,

perhaps thousands, of Purhépechas. See Perlstein Pollard, *Taríacurí's Legacy*. Finally, Altman does not call Guzmán's Indian recruits slaves, instead referring to them as auxiliaries, which can imply a variety of meanings. Altman, *War for Mexico's West*, 22.

7. Weigand, *Orígenes de los caxcanes*, 72–74. Weigand suggests that a principal Caxcan town, Tetitlán, probably had a strong ethnic Caxcan nobility, supported by Huichol commoners. He makes this argument in part because of the proximity of Huichol and Caxcan towns and the fact that the Caxcans were much more warlike than the Huichols.
8. Altman, *War for Mexico's West*, 37. Apparently, Tonalá had a female ruler.
9. Parry, *Audiencia of New Galicia*, 21.
10. Parry, *Audiencia of New Galicia*, 25. Weigand writes that Guadalajara was first moved from what is now Nochistlán, Zacatecas, in 1530. See Weigand, *Orígenes de los caxcanes*, 72–74. Parry suggested 1531 in his work. See also Van Young, *Hacienda and Market*, 19. Because of native resentment and poor placement, the city was subsequently moved three more times.
11. Gerhard, *North Frontier of New Spain*, 42–43. The Spanish Crown eventually recalled Guzmán because of his tactics, which horrified even his own countrymen. Guillermo de la Peña, a noted Mexican anthropologist, put it succinctly: "Guzmán tiene peor fama," as a result of the violence. See de la Peña, *Culturas indígenas de Jalisco*, 37. Parry called Guzmán "a natural gangster," remarking that "such men flourish in times of violence." See Parry, *Audiencia of New Galicia*, 19.
12. Gerhard, *North Frontier of New Spain*, 42, 71; Franz, "Huichol Ethnohistory," 66. Gerhard noted that although Chirinos was in the Huichol area around 1530, "the people there remained 'uncontrollable and savage'" as of 1550.
13. Weigand, *Orígenes de los caxcanes*, 59. The mention of the Guachichiles by Weigand is significant, because this is one of the names by which the Huichols were known during the early colonial period.
14. Altman, *War for Mexico's West*, 125. Altman provides an excellent analysis of the Mixtón War in chapter 5. Encomenderos were Spaniards who received a grant of unpaid Indian labor, or encomienda, in exchange for their service to the Crown in some capacity.
15. Parry, *Audiencia of New Galicia*, 27.
16. Gutiérrez del Ángel, *La peregrinación a Wirikuta*, 23.

17. Parry, *Audiencia of New Galicia*, 27; de la Peña, *Culturas indígenas de Jalisco*, 37. De la Peña suggests that the rebellion was led by the Caxcans and Zacatecos and that the Huichols and Coras also joined in what was essentially a native rebellion. But when reading Weigand's *Los orígenes*, it is unclear as to the participation of the Huichols during the Mixtón rebellion. See Weigand, *Orígenes de los caxcanes*, 81–82.
18. Parry, *Audiencia of New Galicia*, 28.
19. Gerhard, *North Frontier of New Spain*, 49; de la Peña, *Culturas indígenas de Jalisco*, 38.
20. Blosser, "'Force of Their Lives,'" 289, 293–95. Indian troops that served the Crown were known as *flecheros*.
21. Weigand, *Orígenes de los caxcanes*, 81–82. "*La zona nayarita sirvió como escondite para esclavos prófugos, renegados buscados por las autoridades; así como para desaptados, revolucionarios y refugiados.*"
22. Archivo General de Indias (AGI hereafter), Guadalajara, legajo 51.
23. Parry, *Audiencia of New Galicia*, 68. The New Laws attempted to curb excesses on the part of the Spanish against their indigenous laborers. They were extremely unpopular and led to rebellions in parts of the colonies, particularly in Peru.
24. Torres, *Sancta Provincia*, 93. It is likely that the "Huisares" were the Huichols, but we cannot know with certainty. Likewise, the degree of support for the Tepehuan rebellion is unknown.
25. Gerhard, *North Frontier of New Spain*, 76; Blosser, "'Force of Their Lives,'" 290–91. Blosser notes that by 1590, Spaniards and their indigenous allies had established outposts on the "fronteras de Colotlán."
26. Gerhard, *North Frontier of New Spain*, 71.
27. Gerhard, *North Frontier of New Spain*, 49, 76–79. A rebellion, probably led by Huichols, Tepehuanes, and Tepecanos, occurred in 1592; evidence regarding the rebellion is spotty. Loggers in particular were the bane of many indigenous peoples' existences. Negrín, *Acercamiento histórico*, 14.
28. Arlegui, *Chronica de la Provincia*, 81. Father Arlegui said that the Indians were "*tan barbaroso y atrevidos.*"
29. Santoscoy, *Obras Completas*, II:947. See Altman, *The War for Mexico's West*, 16. Here, she explains that the Spanish used "Naguatato or Nahuatato" for someone who could speak or understand Nahuatl, or for someone whose language closely resembled Nahuatl.

30. Santoscoy, *Obras Completas*, II:975, 985. Gerhard noted that the Huichols lived around Huejuquilla (extreme northern Jalisco) by 1649; Huejuquilla is located in the Huichol region that Arias de Saavedra described. See Gerhard, *The North Frontier of New Spain*, 1993, 76. For a more complete description of what Arias Saavedra wrote, see McCarty and Matson, "Franciscan Report," 194–98. Arias de Saavedra spent about twenty years in the area, and his reports offer insight into some of the groups in the area, most notably the Coras (Nayarits).
31. Tello, *Crónica miscelánea*, 757.
32. Rojas, *Los huicholes*, 64–66. See also Liffman, *Huichol Territory*, 32. Finally, Robert Zingg commented that "the community organization of both the Tarahumaras and the Huichols is similar and appears to have resulted from the influence of Catholic missionaries." From Laboratory of Anthropology Archives (LAA hereafter), Zingg, The Huichols (folder 1 of 4), file number 92, MSS.153a.
33. Liffman, *Huichol Territory*, 32. "The Spaniards began erecting the Huichol *repúblicas* of San Andrés, Santa Catarina, and San Sebastián out of the *tukipa* (temple district) land tenure system."
34. Rojas, *Los huicholes en la historia*, 64–66; Zingg, *Huichol Mythology*; Hinton et al., *Indigenous Acculturation*, 12. In Rojas, *Los huicholes en la historia*, see pp. 64–66 for a brief description of the founding of Colotlán and subsequent comunidades in the immediate area. The year 1591 is the point at which Tlaxcalan colonists arrived at Colotlán, in the service of the Crown, to help pacify the northern frontiers.
35. Unfortunately, the reports analyzed in the section below are all that exist on Huichol religion during the colonial period. One document that could yield interesting information about religious practices in the eighteenth century comes from 1768, and was an accusation of idolatry against several Huichols. The accuser was Chief of the Presidio Vicente Cañaveral. This particular document, Archivo General de la Nación (AGN hereafter), Provincias Internas volumen 127, expediente 3, is no longer available to researchers because of deterioration.
36. Lázaro de Arregui, *Nueva Galicia*, 51–52.
37. Lázaro de Arregui, *Nueva Galicia*, 51–52. Many thanks to Tania de Miguel Magro for assisting me with the direct translation into English. "*La yerba que da ánimo y esfuerzo es el peyote, que al que lo toma se lo da por mucho tiempo; y aun los indios*

dicen que adivinan con el, y la verdad es que da una manera de adormecimiento y un calor que hace que el cansancio y otros trabajos se sientan menos, y tomando mucho se privan del sentido de modo que dicen que ven visiones y entonces dicen que adivinan o saben las cosas ocultas que pretenden." In the eighteenth century José de Arlegui recorded a similar observation:

> *La raíz que mas veneran es una, llamada Peyot, la qual muelen y beben en todas sus enfermedades, y no fuera esto tan malo, sino abusaran de sus virtudes, porque para tener conocimiento de los futuros, y saber, como saldrá de las batallas la beben deshecha en agua, y como es tan fuerte, les da una embriaguez, con resabios de locura, y todas las imaginaciones fantásticas, que les sobrevienen con la horrenda bebida, cogen por presagios de sus designios, imaginando, que la raíz les ha revelado sus futuros sucesos, y lo peor es, que no solo los barbaros executan esta diabólica superstición, sino que aun en los indios domésticos dura este infernal abuso.* (Arlegui, *Chronica de la Provincia*, 166)

38. "Illicit Use of Peyote," Mexico City, 1620. *Ramo de Inquisición*, volumen 289, expediente 12. Reprinted in Chuchiak, *Inquisition in New Spain*, 113–14.
39. Arlegui, *Chronica de la Provincia*, 169–71. Unfortunately, Franciscans' commentaries on peyotism and other elements of Huichol spirituality were colored by their Catholicism. This was coupled with Franciscans' inability to speak or understand the Huichol language.
40. McCarty and Matson, "Franciscan Report," 204–5.
41. "They realized it was without a doubt a house of the demon: at the door of the biggest house was a basket with a wax figurine on top of palms, representing a very ugly black man, whose hands were in such a position that it seemed to mean that it protected the door and defended the entrance." See Arlegui, *Chronica de la Provincia*, 169–70.
42. Bugarín, *Visita de las misiones*, 19; Weigand and García de Weigand, "Huichol Society," 22.
43. Meyer, *Atonalisco, Nayarit*, 11.
44. Coronado and Valdés, *Villa Guerrero, Jalisco*. I have been unable to locate a copy of this work. Rojas cites this document extensively in *Los huicholes: documentos*, 43–45. See also Zingg, *Huichol Mythology*, xix. Rojas does not go into much detail regarding this rebellion, but notes that some Huichol villages did have their lands measured the following year; unfortunately, those documents have never been found.

45. Coronado and Valdés, *Villa Guerrero, Jalisco*; Rojas, *Los huicholes: documentos*, 44–45.
46. Coronado and Valdés, *Villa Guerrero, Jalisco*; Rojas, *Los huicholes: documentos*, 46–47.
47. Coronado and Valdés, *Villa Guerrero, Jalisco*; Rojas, *Los huicholes: documentos*, 48. "*Los días 28, 29 y 30 [de septiembre], el Conde recibe sucesivamente a las indias de tres barrios de Colotlán, que se presentan 'con bateas y cestillas de flores y ramilletes con alguna fruta de la tierra y dulces y aves.'*"
48. Meyer, "Introducción: las misiones jesuitas," 17. In his introduction to the sources, Jean Meyer noted that in the eighteenth century, "*en efecto, las misiones todas empezaron con una revolución en el hábitat, una redistribución y concentración de la población en sitios escogidos, tanto para desarraigar a los nayaritas de sus implantaciones anteriores (o sea borrar su geografía religiosa), como para crear un nuevo tipo de hombre: más agricultor, más sedentario.*" ("In effect, all of the missions began with a revolution of the habitat, a redistribution and concentration of the populations into selected sites, more to uproot the Nayaritas from their earlier established practices [in this case religious practices] (or to erase their religious geography), so as to create a new type of man: more farming, more sedentary.")
49. AGI, Guadalajara, 233, legajo 10, fojas 70 and 142–43.
50. Letter from Fray Antonio Margil to the President of the Audiencia of Guadalajara, January 13, 1711. Reprinted in Leutenegger, *Nothingness Itself*, 164–65. Leutenegger edited and translated some of Margil's letters. Whenever possible, I will refer to the specific letters themselves. According to a series of letters between Philip V of Spain and the duke of Albuquerque (who was viceroy at the time), plans had been laid to subjugate the rebellious seven hundred or so families living in the Sierra del Nayar. Fr. Margil was chosen to complete the task. See AGI, Guadalajara, 232, legajo 9, fojas 358–65.
51. Letter from Fray Antonio Margil to the President of the Audiencia of Guadalajara, January 13, 1711. Reprinted in Leutenegger, *Nothingness Itself*, 164–65.
52. Leutenegger, *Nothingness Itself*, 177.
53. Letter from Fray Antonio Margil to Huei Tacat and Other Chiefs of Nayarit, from Guazamota, Mexico, May 9, 1711. Reprinted in Leutenegger, *Nothingness Itself*, 177–80.

54. Letter from Fray Antonio Margil to Huei Tacat and Other Chiefs of Nayarit, from Guazamota, Mexico, May 9, 1711. Reprinted in Leutenegger, *Nothingness Itself*, 180, see notes; see also 181.
55. Letter from Fray Antonio Margil to Huei Tacat and Other Chiefs of Nayarit, from Guazamota, Mexico, May 9, 1711. Reprinted in Leutenegger, *Nothingness Itself*, 181.
56. Letter from Fray Antonio Margil to the President of the Audiencia of Guadalajara, from Guazamota, Mexico, May 25, 1711. Reprinted in Leutenegger, *Nothingness Itself*, 182. Parts of this letter are also reprinted, in Spanish, in Alcocer, *Bosquejo de la historia*, 105–15.
57. Letter from Fray Antonio Margil to the President of the Audiencia of Guadalajara, from Guazamota, Mexico, May 25, 1711. Reprinted in Leutenegger, *Nothingness Itself*, 184–85; Alcocer, *Bosquejo de la historia*, 105–15.
58. Letter from Fray Antonio Margil to the President of the Audiencia of Guadalajara, from Guazamota, Mexico, May 25, 1711. Reprinted in Leutenegger, *Nothingness Itself*, 187; Alcocer, *Bosquejo de la historia*, 105–15.
59. Letter from Fray Antonio Margil to the President of the Audiencia of Guadalajara, from Guazamota, Mexico, May 25, 1711. Leutenegger, *Nothingness Itself*, 188–89.
60. Meyer, "Introducción: las misiones jesuitas" 20. Erasing their sacred, religious geography (*"sea borror su geografía religiosa"*) involved at first realizing that the landscape was important to the Sierra's native peoples and removing them from the elements of their religion that emphasized the importance of place.
61. Meyer, *El Gran Nayar*, 28–29; Alcocer, *Bosquejo de la historia*, 106–7. Alcocer provides a brief history of late seventeenth-century attempts to rid the Coras of the mummies.
62. Blosser, "'By the Force of Their Lives'," 298–300.
63. Meyer, *El Gran Nayar*, 41–43; Alcocer, *Bosquejo de la historia*, 106–8.
64. AGI, Guadalajara 233, legajo 11.
65. *Hacendado*: one who owns a large plot of land for farming or ranching, which is known as a hacienda.
66. See chapter 9 introductory paragraph in Rojas, *Los huicholes: documentos*, 79. Rojas presents no archival citations for this material, and Somoza's name does not appear in further documentation.

67. Tierras y Aguas, Archivo de Instrumentos Públicos de Jalisco (AIPJ hereafter), expediente 21–1. Escobedo's memo has a few mistakes involving the dates of conquest.
68. Tierras y Aguas, AIPJ, expediente 21–1: "*sólo ángeles pueden atravesar.*"
69. Tierras y Aguas, AIPJ, libro 142, expediente 17 and libro 372. Don Juan Sebastián wrote that "*por que los actuales indios están poseyendo aquellas tierras en representación de sus mayores y ascendientes de quienes por su antigüedad, no hay memoria del origen de aquella reducción; de suerte que cuando estos nacieron conocieron como suyos aquellos fundos, que sus bisabuelos y abuelos gozaron de tiempo inmemorial a esta parte.*"

2. *Facing the Young Nation-State*

1. Gutiérrez del Ángel, *La peregrinación a Wirikuta*, 23. Del Ángel suggests that indigenous peoples participated in all wars since the conquest because of land loss. He even argues that the Huichols' participation in *any* war is due to lost land. While I think this is oversimplified, there is certainly truth to his argument.
2. Van Young, "Moving toward Revolt," 182–83. Van Young's study focuses on the central part of Jalisco and the impacts that changes in land tenure had on indigenous peoples and peasants. Because the Huichols' homeland is so distant from this central area, it is hard to use this particular study to understand how they would have experienced this transformative period. See also Taylor, "Banditry and Insurrection," 210.
3. The best work on indigenous participation in the Independence Movement around Guadalajara comes from Archer's study of the period. See Archer, "Indian Insurgents," 84. Here, Archer notes the role of "Encarnación Rojas, the Indian captain from Tlachichilco," who fought valiantly against the Spanish assault at Lake Chapala, just south of Guadalajara.
4. Weigand, *Ensayos sobre el Gran Nayar*, 121. The Huichols themselves have not shared any memories of participation, or at the least, by the time twentieth-century anthropologists visited their villages, nobody could recall fighting in the Wars for Independence. Phil Weigand notes that the Huichols said they participated in the Lozada Rebellion, the revolution, the Cristero Rebellion, and the "Levantimiento" of 1951. This illustrates a long historical memory, as the Lozada Rebellion began in the 1850s and ended in the 1870s. Based upon

the Huichols' rich tradition of oral history, it is conceivable that reminiscences of independence fighting could have been recalled by some Huichol individuals, passed down from their ancestors. Thus far, concrete evidence of such participation has yet to be discovered.

5. López, *Algunos documentos de Nayarit*, 60.
6. López, *Algunos documentos de Nayarit*, 60.
7. López, *Algunos documentos de Nayarit*, 60. This is a remarkable piece of information, because as will become evident by 1848, the Huichols had significant difficulties with the Hacienda de San Antonio de Padua and its hacendado, don Benito del Hoyo. Because of this simple mention of Hacienda San Antonio, in conjunction with the other towns named, it is reasonable to suggest that Minjares and Angles met with Huichols between December 1811 and January 1812.
8. López, *Algunos documentos de Nayarit*, 60; Rojas, *Los huicholes: documentos*, 111. Colotlán is a large cantón, or county. Most documents in the state historical archive about the Huichols come from the eighth cantón.
9. Sandoval Godoy, *Suave patria*, 313; Rojas, *Los huicholes: documentos*, 111–12.
10. Gutiérrez del Ángel, *La peregrinación a Wirikuta*, 23. It is unclear if "Indio" is the man's first name, but unlikely.
11. Sandoval Godoy, *Suave patria*, 313. Apparently, Cañas was a particularly bad seed, though Pérez does not offer much insight into his behavior. He simply notes that he was a "*perverso cabecilla*."
12. Sandoval Godoy, *Suave patria*, 313; Gutiérrez del Ángel, *La peregrinación a Wirikuta*, 23.
13. López, *Algunos documentos de Nayarit*, 67.
14. López, *Algunos documentos de Nayarit*, 67. See also Archivo de la Mitra del Arzobispado de Guadalajara (AMAG hereafter), Bolaños, C/1, expediente 3, 1827–38. Here, Fray Vicente Buenaventura-Cárdenas complained bitterly that when Huichol husbands wanted a younger, prettier wife, they went out and got a new one or traded her for some cows. It is important to keep in mind that these are the observations of priests, and it is unclear if this actually ever occurred. See Buenaventura section, chapter 3. Whether or not Huichols were marrying in their own ceremonies, Catholic ceremonies, or both is hard to say. By the middle of the 1820s, priests rarely noted the ethnic background, *or calidad*, of the spouses being bound in marriage. See, for example: https://familysearch

.org/search/image/index#uri=https://familysearch.org/recapi/sord/collection /1874591/waypoints, "México, Jalisco, registros parroquiales, 1590–1979," database with images, FamilySearch. To find specific images illustrating this point, first select Bolaños, Parish: San José, Matrimonios 1774–1836, and then you can look through images. In this instance, see image 602 of 693. These records were filmed by the Church of Jesus Christ of Latter Day Saints.

15. Baptisms and other Catholic sacraments were provided to interested indigenous participants. Parents did baptize their children and had been doing so in many areas of the Huichol Sierra since at least the end of the eighteenth century. See, for example, Padre Sánchez Martínez's work among indigenous people in https:// familysearch.org/search/image/index#uri=https://familysearch.org/recapi /sord/collection/1874591/waypoints, "México, Jalisco, registros parroquiales, 1739–1978," database with images, FamilySearch. To locate these images, first select Bolaños, Parish: San José, Bautismos 1793–1831, image 94.
16. López, *Algunos documentos de Nayarit*, 69–70.
17. Huichol attitudes toward marriage were rather relaxed by western standards. Based upon the observations of ethnographers during the nineteenth and twentieth centuries, men in certain communities can have multiple wives, so long as they can afford the expense of their care. For instance, Fray Arias y Saavedra noted that during the sixteenth century, men in the province of Chimaltiteco practiced sororal polygamy, in which all daughters might be given to one Indian man. In nearby Xahuanica province, men commonly had two wives. See McCarty and Matson, "Franciscan Report," 207. Grimes and Hinton suggest that some polygyny is practiced. See Grimes and Hinton, "The Huichol and Cora," 803. Finally, Ramón Mata Torres argues that only in Santa Catarina may a man have multiple wives; he also provides an elaborate description of the marriage ceremony, in which the Catholic Church has no part, by and large. Two youngsters, enamored with each other, agree to marry and get their parents' permission. If all parties accept the proposal, the wedding date is set and occurs with little pomp. Problems arise when priests marry young people without the consent of their parents. See chapter 6 and the conclusion for further discussion of Huichol cultural practices such as marriage. See also Mata Torres, *Matrimonio huichol*, 92–93.
18. Hall, *Extracts from a Journal*, 2:225.

19. Hall, *Extracts from a Journal*, 2:225.
20. Hall, *Extracts from a Journal*, 2:226.
21. Hall, *Extracts from a Journal*, 2:227.
22. Fresán Jiménez, *Nierika*, 59–61; Myerhoff, *Peyote Hunt*, 111. The singular form of the word is *mara'akame*.
23. Hall, *Extracts from a Journal*, 2:226–27.
24. See chapter 1.
25. Hall, *Extracts from a Journal*, 2:227.
26. Fresán Jiménez, *Nierika*, 25.
27. http://collections.dartmouth.edu/arctica-beta/html/EAI5-45.html. Unfortunately there is no biography of Lyon. Lyon was an accomplished watercolor artist, painting beautiful scenes of Inuit villages on his expeditions to the Arctic, which occurred just before his death in 1832.
28. Lyon, *Journal of a Residence*, 1:293.
29. Lyon, *Journal of a Residence*, 1:296.
30. Lyon, *Journal of a Residence*, 1:294, 296.
31. Lyon, *Journal of a Residence*, 1:296.
32. Lyon, *Journal of a Residence*, 1:294–96.
33. Lyon, *Journal of a Residence*, 1:295.
34. Lyon does not specify the length of the trial marriage period, nor does he acknowledge whether or not women were allowed to back out of the marriage if they were unsatisfied with the potential match.
35. Lyon, *Journal of a Residence*, 1:297.
36. Letter from Fray Felipe de Jesús María Muñoz to M. R. P Comisario Fr. Bernardino de V. Pérez, 15 diciembre 1848, caja 257. Archivo Histórico Franciscano de Zapopan (AHFZ hereafter). Here, he conducted weddings and baptisms during the first two months of the year.
37. Lyon, *Journal of a Residence*, 1:322.
38. Lyon, *Journal of a Residence*, 1:321.
39. Knowlton, "Dealing in Real Estate," 13.
40. Mallon, "Reflections of the Ruins," 76. In some instances in Mexico, land laws were interpreted in a way that would protect the "humble classes," according to Mallon. This is evident occasionally in northern Jalisco.
41. Tutino, *From Insurrection to Revolution*, 220–21.

42. Reina, *Las rebeliones campesinas*, 15–16; Joseph and Nugent, "Popular Culture and State Formation," 18. For increasing land commodification in general, see Scott, *Seeing Like a State*, 39.
43. "Vecino" technically means neighbors; however, in legal documents pertaining to land in nineteenth-century Jalisco, vecinos meant town inhabitants (that were likely not indigenous). According to the Huichols, however, a vecino was a mestizo outsider, meaning someone who did not have legitimate claims to lands within Huichol domains.
44. Aguirre Loreto, *Colección de acuerdos*, 9.
45. Other restrictions on the fundo legal were as follows: indigenous villages could not parcel out, sell, or rent the lands granted to them by the king (during the colonial period).
46. *Colección de acuerdos*, 1:vi. The initial circular has a date of December 5, 1822, and the follow-up, known as Decree 2, was passed in February 1825.
47. *Colección de acuerdos*, 1:vi.
48. *Colección de acuerdos*, 1:vi. "*Por el decreto número 79 se prohibió a los particulares que hubiesen comprado algunos terrenos de los indígenas, la venta o enajenación que a éstos no se les concedía.*"
49. Knowlton, "Dealing in Real Estate," 23.
50. *Colección de acuerdos*, 1:47.
51. Mallon, "Reflections of the Ruins," 76.
52. *Colección de acuerdos*, 1:vi.
53. Aguirre Loreto, *Colección de acuerdos*, 62.
54. Gabbert, *Becoming Maya*, xi–xiii. Gabbert argues that the term "Maya" is an overarching ethnic term that they would not comprehend as relating to identity. The Mayas, like the Huichols, identify themselves in a local sense, not as a nation or ethnic group.

3. Between Tolerance and Rejection

1. AMAG, Bolaños, expediente 3, 1827–1839.
2. The friar lamented: "*Cuando las mujeres cuando ya están viejas o feas por otras más mozas, dado de ribete a otros maridos una o dos vacas, y hasta por dos votijas de vino y otras coasas de este especié y con decirle a Va. S. Yllma que hasta dentro de la iglesia han fornicado no puede ser más.*" AMAG, Bolaños, expediente 3, 1827–1839.

3. "Dictamen de San Andrés," AHFZ, caja 145; see also "Informe de San Sebastián, 1843," caja 145.
4. "Informe sobre San Sebastian y sus pueblos de visita," AHFZ, caja 145. This sentiment is repeated in a number of reports from this period.
5. "Informe sobre San Sebastián y sus pueblos de visita," AHFZ, caja 145. See also "Informe de San Sebastián, 1843," caja 145; "Estado de la Misión de San Andrés," caja 145.
6. "*Con respecto a las producciones de estos terrenos son varias, abundan las maderas de todas clases, desde la Encina roble, con sus clases de encino blanco y colorado, el pino real, el alazan.*" ("With respect to the production of these lands there are various, woods of various types, from the holm oak, with types of white and red oak, the royal pine, sorrel.") See "Informe sobre San Sebastián y sus pueblos de visita," AHFZ, caja 145.
7. "Informe sobre San Sebastián y sus pueblos de visita," AHFZ, caja 145. About their diet, see another anonymous report, "Informe de Nayarit," AHFZ. This file was not catalogued with the rest, but was provided to me by Fray Carlos Badillo. It is an undated, anonymously written report from before the Reform Era (pre-1855).
8. "Informe sobre San Sebastián y sus pueblos de visita," AHFZ, caja 145.
9. "Informe sobre San Sebastián y sus pueblos de visita," AHFZ, caja 145.
10. "Informe sobre San Sebastián y sus pueblos de visita," AHFZ, caja 145.
11. Benson, *Provincial Deputation in Mexico*, 188.
12. Letter from Jose María Castillo Portugal to Reverendo Padre Provincial, Archivo de Biblioteca Pública del Estado de Jalisco, Manuscritos, volumen 29, legajo 14. Administering the sacraments to Huichols had been occurring since the eighteenth century at the very least; however, it is difficult to tell from parish records the ethnic backgrounds of individuals receiving sacraments such as marriage or baptism. After about 1822 (depending on the parish), priests stopped listing the ethnicity of sacrament recipients.
13. Rojas, *Los huicholes: documentos*, 118. Here, Rojas provides for a citation "Perez Lete I: 302." There is no other bibliographic information. Consultation with archivists at the Archivo Histórico del Estado de Jalisco turned up nothing, nor did an author search of any other repositories.

14. Velázquez, *Colotlán*, 11, 12n32, 36. Velázquez noted that San Sebastián and its pueblos belonged to the Diocese of Durango, but Jose del Valle, "alcalde mayor of Guadalajara" in 1783, wrote that the towns were ministered to by the Franciscans of Zacatecas. Gerhard cites a report by Arlegui, which suggests that "San Sebastián and its visitas were founded from Chimaltitlán [*sic*], but a document of 1731 shows" the towns "as Huichol dependencies of Huejuquilla." He also suggested that "all were abandoned in 1811." I imagine this to mean that Franciscans had abandoned the towns by then. See Gerhard, *North Frontier of New Spain*, 77. In a report he wrote in 1849, José María de F. Sánchez Alvarez seemed bemused by the fact that San Sebastián had *ever* been chosen as a *doctrina*. He claimed that he searched the archives, working diligently for eight days, looking for documents pertaining to the foundation of San Sebastián as a doctrinal town, to no avail. See "Dictámen de San Andrés," AHFZ, caja 145.
15. AMAG, Guadalajara, 1839. Anacleto Cabral was the presbytery and Juan José de Fernándes Palos was the curate at this point (1838–39), though curates rotated frequently in and out of small parishes such as Bolaños. In looking at the parish records from San José, Bolaños, in the span of four years, there were four different authorities. Sometimes both signatures appeared on documents and at other times, only one. See for example "México, Jalisco, registros parroquiales, 1590–1979," database with images, FamilySearch at https://familysearch.org/search/image/index#uri=https://familysearch.org/recapi/sord/collection/1874591/waypoints, Bolaños, San José, Bautismos 1830–1846, images 340, 380, 400.
16. Rojas, *Los huicholes en la historia*, 120.
17. Rojas, *Los huicholes: documentos*, 123.
18. "Informe de San Sebastián, 1843," AHFZ; "Estado de la misión de San Sebastián"; "Informe sobre San Sebastián y sus pueblos de visita," caja 145. "Informe de Nayarit."
19. Letter from Fray Vicente Buenaventura-Cárdenas to Doctor don Diego de Aranda, bishop of Guadalajara, June 1, 1839, AMAG, Bolaños, expediente 3, 1827–39.
20. Letter from Fray Vicente Buenaventura-Cárdenas to Doctor don Diego de Aranda, bishop of Guadalajara, June 1, 1839, AMAG, Bolaños, expediente 3,

1827–39. Buenaventura wrote: "*En este presente año buscando yo por los cerros y por las cuevas sus ídolos los hallé y se los quemé.*"

21. Occasionally a friar would call an idol a "*mono.*" They were not referring to monkeys, but to the humanoid features of the stone and wood idols. Personal conversation with Bruno Calgaro Sandi, November 2008.
22. Letter from Fray Vicente Buenaventura-Cárdenas to Doctor don Diego de Aranda, bishop of Guadalajara, June 1, 1839, AMAG, Bolaños, expediente 3, 1827–39.
23. Letter from Fray Vicente Buenaventura-Cárdenas to Doctor don Diego de Aranda, bishop of Guadalajara, June 1, 1839, AMAG, Bolaños, expediente 3, 1827–39.
24. AMAG, Bolaños, expediente 3, 1827–1839. Buenaventura did not elaborate on who/what Séautara and Juana Móa represented. The names are not reminiscent of any known Huichol deities. Juana Móa, however, implies that the Huichols experienced some transculturation. Twentieth-century German ethnographer Eduard Seler suggested that the name was actually Cuanamoa, Cuainamoa, or Cuainame. See Seler, "Huichol Indians of Jalisco," 188.
25. For the most part, all of the reports written between 1843 and 1856—the last report from this period—were anonymously written, and it is nearly impossible to tell with certainty which of the friars wrote them. Generally, however, based on letters between the Huichol towns and the Colegio Apostólico in Zapopan, where the brothers were based, it is possible to tell which brother was ministering in which town. The letters offer nothing in the way of Huichol voices, even less than the mission reports. For that reason, the letters were left out of this analysis.
26. "Informe de San Sebastián, 1843," AHFZ, caja 145.
27. "Informe de Nayarit," AHFZ.
28. See "Edict of Faith concerning the Illicit Use of Peyote," Mexico City, 1620, AGN, Ramo de Inquisición, volumen 289, expediente 12; "Trials and Testimonies against the Use of Peyote and Other Herbs and Plants for Divination (chapter introductory comments)." Reprinted in Chuchiak, *Inquisition in New Spain*, 113–14, 309. See also n38 in chapter 1.
29. This is the first instance I have ever found in the archival record mentioning the gathering of peyote in San Luis Potosí. The friar wrote:

En lo religiosa conservan un conjunta de supersticiones, usan y celebrant una infinidad de fiestas mescladas de religión e Ydolatría como la del Peyote y otras. Esta da lástima y horror porque desde el mes de septiembre y octubre se previenen para ir en especie de romería desde estos puntos hasta internarse al estado de San Luis Potosí, comienzan por abstenerse de alimentos con la cirucunstancia que los que van la primera vez dese que salen de su rancho o casa van con los ojos bendados hasta que llegan al punto donde cavan el peyote sin permitir que se quite la benda por la idea de que si se la quitan quedan ciegos. Se abstienen los mas de alimentos y de usar sal en lo que toman, llevan varios presents a aquellos puntos. A su venida son muy bien recibidos por todos, principalmente por los que cuidan el calihuey aqui reunidos todos los que fueron permanecen hasta que vienen los que van a llevar noticias y presentes hasta una cueva que existe en la mesa del Nayar venidos que son comienzan su solemnidades, pues ya para esto esta prevenido el mismo peyote fermentado para beberlo a mas del que comen sin fermenter. Una noche antes de concluir la fiesta tres indios mas viejos y de los principales comienzan el canto de mitote, estos permanecen sentados y alrededor de ellos bailan indistintamente . . . usan en la cabeza de plumeros de modo que representan una figura horrorosa . . . La comida se reduce a la carne de venado principalmente del que han matado el día antes de la fiesta . . . De esta fiesta y de otras sin número dire que las idolatrías, la superstición es la reina en ellas. (*"Informe de San Sebastián, 1843,"* AHFZ, *caja 145*)

Peter Furst remarked that pilgrims are blindfolded to protect their eyes from the spiritual gateway at Wirikuta. See Furst, *Rock Crystals*, 75.

30. "Informe sobre San Sebastián y sus pueblos de visita," AHFZ, caja 145. The anonymous author wrote that *"el carácter de los Huicholes, muchos los tienen por dóciles y apacible, porque aparecen apacibles y tímidos, pero en mi concepto, es terribles, caprichoso y tenas, pues aun no olvidan a pesar de la serie prolongada de años que hace desde su conquista muchas ideas de barbarie."*
31. "Informe sobre San Sebastián y sus pueblos de visita," AHFZ, caja 145. The anonymous author does not actually detail crimes he, or anyone else, witnessed. Much of what he wrote was hearsay; yet he believed that all of the terrible stories about the Huichols had a basis in fact. In one sense, he was right: the Huichols *did* worship idols, and the drunkenness of which he spoke might have been a peyote ritual. The state of "embriaguez" was often a catch-all phrase for alcohol-induced drunkenness, or the state of euphoria produced by hallucinogens. Regardless, from the tone of the document, it is clear that the man did want the Huichols to receive some "help."

32. "Informe de San Sebastián, 1843," AHFZ, caja 145.
33. "Informe de San Sebastián, 1843," AHFZ, caja 145. See also "Estado de manifestación, 1843–55," AHFZ, caja 145.
34. "Estado de manifestación, 1843–55," AHFZ, caja 145; "Informe sobre San Sebastián y sus pueblos de visita," AHFZ, caja 145.
35. "Informe de Santa Catarina, 1852," AHFZ, caja 145.
36. "Informe de Santa Catarina, 1852," AHFZ, caja 145.
37. "Informe de Santa Catarina, 1852," AHFZ, caja 145. Several priests and friars were in the región during the series of events that follows: Padres Presidente Vázquez, Zubia, Aguirre, and Vergara. This account was written by Fray Miguel de Jesús María Guzmán.
38. "Informe de Santa Catarina, 1852," AHFZ, caja 145.
39. "Estado de manifestación, 1843–55," AHFZ, caja 145.
40. Archivo General de la Nación (AGN hereafter), GD 120, Justicia Eclesiástica, volumen 156.
41. AGN, GD 120, Justicia Eclesiástica, volumen 156.
42. A note written in May 1850.
43. AGN, GD 120, Justicia Eclesiástica, volumen 156. The only evidence that President José Joaquín de Herrera authorized this comes from a note written by Castañeda in May 1850. At another point, Aranda y Carpinteiro acknowledges that the president undertook the important work of considering the missionaries; by the date of the letter (April 1851) and owing to the extreme political tension of the early 1850s, de Herrera was no longer president. The matter had passed to Mariano Arista. See AGN, GD 120, Justicia Eclesiástica, volumen 167.
44. "Informe sobre San Sebastián y sus pueblos de visita," AHFZ, caja 145.
45. *La Voz de la Patria*, 15 de enero de 1882, "Misiones de los indios." Cited in Casillas Vázquez Flores, *Racismo y poder*, 332–33. The authors reprinted hundreds of newspaper articles about indigenous peoples in Mexico. Wherever possible, I cite the actual newspapers.

4. In Defense of Lands

1. Rojas, *Los huicholes: documentos*, 189. Here, Rojas cites a document from the Colotlán expediente in the Archivo de la Secretaría de la Defensa Nacional (ASDN hereafter). ASDN, Colotlán 5001, as cited in Rojas.

2. See chapter 17 preliminary notes of Rojas, *Los huicholes: documentos*, 189. Rojas claims that since 1817, the hacienda, which belonged to the curate of Huejuquilla, had treated area indigenous villages as a true, or wicked, stepmother. The violent reaction against del Hoyo and his family was predicated by decades of mistreatment.
3. Rojas, *Los huicholes: documentos*, 189.
4. AHJ, G-5-851-899, JAL/3651, expediente VI. "*Ha incendiado un rancho a los indios de Tensompa, ha destruido con sus ganados sus labores de maíz, que ha mandado destruir con ellos.*"
5. ASDN, XI, 481.3, expediente Colotlán 5001, cited in Rojas, *Los huicholes: documentos*, 189–90. See also Brittsan, *Popular Politics*, 29.
6. For an excellent analysis of the Lozada Rebellion, see Brittsan, *Popular Politics*. See also Meyer, *La tierra de Manuel Lozada*; Barba González, *Manuel Lozada*; Aldana Rendón, *La rebelión agraria*. As Beatriz Rojas noted in her brief introductory notes to the documents on the Lozada Rebellion, there is only some isolated testimony regarding their participation. See Rojas, *Los huicholes: documentos*, 189.
7. For an excellent analysis of indigenous and peasant perspectives, see Guardino, *Peasants, Politics*. Though he ends his book with the Reform Era, and deals with the state of Guerrero, an important theme is that indigenous peoples supported or rejected Liberal and Conservative political ideology depending on local circumstances.
8. For the privatization of church lands, for instance, see Bazant, *Alienation of Church Wealth*. This idea was similar to that proposed by Thomas Jefferson in the early 1800s, in which yeoman farmers would be the building blocks of the United States.
9. The ley Lerdo, promulgated in 1856, effectively canceled the *ejido*, a legal protection of Indian village lands that had existed almost as long as Spain ruled in the Americas.
10. These midcentury reforms triggered the Reform Wars, which consumed Mexico after 1857 and pitted Liberal against Conservative factions. The Liberals, who sought to modernize Mexico through a series of land, religious, and citizenship laws, had fled Mexico City for the safety of Veracruz, home of the Mexican customs house. Here, Juárez took control of the Liberal Party and ruled from exile, while Conservatives commanded the country from Mexico

City. A full-scale civil war engulfed Mexico City when Liberals regained power, however weakly, in 1860.

11. Rojas, *Los huicholes en la historia*, 70, 94. In her history of the Huichols, Rojas mentioned that Captain Escobedo conquered the Huichols of Santa Catarina and San Sebastián sometime in the middle of the seventeenth century, and they began accepting some elements of Spanish colonial life. Her supposition for this comes from testimony given by Escobedo's son, in the 1730s, which corresponds to documentation that she found in CONDUMEX and the Archivo de Instrumentos Públicos, which I have been unable to locate. On p. 94 she notes that "*para estas fechas, ya no nos cabe ninguna duda, San Andrés, Santa Catarina, y San Sebastián existen como pueblos organizados y tienen sus gobernadores y principales.*" See also Liffman, *Huichol Territory*, 32.
12. Weigand, *Ensayos sobre el Gran Nayar*, 122. Weigand wrote: "*Medida que afectaría el sistema franciscano entre los Huichols y pondría fin al sistema de comunidades establecido por la corona española, exponiendo aún más las tierras comunales Huichols a los colonos y ganaderos vecinos.*" For a brief discussion on the technicalities of ley Lerdo, see Tutino, *From Insurrection to Revolution*, 260–62. See also Burns, *Poverty of Progress*, 5–17. Burns suggests that the Liberal constitutions of the mid-nineteenth century turned land into "a commodity to be bought and sold." This is part of what James Scott argues as well. See n14, this chapter.
13. See chapter 2. Jean Meyer points out that it was not the Reform Laws alone that sparked the Lozada Rebellion, because indigenous communities had experienced legal problems over land since the 1820s. Deaton, "Decade of Revolt," 46.
14. *Colección de acuerdos, órdenes y decretos*, 2:170–72. Such was the case in Mezquitic during November and December in 1850. See also Scott, *Seeing Like a State*, 4–5, 39. Scott argues that "as long as common property was abundant and had essentially no fiscal value, the illegibility of its tenure was no problem. But the moment it became scarce (when 'nature' became 'natural resources'), it became the subject of property rights in law, whether in the state or of the citizens." This is precisely the issue for the Huichols: to them, land had spiritual importance and was the avenue through which communities sustained themselves; for nonindigenous Mexicans, land increasingly had value for mining, railroad, and agricultural operations.

15. *Colección de acuerdos, órdenes y decretos*, 2:187–90 and 227–28. Meyer, *Esperando a Lozada*, 131.
16. Jalisco, Gobierno del Estado, Circular, 1856 febrero 7. AHJ, G-9–856 JAL/3565.
17. Jalisco. Gobierno del Estado, Circular, 1856 febrero 7. AHJ, G-9–856 JAL/3565.
18. Jalisco. Gobierno del Estado, Circular, 1856 febrero 7. AHJ, G-9–856 JAL/3565
19. *Colección de acuerdos, órdenes y decretos*, 3:28–29. Ignacio Herrera y Cairo served as acting governor of Jalisco in place of Santos Degollado. Miguel Contreras Medellín was trained as an attorney and served as Herrera y Cairo's secretary during the former's term as governor. The unnamed attorney was appointed by this commission in June 1856.
20. Aguirre Loreto, *Colección de acuerdos*, 33. Interestingly, this area had been divided in thirds by order of the town council of Tepic in early 1828. Regarding Lozada's ethnic background, see Brittsan, *Popular Politics*, 12 and Liffman, *Huichol Territory*, 45.
21. Van Oosterhout, "Confraternities and Popular Conservatism," 102. Van Oosterhout suggests that Lozada's rebellion hinged more on religion than on land. While religion may have played an important role, for the Huichols who participated, land was a more pressing issue.
22. For a discussion of José María Leyva Pérez see Hu-DeHart, *Yaqui Resistance and Survival*. See also Burns, *Poverty of Progress*, 110–11. For a discussion of José María Barrera see Rugeley, *Yucatán's Maya Peasantry*, 61, 109. On p. 109 Rugeley suggests that Barrera, a mestizo, may have been the founder of the Speaking Cross phenomena.
23. It is not my intent to recreate the entirety of the Lozada conflict. I only want to emphasize the limited participation that the Huichols had, based on the anecdotal evidence that exists. Archivo de la Comisión Nacional para el Desarrollo de los Pueblos Indígenas (ACDI hereafter, formerly known as INI). Biblioteca Juan Rulfo, FD 18/12. *Cora, Huichol, Tepehuano en Jalisco, Nayarit, Durango*. Author and date unknown, written some time after the 1970 Mexican census. "*Los Huicholes siempre se han opuesto a todo lo que les es extraño.*"
24. Brittsan, *Popular Politics*, 54, 66.
25. Seguridad Pública. "*Con indios de Bolaños, Jesús María, San Lucas y Chimaltitán rancheros e indios mal armados de lanzas y garrotes y algunos güicholes con flechas.*" AHJ, G-15–857, JAL/1348.

26. Colotlán, Gobierno Político, Oficio, 1861 septiembre 2, AHJ, G-15-861, MEZ/1336.
27. Memo, 18 de junio de 1861, CARSO (formerly CONDUMEX). The memo promulgates a 5 June 1861 decree by Juárez that proclaimed the above-mentioned men to be bandits. The reward for their deaths was $10,000, and if the killer happened to be wanted for a crime, he would be pardoned. See also Gutierrez Contreras, *Tierras para los indígenas*, 10–11.
28. "Letter from Mexico," *San Francisco Bulletin*, November 9, 1869.
29. "Letter from Mexico. Unsettled Condition of the Country—Revolution in Pueblo [*sic*]—Other Letters," *San Francisco Bulletin*, January 17, 1870. See also "Mexico: A Declaration of Independence by Northwestern States—Lozada and Vega the Leaders," *New York Times*, February 26, 1870.
30. Early 1871 once again found Mexico in the state of political turmoil that had been brewing since the expulsion of the French. Liberal supporters of Juárez and Sebastián Lerdo de Tejada faced a challenge from a faction led by General Porfirio Díaz. After failing to overthrow the Lerdista government during the La Noria Revolt (1871–72), launched from Díaz's home state of Oaxaca, Díaz sought refuge in the breakaway province of Tepic as he fled north for the safety of Texas. For the sketchy account of this meeting, see Bancroft, *History of Mexico*, 6:382; Gutierrez Contreras, *Tierras para los indígenas*, 12–13. Contreras cites a biography of Díaz, written by don Nemesio Garía Naranjo, which states that "*el General Díaz se vio obligado a salir de Oaxaca, para ir a refugiarse a Tepic y luego a peregrinar obscuramente por el Estado de Chihuahua.*" Alberto María Carreño, who edited and published documents from the Archivo Porfirio Díaz, does not know what to make of the documents. See Carreño, *Archivo del General Porfirio Díaz*, 10:26. As the story goes, Díaz and Lozada went on a day trip to the Santiago River, whereby Díaz bathed and Lozada fished with dynamite. So close was their relationship, according to the narrator, that when the dynamite blew up too early and injured Lozada, Díaz was the first to provide medical care. The story comes from Everardo Peña Navarro's *Breve monografía de Lozada*, reprinted in Carreño, *Archivo del General Porfirio Díaz*, 10:27. "*Cierto día Lozada y el General Porfirio Díaz se encontraban a la orilla del río de Santiago; mientras don Porfirio tomaba un baño, Lozada se dedicó a pescar con dinamita. Uno de los cartuchos explotó antes de tiempo, por lo que perdió un ojo. Don Porfirio le hizo la primera curación.*" ("One day Lozada and General Porfirio Díaz encountered one another at the

mouth of the Santiago River; while don Porfirio was taking a bath, Lozada dedicated himself to fishing with dynamite. One of the cartridges exploded before it should have, for which he [Lozada] lost an eye. Don Porfirio gave him the first treatment.")

31. Corona, "Parte detallada de la batalla de la Mohonera," Ignacio L. Vallarta Papers, box 3, folder 14, Benson Latin American Collection (hereafter BLAC), the University of Texas at Austin Libraries.
32. Corona, "Parte detallada de la batalla de la Mohonera," Ignacio L. Vallarta Papers, box 3, folder 14, BLAC. For a detailed description of the invasion from start to finish, including analysis, see *Juan Panadero*, 23 de enero, 26 de enero, and 31 de enero de 1873.
33. "A Band of Revolutionists Suppressed—Capture of Notorious Lozada," *New York Times*, July 24, 1873.
34. Ignacio L. Vallarta Papers, box 3, folder 14, BLAC. Corona wrote a brief note mentioning the death of Lozada: "*El feroz bandido murió con entereza y ferocidad, pues ya en momentos de ser ejecutado, dijo que no se arrepentía de lo que había hecho en este Distrito.*" Lozada died the morning of either the nineteenth or the twentieth; documents disagree. Corona noted the execution on the twentieth, but two newspapers reported the death as having occurred on the nineteenth. See "Más sobre Lozada," *Juan Panadero*, 24 de junio de 1873. This gives a report of the death sentence.
35. Ignacio L. Vallarta Papers, box 3, folder 14, BLAC. Lozada said, "*Nunca cometido un crimen, que todo lo que había hecho era por la felicidad de los pueblos y que algún día conocerían la falta que hacía para el progreso de México.*"
36. Reina, *Las rebeliones campesinas*, 25.
37. Garner, *Porfirio Díaz*, 42, 187–88. Garner suggests that Díaz was more sensitive to the issue of pueblo land privatization than he has previously been given credit for. Garner's work provides another view of Díaz, but one that unfortunately fails to take into account the effects that Porfirian land policies had on indigenous villages outside of Díaz's home state of Oaxaca.
38. Between 1880 and 1884, Manuel González, a puppet replacement for Díaz, took the helm of Mexico.
39. Cosio Villegas, *Historia moderna*, 187–88. An undated, untitled newspaper clipping from Michoacán, found in the Archivo Porfirio Díaz (APD hereafter when

referencing the archive, as opposed to the Carreño-edited volumes), provided a sense of local attitudes on the issue, and it appears to have been printed after the passage of the law. See "Michoacán: circular sobre terrenos baldíos," APD, document #009839.

40. Cosio Villegas, *Historia moderna*, 188.
41. Scott, *Seeing Like a State*, 14–22. In this section of the book, Scott examines the importance of timber lands management and how states (in this case, Germany) managed and valued land.
42. Colotlán, Jefatura Política del 8° cantón, expediente, 1887–1888, AHJ, G-9-887, CON/3455. All of the Huichol towns fall under the jurisdiction of either Colotlán or Mezquitic of the eighth cantón of Jalisco. The jefe político of Tepic (for whom Antonio Fuentes was presumably a secretary) got involved because the bothersome party of vecinos lived in the town of Huajimic, part of the seventh cantón.
43. AHJ, G-9-887, CON/3455.
44. Catalino Arriaga Albáñez was a representative for the Huichol governor, Brigido Aguilar. Indeed, as was evident during the final phase of the Lozada conflicts, resolving any issues between the state government of Jalisco and the military district of Tepic was fraught with problems. Juárez had made Tepic a military district in 1867.
45. Letter from the jefe político of Colotlán to Brigido Aguilar, AHJ, G-9-887, CON/3455. Correa y Chacón does not mention what the Navarrete family members actually did, just that they had committed annoyances in action and in word (*vejaciones de hecho y de palabra*).
46. Jalisco, Secretaría del Supremo Gobierno del Estado, carta, 1888 abril 9, AHJ, G-9-888, MEZ/1787. I assume that because Medrano declared the lands "terrenos baldíos" the case was no longer within the jurisdiction of the local authorities.
47. Colotlán, Jefatura Política del 8° cantón, 1876, AHJ, G-15-876, CON/1078. "*Varios indígenas de los pueblos de la Soledad Tensompa y San Nicolás.*"
48. Franz, "Huichol Ethnohistory," 82. Franz notes that increasing development in other areas meant that pressure from outsiders increased too, including from other Huichol towns.
49. Jalisco, Secretaría del Supremo Gobierno del Estado, carta, 1888 mayo 28, AHJ, G-9-888, CON/1803.

50. AHJ, G-9-888, CON/1803. It actually seemed as though the government wanted to help in this instance.
51. AHJ, G-9-888, CON/1803.
52. See chapter 2.
53. Cruz, Rosalio de la et al., Ocurso, 1888 octubre 20: "*Le dispone que el Ingeniero Rosendo Corona arregle las diferencias sobre limites entre los indígenas de Santa Catarina y San Andrés.*" AHJ, G-5-888, HUA/798.
54. Craib, *Cartographic Mexico*, 145–56. Craib noted that "both landowners and campesinos were particularly wary of the sight of military engineers with land-measuring instruments, accompanied by a military escort."
55. AHJ, G-5-888, HUA/798. During the Porfirian era, mapping lands and demarcating boundaries was believed to be an effective way of pacifying unhappy indigenous peoples. Díaz "viewed both operations—forced settlement and the land division—as essential components to the pacification and civilizing of the Yaqui." The same can be surmised for the Huichols in Jalisco. Craib, *Cartographic Mexico*,166.
56. AHJ, G-9-888, HUR/3458.
57. The Hacienda San Antonio de Padua was located in Zacatecas, but another troublesome property, the Hacienda Hipazote, was in Jalisco. Border problems had plagued relations between Jalisco and Zacatecas since the 1860s.
58. AHJ, G-9-888, HUR/3458. The Reglamento por los Indígenas de Tlajomulco was established on October 2, 1871, to protect native resources, though I could not find any more information on the matter. The Comisión Repartidora de terrenos de indígenas de Huejucar implemented the Reglamento to guard their forest reserves.
59. Colotlán, Jefatura Política del 8° cantón, Oficio, 1889 marzo 30, AHJ, G-9-889, CON/1959.
60. Colotlán, Jefatura Política del 8° cantón, Oficio, 1889 marzo 30, AHJ, G-9-889, CON/1959.
61. Hinton, "Cultural Visibility and the Cora," 37. It is unclear how the Cora elder meant this comment to be taken. However, the Huichols "squawking" brought attention to themselves, and thus they retained a significant amount of their land.
62. Jefatura Política del Territorio de Tepic, Oficio, 1889 diciembre 4, AHJ, G-9-889, CON/3456.

63. Weigand, "Role of Huichol Indians," 168.

64. Cited in Rojas, *Los huicholes: documentos*, 219–22. I searched for this document in the archives and found only a portion, G-9-889, CON/3456, most of which was barely legible. Rojas also consulted G-9-890, CON/508, but the archivist in Guadalajara could not locate this file.

65. For more information on the ideas of positivism, as they pertained to Mexican indigenous peoples, see Hale, *Transformation of Liberalism*, chap. 7.

66. Cited in Rojas, *Los huicholes: documentos*, 222. Document number is apparently AHJ, G-9-890, CON/508.

67. Cited in Rojas, *Los huicholes: documentos*, 226. Document number is AHJ, G-9-892, CON/3477. This, among a few other documents, was not located during my research.

68. Coyle, *From Flowers to Ash*, 90. According to Liberals, "lands were wasted in the hands of Indians, described as 'savages who cut the tree at its base in order collect its fruits with greater ease.'" They also suggested indigenous peoples were "eternal enemies of progress."

69. Casillas and Vázquez Flores, *Racismo y poder*, 99.

70. Powell, "Mexican Intellectuals," 21. See Pimentel, *Obras completas*, 3:144. Pimentel wrote: "*Para conseguir la transformación de los indios lo lograremos con la immigración europea; cosa también que tiene dificultades que vencer; pero definitivamente menores que la civilización de la raza indígena.*"

71. Powell, "Mexican Intellectuals," 21.

72. Burns, *Poverty of Progress*, 30.

73. *El Imperio*, 7 de octubre de 1865. Cited in Casillas and Vázquez Flores, *Racismo y poder*, 189.

74. *Juan Panadero*, 8 de diciembre de 1872.

75. Vanderwood, *Power of God*, chap. 4.

76. "El cantón de Tepic," *Juan Panadero*, 17 de abril de 1881.

77. *Juan Panadero*, 13 de agosto de 1874. Incidentally, the author acknowledged that the religious institutions seemed to be succeeding, but those methodologies were only tried *after* the United States grew tired of exterminating indigenous peoples.

78. Cosio Villegas, *Historia moderna*, 273. "*De no ser por los curas, concluía, ya habrían vuelto al salvajismo.*"

79. Colonization projects had occurred in other regions of Latin America. For a discussion on the Tipú of Belize, see Jones, *Maya Resistance.*
80. "Censo de la República Mexicana," *Juan Panadero*, 29 de abril de 1883. See also Hale, *Transformation of Liberalism*, 220. Hale quotes Justo Sierra's data here, which gives a figure of 3.97 million, or 38.02 percent of the population in 1889.
81. Letter from President Manuel González to General Guillermo Carbó, Guaymas, Sonora. 26 de febrero 1883, APD, folio 000025. Cosio Villegas, *Historia moderna*, 273.
82. Casillas and Vázquez Flores, *Racismo y poder*, 99. Most Mexicans clung to the Liberal belief that communal landholdings stunted economic growth. Cosio Villegas, *Historia moderna*, 273.
83. Cosio Villegas, *Historia moderna*, 597.
84. AHJ, G-9–888 CON/1803. This law stated that Huichols "*usarán pantalones conforme a sus circunstancias pencunarias.*" It also forced the Huichols to wear underwear, but it is unclear how officials enforced this aspect of the law, and *who* did the enforcing.
85. Cosio Villegas, *Historia moderna*, 396. Norwegian botanist Carl Lumholtz, whom we will meet in the next chapter, remarked that fining a person who made between 31 and 37 centavos per day for wearing traditional clothing was unjust. The clothing, he noted, was hygienic and decent and Lumholtz saw no need to try and force them into western clothing in some vain attempt at feigned civilization.
86. Cosio Villegas, *Historia moderna*, 491.
87. Rojas, *Los huicholes: documentos*, 231. I have yet to come across old land titles for San Andrés, but seeking titles was a common request.
88. Negrín, *Acercamiento histórico*, 19. Negrín and others note that parts of San Sebastián and Santa Catarina became part of the Hacienda la familia Torres by the end of the nineteenth century. Though San Andrés had a school, this did not make leaders there comfortable or content, because they feared what the future brought. See also Rojas, *Los huicholes: documentos*, 230–32.
89. Cited in Rojas, *Los huicholes: documentos*, 223. Document number is AHJ, G-9–892, CON/3477.
90. Cited in Rojas, *Los huicholes: documentos*, 223. Document number is AHJ, G-9–892, CON/3477.

5. Foreign Scholars as Tools of Resistance

1. "The Artist Savages of Mexico: Professor Lumhotlz' Story of the Huichol or Vi-ra-ri-ka Indians. Curios [*sic*] rites of their fire-god and deer-god worship. A Nation of Liars," *Dallas Morning News*, December 6, 1903.
2. Lumholtz was born in Norway in 1851 and initially chose the ministry as his intended career path; while recovering from an illness, he developed an interest in botany. See Bowden, "Learning Nothing, Forgetting Nothing," 361; Eek, "Secret of Cigar Box," 369. Born in Le Havre, France, in 1859, Diguet received an education at the Musée d'Histoire Naturelle in Paris, which exposed him to the burgeoning fields of ethnography and anthropology. See Debroise, *Mexican Suite*, 126; Darling, "Diguet's Studies of West Mexico," 181. The German ethnographer and linguist Konrad Theodor Preuss became fascinated with the works of Lumholtz and Diguet. Born in Prussia in 1869, Preuss originally intended on completing an education in the seminary; though he never finished his theological studies, his interest in religion influenced his work later in life. See Schaefer and Furst, "Introduction to Chapter Four," 88–89; Preuss, *Fiesta, literatura y magia*, 22.
3. Letter dated 3 May 1895 from Jesús María, Jalisco, American Museum of Natural History, New York, Department of Anthropology Archives (AMNH hereafter), Acc# 1895–8, Cat#s 65/i-163. Lumholtz wrote that the Coras "won't allow whites onto their lands and . . . don't like strangers."
4. Lumholtz, "Huichol Indians," 89. Back shields are not used for war, but are instead a small circular shield used in religious ceremonies, or as talismans to protect one's home or person. They are frequently decorated with frightening beasts, such as mountain lions in the aforementioned case.
5. Letter to Morris K. Jesup, 27 September 1895. AMNH, Acc# 1895–8, Cat#s 65/i-163. See also Lumholtz, "Huichol Indians," 80. Lumholtz does not divulge how he knew they were "civilized" or why they planned to kill him. "The Artist Savages of Mexico. Professor Lumholtz' Story of the Huichol or Vi-ra-ri-ka Indians," *Dallas Morning News*, December 6, 1903. Apparently, the alcalde of Santa Catarina warned Lumholtz that if he proceeded, he did so at great risk.
6. Lumholtz, "Huichol Indians," 81.
7. Lumholtz, "Huichol Indians," 81.
8. Lumholtz, "Explorations in Mexico," 127.

9. Lumholtz, "Explorations in Mexico," 127; Lumholtz, *Unknown Mexico*, 2:2.
10. Letter to Morris K. Jesup, 3 July 1894. Letter from John Winser, 6 November 1894. Letter from John Winser, 16 November 1894. AMNH, Acc# 1895–8, Cat#s 65/i-163. Part of Lumholtz's job in Mexico was to collect specimens of public and academic interest for the American Museum of Natural History; it seems as though he spent much of 1894 and early 1895 doing just that. While the vases and "Aztek" pottery that Lumholtz procured were of interest to John Winser, secretary of the Museum of Natural History, human remains and photographs were much more important.
11. Zingg, *Huichol Mythology*, xxi. Zingg suggested that mummy worship still occurred when he visited the Huichols in the 1930s, so there is no reason to suggest that Lumholtz was exaggerating in his letter to his colleagues in New York.
12. See Arlegui, *Chronica de la Provincia*, 169–71. See also AMAG, Bolaños, expediente 3, 1827–39.
13. Letter from F. W. Putnam (Peabody Museum of Anthropology), 23 January 1895, AMNH, Acc# 1895–8, Cat#s 65/i-163. On some of his expeditions Lumholtz was accompanied by Aleš Hrdlička, a young Czech anthropologist. Hrdlička commented that "the principal motive of my search was the physical remains of the prehistoric people," suggesting that gathering skulls and skeletons was an exercise "to save it from destruction, or, what is but little better, dispersion." See Hrdlička, "Region of Ancient 'Chichimecs,'" 386. Reginald Horsman suggests that the obsession with skulls among American and European scholars stemmed from a long-standing nineteenth-century belief that by examining skulls, the racial inferiority of American indigenous peoples and Africans could be assessed. See Horsman, "Scientific Racism." In reality Lumholtz was in a bind with his superiors. For a discussion of skull and body measurements, used by nineteenth-century scientists to determine "the inaptitude of the Indian for civilization," see Gould, *Mismeasure of Man*, 89, 140, 144.
14. Letter from F. W. Putnam, 23 January 1895; Letter to F. W. Putnam, 27 September 1895. AMNH, Acc# 1895–8, Cat#s 65-i-163.
15. Letter to Morris K. Jesup, 22 March 1896. AMNH, Acc# 1896–11, Cat#s 65/164–583. Recall the description reported by Arlegui of a mummified body in a temple. See chapter 1. Later in his expedition Lumholtz witnessed either a serious evolution among the Huichols in a short period, or the Huichols had little fear of

the dead and had only made idle threats. Upon his departure from the area at a later (undated) period, some Huichols gave him a gift of skulls to take with him on his travels. Perhaps there is a third scenario, that Lumholtz took the skulls without the knowledge of the Huichols? Considering the violent rebellion that the Huichols and Coras fought over the destruction of ancestral mummies in the 1720s, his story is highly suspect. See Lumholtz, *Unknown Mexico*, 2:285.

16. Preuss, "Ride through the Country," 25. Tozzer Library.
17. Preuss, "Ride through the Country," 25. Tozzer Library.
18. Lumholtz, *Unknown Mexico*, 2:6–9. However interested he may have been in Huichol cosmology, Lumholtz's initial writings reveal a man thoroughly dismayed upon the realization that this festival sought more rain; upon his initial arrival, a horrific thunderstorm with torrential downpour welcomed him.
19. Lumholtz, *Unknown Mexico*, 2:6–9.
20. Letter to Morris K. Jesup, 27 September 1895. AMNH, Acc# 1865–8, Cat#s 65/i-163. Lumholtz, "Explorations in Mexico," 136.
21. Lumholtz, "Explorations in Mexico," 136.
22. Lumholtz, "Explorations in Mexico," 136, 137. Lumholtz commented that "from his birth to his death his actions are governed by the belief in his native deities." See Lumholtz, "Huichol Indians," 84.
23. Lumholtz, *Unknown Mexico*, 2:148.
24. Lumholtz, *Unknown Mexico*, 2:171. For a modern commentary on Huichol attitudes towards saints vis-à-vis their own deities, see Basauri, *La población indígena de México*, 3:67. Here he says "'*Veneran a los santos como a otras deidades y guardan firmemente arraigadas en su entendimiento las creencias, costumbres y ceremonias antiguas.*'" ("'They venerate the saints as they do other deities and firmly remain rooted in their understanding of beliefs, customs, and ancient ceremonies.'")
25. Myerhoff, "Deer-Maize-Peyote," 68. Lumholtz called it a trinity (as did Fernando Benítez), but Myerhoff suggests it is much more than that. She argues it is simply a cycle. Liffman agrees, suggesting that it links different parts of the year (hunting, gathering, farming). See Liffman, *Huichol Territory*, 76.
26. Diguet, *Por tierras occidentales*, 144–45. The placement of deer, peyote, and maize within a symbolic cyclical calendar was an idea that Diguet touched upon, but did not develop as completely as future generations of scholars would eventually do.

27. Diguet, *Por tierras occidentales*, 145.
28. Fresán Jiménez, *Nierika*, 39.
29. Recall that I have recreated this story in the prologue. Diguet called the deity Majakuagy, a corruption of the Huichol name currently spelled Maxa Kwaxi. There is no mention of Kauyaumari. As Myerhoff explained, the concept of semidivine/divine transformation may have escaped the Frenchman, as it is a difficult concept for foreigners to comprehend. Instead of repeating Diguet's mistakes, I will substitute Kauyaumari as the individual whose conflicts with unnamed enemies left him stricken in the desert. Tamatsi Maxa Kwaxi was the deer deity who took pity on the mara'akame and his people, providing them with peyote. See Myerhoff, *Peyote Hunt*, 85. Incidentally, Preuss recognized Kauyaumari as a semidivine trickster. See Preuss, "Die Hochzeit des Maises."
30. Diguet, *Por tierras occidentales*, 144–45, 147. "*Cuando Majakuagy expuso sus doctrinas, sufrió toda clase de persecuciones por parte de sus enemigos; él y sus discípulos tuvieron que huir; los encargados de perseguirlos los desvalijaron y les destruyeron los utensilios que les servían para alimentarse en un lugar llamado Rhaitomuany. Los dioses compadecidos de su desgracia, convirtieron los residuos de los utensilios en peyote, proveyéndolos de esto modo, de una planta con propiedades sobrenaturales, que tiene la virtud de defenderlos del hanbre y de la sed durante un tiempo considerable.*" Because Diguet's native language was French, he spelled Huichol words like Maxa Kwaxi as "Majakuajy." I use the spelling regulated by twentieth-century anthropologists such as Peter Furst, who worked extensively with Diguet's sources.
31. Lumholtz, *Unknown Mexico*, 2:126–29.
32. Lumholtz, *Unknown Mexico*, 2:130, 156.
33. See n1, prologue. I have corrected Diguet's apparent mistake, based upon Myerhoff's observations and work.
34. For a list of towns that the Huichols pay homage to, see Diguet, *Por tierras occidentales*, 155–56; Fresán Jiménez, *Nierika*, 39.
35. Myerhoff, "Deer-Maize-Peyote," 68; Lumholtz, "Explorations in Mexico," 138–39.
36. Furst, *Rock Crystals*, 63–64. Here, Furst suggests that Lumholtz believed this to be a type of patriotism — not the one we usually associate with nation-state pride, but of ethnic pride. Furst's subject, a Huichol mara'akame named Ramón Medina, said that the pilgrimage means "being Huichol . . . to have one's life." Lumholtz noted that peyote promoted group health. Lumholtz, "Explorations

in Mexico," 138; Fresán Jiménez, *Nierika*, 39. Here, the Spanish says "*primordial casa ceremonial.*"

37. *Kurz, es ist die heilige Hirschjagd der Götter, die hier in dem Peyote-suchen, nachgeahmt wird, und diese Hirschjagd im Lande des Peyote, am Orte des Sonnenaufgangs, erfährt sowohl am Feste des Maisröstens im März, das den Abschluß für den kultischen Zustand der Peyote-sucher bildet, wie am Junifeste des Essens von Gebäck aus rohem Mais (haxari kuaixa) andere Darstellungen in verschiedenen Formen. Leute werden als Hirsche am Festorte selbst in die Schlingen gejagt, ganz in der Weise, wie eine wirkliche Hirschjagd verläuft, oder der Sonnengott tayau, "unser Vater", und eine Abart des Feuergottes tatusi maxa kuaxi, "Urgroßvater Hirschschwanz", verfolgen kurz vor Tagesanbruch den Darsteller des Hirsches nach parizakutsie, dem Orte des Sonnenaufgangs, oder es findet ein Wettlauf nach den Federn des Blauhähers und nach Hirschschwänyen, wiederum nach dem genannten Orte statt, wobei die Federn nur ein anderer Ausdruck für Hirschgeweihe sind.* (Preuss, "Die religiösen Gesänge," 385)
38. Preuss, "Die religiösen Gesänge," 372.
39. Preuss, "Die Hochzeit des Maises," 188. "*Auch gibt es nicht einzelne Gesänge bestimmten Inhalts, sondern ein einziger Gesang währt die ganze Nacht, ein anderer den ganzen folgenden Tag, wenn das Fest so lange dauert. Das ist nur möglich durch breite Ausführung jedes einzelnen Gedankens und seine Anwendung auf die vielen Götter aller vier bis sechs Weltrichtungen.*"
40. "Die Hochzeit des Maises,"189, IAI.
41. Lumholtz had expected to find the Huichols living in a state of "primitive simplicity," when in fact their social, political, and religious structures were fairly complicated. See Lumholtz, "Explorations in Mexico," 136. Lumholtz, *Unknown Mexico*, 2:245–46. He commented that this had been the case since the colonial times. While I failed to find evidence of these offices from that early, Franciscans noted the ceremony of the changing of staff, or *cambia de varas*, in "Estado de la misión de San Sebastián," AHFZ, caja 145. See chapter 3.
42. Lumholtz, *Unknown Mexico*, 2:245–46. Women also served as tenanches in San Luis de Mezquitic, San Luis Potosí, during colonial times. Personal communication with Laurent Corbeil, July 15, 2015.
43. Lumholtz, *Unknown Mexico*, 2:246–49.
44. Diguet, *Por tierras occidentales*, 129.

45. Diguet, *Por tierras occidentales*, 129. It is entirely possible that there was a hierarchy of sorts, but not a nobility to speak of. Those individuals who held religious or secular office might have been held in higher esteem, as mara'akate were (and still are) incredibly important members of society.
46. Lumholtz, *Unknown Mexico*, 2:59.
47. Gabbert, *Becoming Maya*, xi–xii.
48. Lumholtz, *Unknown Mexico*, 2:263.
49. Diguet, *Por tierras occidentales*, 168. "*El carácter de los indígenas también llegó a cambiar. Aquellos que vivían en el distrito de San Andrés eran más abiertos y más accesibles a las ideas traídas por los españoles; al contact con los misioneros, abandonaron con bastante facilidad sus antiguas costumbres; actualmente los cristianos son más numerosos entre ellos.*" Huicholes in San Andrés may not have been more Christianized necessarily, but proximity to the Spanish/Mexicans certainly made them more easily approached, as evidenced by Lumholtz as well.
50. Juan Negrín, personal communication, November 3, 2008. Owing to a rise in tourism, "the community of Santa Catarina worried that the government is going to try to force road improvement down its throat again, in order to further its 'eco-touristic' program in the area." So while Huichols in Cuexcomatitán might have been willing to talk to Lumholtz or Diguet, I think this was likely because they did not perceive either man as existential threats. Lumholtz and his donkeys and dog were not agents of the state.
51. Diguet, *Por tierras occidentales*, 163–64. Regarding Santa Catarina: "*En el distrito de Santa Catalina, se enorgullecen de ser los que mejor conservaron las antiguas tradiciones, los indios, aunque bastante abiertos al progreso, no abandonan fácilmente sus antiguas costumbres.*" And San Sebastián: "*Finalmente los indios del distrito de San Sebastián siempre se manifestaron como los menos inteligentes y los más atrasados de toda la población huichol.*"
52. Diguet, *Por tierras occidentales*, 128–29. Diguet uses the phrase "social disorganization," but does not elaborate on what he actually meant. He was likely influenced at this point by Émile Durkheim. See Durkheim, *Rules of Sociological Method*. Durkheim was influenced by positivist philosopher Auguste Comte and studied society in reaction to the modernizing world. It should go without saying that decades of Liberal land policies, plus rebellions, disrupted normal society in the Sierra Madre Occidental.

53. Diguet, *Por tierras occidentales*, 124.
54. "Art of a Strange People," *New York Times*, November 4, 1903.
55. "Ark Landed in Mexico," *Los Angeles Times*, October 28, 1903.
56. "The Artist Savages of Mexico . . . A Nation of Liars," *Dallas Morning News*, December 6, 1903.

6. A Revolution Comes to the Huichols

1. Elsie Clews Parson and Ralph L. Beals, "Notes on the Coras and Huichol." Smithsonian Institution-NAA, Ralph Leon Beals Papers, Manuscripts of Writings and Lectures, Unpublished Manuscript on Huichols and Coras, box 86.
2. Zingg Huichol Film Footage, 1933–34, Human Studies Film Archive, Smithsonian Institution-NAA.
3. Lumholtz, "Explorations in Mexico," 139. Indigenistas were intellectuals who, in the early post-revolutionary period, pushed an agenda of assimilation of Mexico's indigenous populations.
4. Burciaga Campos, "Revolución mexicana," 55. "*Además, los perjuicios racistas no habían disminuido; al contrario, aumentaron durante y después del fragor de la lucha revolucionaria y fomentaron la discriminación.*" ("Additionally, racist prejudices had not diminished; on the contrary, they grew and fomented during and after the heat of the revolution.") See also Cumberland, *Mexican Revolution*, 6. This might be an overly simplified notion, but it is nevertheless the prevailing attitude of the time.
5. For a good discussion of the emergence of discontent toward Díaz, see Osorio, "Villismo," 89.
6. Burciaga Campos, "Revolución mexicana," 55. "*En el caso de los huicholes, pueblo traicionalmente reacio al contacto con los mestizos, se puede encontrar otra razón para no atraer la atención de las autoridades nacionales y regionales. Su aislamiento geográfico debió ser suficiente para ello.*" ("In the case of the Huichols, a people traditionally opposed to contact with mestizos, there is another reason not to attract the attention of regional and local authorities. Their geographic isolation should have been sufficient.") In this instance I disagree with Burciaga Campos in terms of his suggestion that isolation helped keep them out of the revolution. I suggest, as will become clear throughout this chapter, that other issues divided the Huichols in typical fashion. As should be evident based on

chapters 4 and 5, with the expansion of the state into the Sierra Madre and the increasing presence of outsiders, the Huichol homeland was not exactly isolated in the traditional sense by 1910. However, it was also not exactly on major highways or railways taken by revolutionary soldiers.

7. Some of the source material cited throughout part of this chapter comes from oral testimonies conducted by Robert M. Zingg, who worked in the Tuxpan de Bolaños during the 1930s. He interviewed survivors of the revolution. This is the only evidence of revolutionary activity for much of this period and has been cited and recited by anthropologists and other scholars.
8. See chapter 5.
9. In 1900, for example, a very short piece from the presidente municipal of Mesquitic [*sic*] noted that the Huichols of San Andrés did not appear, as ordered, to name a commission to divide their lands. Having title to their properties might not have prevented land divisions, as the 1857 Constitution and the 1884 Land Law technically prohibited communal properties; however, the borders of their physical territory—at least according to the Mexican government—would be definitive if San Andrés could produce a title. Additionally, the lands that San Andrés used would also be marked, thereby invalidating claims of "vacant lands" by unscrupulous outsiders. By 1901, they asked to look for it in various archives. See AHJ, G-9-900, C/515.
10. *Archivo de Buscas*, AGN, expediente 65, 1901–1904. Submitted by Gobernador Juan Ignacio de la Cruz and Interim Alcalde Santos Torre de la Cruz, 11 de enero 1901. This period of Huichol unity, real or imagined, did not last particularly long, as was typically the case. In regards to the title, Paul Liffman suggests that San Andrés received title to their lands in 1725, though the town "was demarcated in February 1809, just before the Mexican independence movement erupted." See Liffman, *Huichol Territory*, 83.
11. Receptoría de rentas, 1901–1905, AHJ, G-9-901, MEZ/3566. A complaint levied by Francisco Gabriel, governor of Santa Catarina, on December 20, 1901, was too late; a fraction of Santa Catarina's land had been sold to pay off debts they owed. This was done, as the document states, despite the fact that indigenous officials did not verify payment of 360 pesos for the land.
12. Weigand, *Ensayos sobre el Gran Nayar*, 123; Negrín, *Acercamiento histórico*, 19. Finally, I found a curious document in the Archivo Histórico del Estado de Jalisco

that described the hardships the Huichols of Santa Catarina faced because they could not come up with rent payments. It was never evident to whom they paid the rent, but their plight is clear from the letter they wrote in 1901, asking to be relieved of rent payments. The government paid little attention, and the matter apparently received no further review. Receptoría de rentas, 1901–1905, AHJ, G-9-901 MEZ/3566, Mezquitic.

13. Rojas, *Los huicholes en la historia*, 190; Coyle, *From Flowers to Ash*, 95.
14. Gobierno del Estado, 8 de diciembre de 1909, AHJ, G-9–909, C/501.
15. Gobierno del Estado, marzo de 1908, AHJ, G-15–908. C/1223. "*Y como esa superioridad debe tener en cuenta, que el medio mas eficaz para la civilización de estos pueblos de indígenas es el contacto con la gente blanca y el número de individuos blancos asciende a unos cien.*"
16. Osnaya Velázquez, *Los misioneros Josefinos*, 10-11.
17. Letter from Juan Antonio Martínez to José María Vilaseca (*Carta de Juan Antonio Martínez a José María Vilaseca*), San Sebastián Tescuautla, 5 de febrero de 1902. Original: Archivo General de los Misioneros Josefinos (AGMJ hereafter), FUN-01-MJ-M, cited in Osnaya Velázquez, *Los misioneros Josefinos*, 21.
18. Letter from Macario Ramírez a José María Vilaseca (*Carta de Macario Ramírez a José María Vilaseca*), San Andrés Cohamiata, 7 de diciembre de 1902, reprinted in *El Propagador* 32 (1902), cited in Osnaya Velázquez, *Los misioneros Josefinos*, 31.
19. Letter from Macario Ramírez a José María Vilaseca (*Carta de Macario Ramírez a José María Vilaseca*), San Andrés Cohamiata, 7 de diciembre de 1902, reprinted in *El Propagador* 32 (1902), cited in Osnaya Velázquez, *Los misioneros Josefinos*, 31.
20. Letter from José Román Frías to José María Vilasca (*Carta de José Román Frías a José María Vilaseca*), San Antonio, 20 de marzo de 1920, cited in Osnaya Velázquez, *Los misioneros Josefinos*, 22.
21. Report from Calixto Guerrero, "Las misiones de infieles en el Nayarit." Cited in Osnaya Velázquez, *Los misioneros Josefinos*, 24. Original: AGMJ, FUN-01-MJ-G, *El Propagador* 40 (1910).
22. Report from Calixto Guerrero, "Las misiones de infieles en el Nayarit," Cited in Osnaya Velázquez, *Los misioneros Josefinos*, 54. Original: AGMJ, FUN-01-MJ-G, *El Propagador* 40 (1910).
23. "Reglamento de la Asociación de Nuestra Señor del Refugio, establecida en el Venerable Santuario del Señor de Plateros," 4 de julio de 1912. Report from

Calixto Guerrero, "Las misiones de infieles en el Nayarit," Cited in Osnaya Velázquez, *Los misioneros Josefinos*, 59. Original: AGMJ, FUN-01-MJ-G, *El Propagador* 40 (1910).

24. See P. Robles and Velasco, *Ensayo Catequístico*, 3, AHFZ. The short missal contains basic religious instruction for the Huichols, asking such questions as: "*Padre: 'Diced hermano, ¿cuántos Dioses hay?' Respondente: 'Un solo Dios verdadero.'*" In Huichol, this was translated as: "*Padre: 'Ihuá, ne ne tinió tachatúa, ¿quiapátu yúzite me pu chuáhue?' Respondente: 'Chehuítu yucháu Yúzi quientihuayácu.'*"
25. Osnaya Velázquez, *Los misioneros Josefinos*, 60–61.
26. Miguel de la Mora, "Estado de las misiones del Nayarit entre los indios huicholes," marzo de 1912. Original: AGMJ, Misión de los Huicholes, Santuario de Plateros, 1912. Cited in Osnaya Velázquez, *Los misioneros Josefinos*, 61.
27. Rojas, *Los huicholes: documentos*, 219, 241. For clarification on Huichol unity prior to the revolution, see above.
28. Rojas, *Los huicholes: documentos*, 241.
29. Coyle, *From Flowers to Ash*, 183. Coyle is an anthropologist who studies the Náyari, more commonly known as the Coras. As mentioned in previous chapters, occasionally their history intertwines with the Huichols', and sometimes the two overarching groups found common ground during periods of regional or national crisis. Coyle notes that for the revolutionary period as it pertains to the Náyari, the source material came from oral testimonies; he commented that "it was difficult to know whether 'the revolution' of which older people spoke referred to any clearly delimited period."
30. Gobierno del Estado, 29 de agosto de 1912, AHJ, G-9-912, expediente 3026, C/G 1414.
31. Gobierno del Estado, noviembre de 1912, AHJ, G-9-912, expediente 3616, C/G 1422.
32. Negrín, *Acercamiento histórico*, 19. Negrín writes: "*La revolución no afectó la región Huichol hasta que los mestizos se declararon por Villa.*" See Weigand, "Differential Acculturation," 13. Nevertheless, many Huichols supported Villa. Others, as we will see, chose another path. See below.
33. Rojas, *Los huicholes en la historia*, 162. It is not clear where Rojas gets her evidence. I have yet to find any documentation supporting this. Gutiérrez del Ángel, *La peregrinación a Wirikuta*, 23.

34. Rojas, *Los huicholes en la historia*, 160–65. In *Los huicholes: documentos* (p. 241), Rojas notes that "*de 1914 a 1920 ningún documento corresponde a los violentes años de dominio villista en la sierra y de la participación de los huicholes en la revolución, de su exilio, y de la violencia suscitada entre los mismos pueblos por haber tomado partidos diferentes.*"

35. Gobierno del Estado. 24 de marzo de 1912. AHJ, 1912, expediente 1836, C/1396. "'*Manifieste Ud. a los peticioneros que los Zapatistas ninguna bandera política tienen, pues los fines que persiguen es el despojo y el robo.*'"

36. Coyle, *From Flowers to Ash*, 183. See also Rojas, *Los huicholes en la historia*, 163; Weigand, *Ensayos sobre el Gran Nayar*, 121. Rojas writes, "*Como la region fue villista, fueron predominantemente villistas.*"

37. Katz, *Pancho Villa*, 442.

38. Rojas, *Los huicholes en la historia*, 162. Unfortunately, as mentioned earlier, this work by Rojas is often all I have to work with in terms of "specifics" in this middle period of the revolution. For a dated, but excellent, biography of Victoriano Huerta, see Meyer, *Huerta*.

39. Meyer, *Huerta*, 2, 3n2. For information on the military campaigns against the Yaquis and Mayas, see pp. 7–14. For his comments about his Huichol identity, see 163n17. He reportedly said, "'*Yo soy indio huichol.*'" Meyer remarked that critics of Huerta said that his "unbridled use of force [during his reign] is branded as an inheritance from the Huichol Indians, 'that savage race of butchers.'" See Meyer, *Huerta*, 128. That particular quote comes from Manero, *Por el Honor*, 43.

40. Gobernación, noviembre de 1912, AHJ, 1912, expediente 3616, C/G 1422.

41. Gobierno del Estado, 24 de enero de 1913, AHJ, 1913, expediente 841, C/G 1496.

42. Gobernación, 30 de abril de 1914, AHJ, expediente 2210, C/G 1633. Martínez wrote, "*Como en el mes de Noviembre de 1913, no hubo en éste lugar, elecciones para Comisarios Judiciales para el año actual, por haberse acercado los revoltosos, ruego á ese Superioridad si lo cree prudente, se sirva gestionar del Supremo, el nombramiento provicional de dichos funcionarios, interin se hace la elección en Noviembre, del año actual; para cuyo efecto me permit proponer para propietario al C. Macario Venegas y para suplente al C. José Madera Torres.*"

43. Negrín, *Acercamiento histórico*, 19. It is not entirely clear to which town Negrín is referring in this instance, though one could make the argument that most Huichols wanted nonindigenous Mexicans out of their territory.

44. Zingg, *Los huicholes*, 1:133. Zingg commented that "*Patricio González, quien por su crueldad y dureza mereció el apodo que le dieron los indios, de Patricio Mesquite, porque la madera de este árbol es sumamente dura y refractaria. . . . Los comerciantes mexicanos cuentan muchas relatos de sus crímenes.*" See also Weigand, "Differential Acculturation," 13. It is unclear what rebel army Mesquite supported: Zingg says nothing in this regard, except that "*los soldados federales finalmente cayeron sobre Patricio Mesquite luego que la paz fue restablecida y lo ejecutaron, bajo la aplicación de la ley fuga.*" See Zingg, *Los huicholes*, 133. However, Rojas suggests that he was a Villista, and even worse, that he attacked his own people, because of course, he was Huichol: "*Cuenta la tradición que hasta un general villista tuvieron, el general Mezquite* [sic], *azote primero de la region y después de sus propios hermanos.*" See Rojas, *Los huicholes en la historia*, 163. Finally, Negrín remarked that he was a Carrancista, at least for a little while: "*Entonces los Huicholes bajo el liderazgo del General Mezquite, un cacique huichol, optaron por Carranza . . . los huicholes ganaron varias batallas y los mestizos eventualmente huyeron de la zona huichol.*" See Negrín, *Acercamiento histórico*, 19.
45. Rojas, *Los huicholes en la historia*, 164; Coyle, *From Flowers to Ash*, 183. Rojas writes, "*a estas alturas, villismo y bandolerismo eran casi una misma cosa.*"
46. Rojas, *Los huicholes en la historia*, 164. She wrote that "*también al general Santiago, originario de Colotlán, le tocó organizar la campaña contra el villista Rafael Buelna, que había montado su cuartel general en la región de Jesús María y desde allí dominaba gran parte de esta zona de la Sierra Madre. Hasta finales de 1919 pequeñas bandas de villistas siguieron molestando en la región.*" Curiously, a Josephine missionary claimed that "*el Coronel Villista Félix Díaz*" arrived in San Sebastián in May 1916. I have not found any information corroborating Calixto Guerrero's report, which appeared in October 1917. He does mention that the government, in order to finish off the rebels (presumably Villista rebels), armed the Huichols and named one as their leader. *Informe de Calixto Guerrero sobre la Misión de Nayarit, Plateros*, 22 de octubre de 1917. Original: AGMJ, FUN-01-MG-G, cited in Osnaya Velázquez, *Los misioneros Josefinos*, 62–63.
47. Zingg, *Huichol Mythology*, xvi. The assumption, based on other authors, is that San Andrés Huichols supported the constitutional government.

48. Zingg, *Los huicholes*, 1:133.
49. Zingg, *Los huicholes*, 1:133. Zingg reported that "*entre los nativos de Tuxpan y los comerciantes mexicanos, los habitants de San Sebastián tienen fama de ser violenos y peligrosos . . . . Durante la revolución, toda la comunidad fue hervidero de auto-procalamados revolucionarios, quienes con el pretexto de que no existía ningún orden en México, mataban y saqueaban a otros indios.*"
50. Zingg, *Pfeiffer Expedition*, xlvi; Zingg, *Los huicholes*, 1:133; Rojas, *Los huicholes en la historia*, 164.
51. Zingg, *Los huicholes*, 1:133; Rojas, *Los huicholes en la historia*, 164–65. Zingg's visit to the Sierra Huichols came a little more than two decades after the outbreak of the revolution.
52. Gobierno del Estado, 31 de diciembre de 1920, AHJ, G-9-920, C/G 518. It is unclear whether this is the same Ignacio de la Cruz that wrote on behalf of the four principal Huichol towns in 1901 (see above). What is curious in demonstrating Huichol knowledge of national political etiquette is that de la Cruz ended his request with the common closing of "*Sufragio efectivo, no Relección*" ("effective suffrage and no re-election").
53. Gobierno del Estado, 27 de febrero de 1921, AHJ, G-9-920, C/G 518.
54. Gobierno del Estado, 17 de febrero de 1921, AHJ, G-9-920, C/G 518.
55. Meyer, *Huerta*, 163. Meyer wrote that "national unity was no more than an illusion when millions of Indians were so far removed from the rest of the community by language, customs, diet, and life expectancy. The administration, headed by a president [Huerta] whose Indian background was obvious to everyone who even glimpsed his picture, did not initiate a well-defined program of incorporating the Indian systematically into the mainstream of society, but neither was the Indian systematically denigrated and scorned as he had been in the past." Perhaps Huichols recognized this in Huerta; they were, after all, aware of national developments despite their geographical distance.
56. Zingg, *Huichol Mythology*, xxvi.
57. Interestingly in 1938 the ejido president of San Andrés Cohamiata, Juan Antonio Carrillo, sent a telegram to a "Señor Presidente" complaining that their neighbors in Santa Catarina had intended to invade their land. In a subsequent telegram, from February 1939, Carrillo asked for an engineer to be sent out to

measure their lands. See Signatura antigua: Lázaro Cárdenas del Río, AGN, caja 0218, expediente 404.1/743.

58. Several excellent studies of the Cristero Rebellion exist, including a seminal, three-volume work by Jean Meyer. See Meyer, *La cristiada*. See also Butler, *Popular Piety*; Purnell, *Popular Movements*.
59. Cristeros were rebels who took their name from "Cristo Rey," Christ the King, and fought in support of the Catholic Church against anticlerical reforms of the 1917 Mexican Constitution. The agraristas were a rural militia, drawn up in support of the government. Weigand, "Role of Huichol Indians," 170–71. Schaefer, "Cosmos Contained." Some Huichols who lived in Tuxpan fled to the mestizo settlement of Bolaños to escape the fighting. See Zingg, *Huichol Mythology*, xlvi. See also Shelton, "Recollection of Times Past," 357.
60. Zingg, *Huichol Mythology*, xxvi. Zingg claims that San Sebastián's attitude toward the government emerged because of government policies of acculturation that existed after the Mexican Revolution.
61. Weigand, "Role of Huichol Indians," 170. He asserts that Huichols only fought for other Huichols when "all comunidades were equally threatened." For a brief discussion of San Sebastián, see Zingg, *Huichol Mythology*, xxvi; Tuck, *Holy War in Los Altos*, 14; Bailey, *Viva Cristo Rey*, 112.
62. Letter from Jay C. Fikes to Curtis Schaafsma, July 11, 1982, LAA. Here Fikes was relating to the Zingg manuscript, n.d., 345.
63. Burciaga Campos, "Revolución mexicana," 56. Burciaga Campos notes: "*entonces la migración aftecó a la cultura huichola del estado de Jalisco; por ello fueron fundadas otras comunidades en los vecinos estados de Durango y Nayarit.*"
64. Klineberg, "Notes on the Huichol," 447; Zingg, *Huichol Mythology*, xxix. See also "Notes on the Cora and Huichol," Smithsonian-NAA, Ralph Leon Beals Papers, Manuscript of Writings and Lectures, Unpublished MS on Huichols and Coras, box 86.
65. Klineberg, "Notes on the Huichol," 447. Klineberg noted that though fiestas are invariably social, there was a spiritual component even to the most mundane festival.
66. J. Alden Mason, "The Tepehuan and the other Aborigines of the Mexican Sierra Madre Occidental," 295, BLAC, General Libraries, Campbell W. Pennington Papers, box 14, folder 4.

Conclusion

1. Regional Wixárika Council for the Defence of Wirikuta, "Wixárika people deliver letter to Mexican President Calderón and shareholders of First Majestic Silver"; "Urgent Letter from the Wixárika People to the President of Mexico and to all the Peoples and Governments of the World, May 9, 2011, México DF," *MiningWatch Canada* (blog), May 20, 2011, http://miningwatch.ca/blog/2011/5/20/wix-rika-people-deliver-letter-mexican-president-calder-n-and-shareholders-first#sthash.UWcLXFzS.dpbs
2. Fresán Jiménez, *Nierika*, 22–27. See also Meyer, "Introducción: las misiones jesuitas," 20. Letter from Fray Vicente Buenaventura-Cárdenas to Doctor don Diego de Aranda, bishop of Guadalajara, June 1, 1839, AMAG, Bolaños, expediente 3, 1827–1839.
3. Furst, *Rock Crystals*, 1.
4. See chapter 4, the conflict between San Andrés and Santa Catarina that draws the attention of officials in 1888, for example.
5. Zingg, "The Huichols," LAA, Manuscripts Collection, folder 1 of 4, file number 92, MSS.153a. Zingg wrote that "the lack of tribal solidarity is no more strikingly shown than in Huichol participation in the Mexican revolutions. Rather than exerting any influence on revolution as the Cora and Yaqui Indians have done, the Huichols turn against each other."
6. Hu-DeHart, *Yaqui Resistance and Survival*; Erickson, *Yaqui Homeland*; Rugeley, *Rebellion Now and Forever*.
7. AGN, Secretaría de Educación Pública (SEP), Dirección General de Educación Primaria en los Estados y Territorios, Año 1936, referencia 311, expediente 14, Delegación Nayarit, "Inspección y Informes."
8. See *La Prensa Libre*, Tepic, 4 de abril 1936, located in AGN-SEP, Dirección General de Educación Primaria en los Estados y Territorios, Año 1936, referencia 311, expediente 14, Delegación Nayarit, "Inspección y Informes."
9. The SEP archives had been moved, as of about 2012, to the AGN. They are not particularly well catalogued, making research complicated. I looked through roughly fifty boxes of files, and found evidence for Huichol schools in about six files; most of these schools were established in the 1960s and 1970s.

10. Dawson, *Indian and Nation*, 70, 86; Lewis, "Mexico's National Indigenist Institute," 612. Dawson notes that these indigenistas from the 1930s and 1940s believed that groups like the Huichols were not inferior biologically, but instead victims of economic and social policies that kept them oppressed.
11. Fábila, "Situación de los huicholes de Jalisco," 1–8, 65–69, 80–86, 89–90. Fábila originally worked among the Yaquis. See de la Peña, "Social and Cultural Policies," 726.
12. Anónimo, "Cora, Huichol, Tepehuano en Jalisco, Nayarit, Durango," Biblioteca Juan Rulfo CDI, México DF, sin fecha.
13. Anónimo, "Cora, Huichol, Tepehuano en Jalisco, Nayarit, Durango," Biblioteca Juan Rulfo CDI, México DF, sin fecha, 4, 7.
14. Juan Negrín, "Wixárika: An online archive of Huichol Art, History, and Culture," http://wixarika.mediapark.net/en/index.html.
15. "Battle for 'the birthplace of the sun' in Mexico," *Al Jazeera*, October 28, 2011.
16. "Battle for 'the birthplace of the sun' in Mexico," *Al Jazeera*, October 28, 2011.
17. Juan Negrín, "Spring 2010 Newsletter" in "Wixárika: An online archive of Huichol Art, History, and Culture," http://wixarika.mediapark.net/en/documents/NewsletterSpring2010.pdf; Press release from Asociación Jalisciense de Apoyo a Gropos Indígenas, http://wixarika.mediapark.net/en/documents/PressRelease2242010.pdf.
18. Spoken by Leonardo Carrillo Gonzalez, an elder peyote-gatherer, or jícarero, from the Huichol town of Pochotita. Excerpt taken from "El puento sobre el río Chapalagana," *Pueblos de México*, a documentary series produced by Universidad Nacional Autónoma de México (UNAM). See http://www.nacionmulticultural.unam.mx/portal/galeria_audiovisual/serie_pueblos.html.

BIBLIOGRAPHY

Archives

ACDI/INI. Archivo de la Comisión Nacional para el Desarrollo de los Pueblos Indígenas, Mexico City.

AGI. Archivo General de Indias, Seville.

AGMJ. Archivo General de los Misioneros Josefinos.

AGN. Archivo General de la Nación, Mexico.

AGN-SEP. Archivo General de la Nación, Secretaría de Educación Pública.

AHEJ-Archivo Histórico del Estado de Jalisco

AHFZ. Archivo Histórico Franciscano de Zapopan, Colegio Apostólico de Guadalupe, Zacatecas.

AHJ. Archivo Histórico del Estado de Jalisco.

AIPJ. Archivo de Instrumentos Públicos Jalisco.

AMAG. Archivo de la Mitra del Arzobispado de Guadalajara.

AMNH. American Museum of Natural History, Department of Anthropology Archives, New York.

APD. Archivo Porfirio Díaz.

ASDN. Archivo de la Secretaría de la Defensa National.

BLAC. Benson Latin American Collection, the University of Texas at Austin Libraries.

CARSO (formerly CONDUMEX). Archivo del Centro de Estudios de Historia de México.

IAI. Ibero-Amerikanisches Institut, Berlin.

LAA. Laboratory of Anthropology Archives, Santa Fe NM.

Smithsonian-BOE. Smithsonian Institute, Bureau of Ethnology, Washington DC.

Smithsonian-NAA. Smithsonian Institute, National of Anthropology Archives, Washington DC.

Tozzer Library, Harvard College Library, Harvard University, Cambridge MA.

Published Works

Aguirre Beltran, Gonzalo. *Regions of Refuge*. Washington DC: Society for Applied Anthropology, 1979.

Aguirre Loreto, Ignacio, ed. *Colección de acuerdos, órdenes y decretos sobre tierras, casas y solares de los indígenas, bienes de sus comunidades y fundos legales de los pueblos del estado de Jalisco*. Zapopan: El Colegio de Jalisco, 1993.

Alcocer, Fray José Antonio. *Bosquejo de la historia del Colegio de Nuestra Señora de Guadalupe y sus misiones: año de 1788*. Edited by Rafael Cervantes. México DF: Editorial Porrúa, 1958.

Aldana Rendón, Mario A. *La rebelión agraria de Manuel Lozada, 1873*. México DF: Fondo de Cultura Económica, 1983.

Altman, Ida B. *The War for Mexico's West: Indians and Spaniards in New Galicia, 1524–1550*. Albuquerque: University of New Mexico Press, 2010.

Archer, Christon I. "The Indian Insurgents of Mezcala Island on the Lake Chapala Front, 1812–1816." In *Native Resistance and the Pax Colonial in New Spain*, edited by Susan M. Schroeder, 84–128. Lincoln: University of Nebraska Press, 1998.

Arlegui, José de. *Chronica de la Provincia De NSPS Francisco de Zacatecas: compuesta por el M. R. P. Fr. Joseph Arlegui*. México DF: J. Bernardo de Hogal, 1737.

Bailey, David C. *Viva Cristo Rey: The Cristero Rebellion and the Church-State Conflict in Mexico*. Austin: University of Texas Press, 1974.

Bancroft, Hubert Howe. *History of Mexico, Volume 6: 1861–1887*. San Francisco: History Co., 1888.

Barba González, Silvano. *Manuel Lozada*. México DF, 1956.

Basauri, Carlos. *La población indígena de México*. Vol. 3. 3 vols. México DF: Secretaría de Educación Pública, 1940.

Bazant, Jan. *Alienation of Church Wealth in Mexico: Social and Economic Activities of the Liberal Revolution, 1856–1875*. Edited and translated by Michael P. Costeloe. Cambridge: Cambridge University Press, 1971.

Benítez, Fernando. *In the Magic Land of Peyote*. Texas Pan American Series. Austin: University of Texas Press, 1975.

Benson, Nettie Lee. *The Provincial Deputation in Mexico: Harbinger of Provincial Authority*. Austin: University of Texas Press, 1992.

Blosser, Bret. "'By the Force of Their Lives and the Spilling of Blood': Flechero Service and Political Leverage on a Nueva Galicia Frontier." In *Indian Conquistadors: Indigenous Allies in the Conquest of Mesoamerica*, edited by Laura E. Matthew and Michel R. Oudijk, 289–316. Norman: University of Oklahoma Press, 2007.

Bowden, Charles. "Learning Nothing, Forgetting Nothing: On the Trail of Carl Lumholtz." *Journal of the Southwest* 49, no. 4 (2007): 357–68.

Brittsan, Zachary. *Popular Politics and Rebellion in Mexico: Manuel Lozada and La Reforma, 1855–1876*. Nashville TN: Vanderbilt University Press, 2015.

Bugarín, José Antonio. *Visita de las misiones del Nayarit 1768–1769*. Edited by Jean A. Meyer. México DF: Centro de Estudios Mexicanos y Centroamericanos: Instituto Nacional Indigenista, 1993.

Burciaga Campos, José Arturo. "Revolución mexicana y transformaciones culturales del arte del pueblo huichol en el contexto occidental de México." In *Independencia, revolución, y derecho: catorce miradas sobre las revoluciones de México*, edited by Oscar Cuevas Murillo and José Enciso Contreras, 49–63. Zacatecas: Universidad Autónoma de Zacatecas, 2012.

Burns, E. Bradford. *The Poverty of Progress: Latin America in the Nineteenth Century*. Berkeley: University of California Press, 1980.

Butler, Matthew. *Popular Piety and Political Identity in Mexico's Cristero Rebellion: Michoacán, 1927–1929*. Oxford: Oxford University Press, 2004.

Campbell, Howard. *Zapotec Renaissance: Ethnic Politics and Cultural Revivalism in Southern Mexico*. Albuquerque: University of New Mexico Press, 1994.

Carreño, Alberto María. *Archivo del General Porfirio Díaz*. Vol. 10. México DF: Editorial Elede, 1951.

Casillas, Horacio Hernández, and Erika Julieta Vázquez Flores. *Racismo y poder: la negación del indio en la prensa del siglo XIX*. México DF: Instituto Nacional de Antropología e Historia, 2007.

Chuchiak, John F., IV, ed. *The Inquisition in New Spain, 1536–1820*. Baltimore MD: Johns Hopkins University Press, 2012.

Colección de acuerdos, órdenes y decretos sobre tierras, casas y solares de los indígenas, bienes de sus comunidades y fundos legales de los pueblos del estado de Jalisco. Vol. 1. 6 vols. Guadalajara: Gobierno del Estado, 1849.

Colección de acuerdos, órdenes y decretos sobre tierras, casas y solares de los indígenas, bienes de sus comunidades y fundos legales de los pueblos del estado de Jalisco. Vol. 2. 6 vols. Guadalajara: Gobierno del Estado, 1868.

Colección de acuerdos, órdenes y decretos sobre tierras, casas y solares de los indígenas, bienes de sus comunidades y fundos legales de los pueblos del estado de Jalisco. Vol. 3. 6 vols. Guadalajara: Gobierno del Estado, 1868.

Coronado, Juan Zambrano, and Nicolás Valdés. *Villa Guerrero, Jalisco*. Vol. 2. Guadalajara, 1982.

Corr, Rachel. "Ritual Knowledge and the Politics of Identity in Andean Festivities." *Ethnology* 42, no. 1 (2003): 39–54.

Cosio Villegas, Daniel. *Historia moderna de México: el Porfiriato, la vida social*. México DF: Editorial Hermes, 1957.

Coyle, Philip E. *From Flowers to Ash: Náyari History, Politics, and Violence*. Tucson: University of Arizona Press, 2001.

Craib, Raymond B. "A Nationalist Metaphysics: State Fixations, National Maps, and the Geo-Historical Imagination in Nineteenth-Century Mexico." *Hispanic American Historical Review* 82, no. 1 (February 2002): 33–68.

———. *Cartographic Mexico: A History of State Fixations and Fugitive Landscapes*. Latin America Otherwise: Languages, Empires, Nations, series edited by Walter D. Mignolo, Irene Silverblatt, and Sonia Salidívar-Hill. Durham NC: Duke University Press, 2004.

Cumberland, Charles. *Mexican Revolution: Genesis under Madero*. Austin: University of Texas Press, 1952.

Darling, J. Andrew. "Review: Diguet's Studies of West Mexico." *Journal of the Southwest* 42, no. 1 (2000): 181–85.

Dawson, Alexander S. *Indian and Nation in Revolutionary Mexico*. Tucson: University of Arizona Press, 2004.

Deaton, Dawn Fogle. "The Decade of Revolt: Peasant Rebellion in Jalisco, Mexico, 1855–1864." In *Liberals, the Church and Indian Peasants: Corporate Lands and the Challenge of Reform in Nineteenth-Century Spanish America*, edited by Robert S. Jackson, 37–64. Albuquerque: University of New Mexico Press, 1997.

Debroise, Olivier. *Mexican Suite: A History of Photography in Mexico*. Austin: University of Texas Press, 2001.

Diguet, Léon. *Por tierras occidentales entre sierras y barrancas*. México DF: Centro de Estudios Mexicanos y Centroamericanos de la Embajada de Francia en México Instituto Nacional Indigenista, 1992.

Durkheim, Émile. *The Rules of Sociological Method*. Translated by Sarah A. Solovay and John H. Mueller. 8th ed. Chicago: University of Chicago Press, 1938.

Eek, Ann Christine. "The Secret of the Cigar Box: Carl Lumholtz and the Photographs from His Sonoran Desert Expedition, 1909–1910." *Journal of the Southwest* 49, no. 4 (2007): 369–418.

Eisenstadt, Todd A. "Indigenous Attitudes and Ethnic Identity Construction in Mexico." *Mexican Studies/Estudios Mexicanos* 22, no. 1 (Winter 2006): 107–30.

Erickson, Kirstin C. *Yaqui Homeland and Homeplace: The Everyday Production of Ethnic Identity*. Tucson: University of Arizona Press, 2008.

Evans, Susan Toby, and David L. Webster, eds. *Archaeology of Ancient Mexico and Central America Encyclopedia*. New York: Garland, 2001.

Fábila, Alfonso. "Situación de los huicholes de Jalisco." México DF: Instituto Nacional Indigenista, Biblioteca Juan Rulfo, 1958.

Faudree, Paja. *Singing for the Dead: The Politics of Indigenous Revival in Mexico*. Durham NC: Duke University Press, 2013.

Franz, Allen R. "Huichol Ethnohistory: The View from Zacatecas." In *People of the Peyote: Huichol Indian History, Religion, and Survival*, edited by Stacy B. Schaefer and Peter T. Furst, 63–87. Albuquerque: University of New Mexico Press, 1997.

Fresán Jiménez, Mariana. *Nierika, una ventana al mundo de los antepasados*. México DF: CONACULTA-FONCA, 2002.

Furst, Peter T. "Introduction to Chapter Four." In *People of the Peyote: Huichol Indian History, Religion, and Survival*, edited by Stacy B. Schaefer and Peter T. Furst, 88–93. Albuquerque: University of New Mexico Press, 1996.

———. *Rock Crystals & Peyote Dreams: Explorations in the Huichol Universe*. Salt Lake City: University of Utah Press, 2006.

Gabbert, Wolfgang. *Becoming Maya: Ethnicity and Social Inequality in Yucatán Since 1500*. Tucson: University of Arizona Press, 2004.

Garner, Paul. *Porfirio Díaz*. Harlow England: Pearson, 2001.

Gerhard, Peter. *The North Frontier of New Spain*. 2nd ed. Norman: University of Oklahoma Press, 1993.

Gould, Stephen Jay. *The Mismeasure of Man*. Rev. ed. New York: W. W. Norton, 2008.

Grimes, Joseph E., and Thomas B. Hinton. "The Huichol and Cora." In *The Handbook of Middle American Indians, Ethnology, Part 2*, edited by Evon Z. Vogt, Vol. 8, 792–813. Austin: University of Texas Press, 1969.

Guardino, Peter F. *Peasants, Politics, and the Formation of Mexico's National State: Guerrero, 1800–1857*. Stanford CA: Stanford University Press, 1996.

Gutierrez Contreras, Salvador. *Tierras para los indígenas y autonomía de Nayarit: fueron del ideal de Lozada*. Compostela: NAY, 1954.

Gutiérrez del Ángel, Arturo. *La peregrinación a Wirikuta: el gran rito de paso de los huicholes*. México DF: Instituto Nacional de Antropología e Historia, Universidad de Guadalajara, 2002.

Gutiérrez Pulido, Humberto, Moníca Mariscal Gonzáópez, Pedro Pablo Almanzor García, Marcela del Carmen Ayala López, Viviana Gama Hernández, Gabriela Lara Garza, and Mario Gerardo García Navarro. "La población indígena de Jalisco." In *Desarrollo humano y demografía de grupos vulnerables en Jalisco*, 105–12. Guadalajara: Gobierno de Jalisco, 2010, http://docplayer.es/23341733-Desarrollo-humano-y-demografia-de-grupos-vulnerables-en-jalisco.html.

Hale, Charles A. *The Transformation of Liberalism in Late Nineteenth-Century Mexico*. Princeton NJ: Princeton University Press, 1989.

Hall, Basil. *Extracts from a Journal Written on the Coasts of Chili, Peru and Mexico, in the Years 1820, 1821, 1822*. Vol. 2. Edinburgh: Constable, 1825.

Hinton, Thomas B. "Cultural Visibility and the Cora." In *Themes of Indigenous Acculturation in Northwest Mexico*, edited by Thomas B. Hinton, Phil C. Weigand, and N. Ross Crumrine, 1–3. Tucson: University of Arizona Press, 1981.

Hinton, Thomas B., Phil C. Weigand, and N. Ross Crumrine, eds. *Themes of Indigenous Acculturation in Northwest Mexico*. Tucson: University of Arizona Press, 1981.

Horsman, Reginald. "Scientific Racism and the American Indian in the Mid-Nineteenth Century." *American Quarterly* 27, no. 2 (1975): 152–68.

Hrdlička, Aleš. "The Region of the Ancient 'Chichimecs,' with Notes on the Tepecanos and the Ruin of La Quemada, Mexico." *American Anthropologist* 5, no. 3 (1903): 385–440.

Hu-DeHart, Evelyn. *Yaqui Resistance and Survival: The Struggle for Land and Autonomy, 1821--1910*. Madison: University of Wisconsin Press, 1984.

Jones, Grant D. *Maya Resistance to Spanish Rule: Time and History on a Colonial Frontier*. Albuquerque: University of New Mexico Press, 1989.

Joseph, Gilbert M., and Daniel C. Nugent. "Popular Culture and State Formation in Revolutionary Mexico." In *Everyday Forms of State Formation: Revolution and the Negotiation of Rule in Modern Mexico*, edited by Gilbert M. Joseph and Daniel C. Nugent, 3–23. Durham NC: Duke University Press, 1994.

Katz, Friedrich. *The Life and Times of Pancho Villa*. Stanford CA: Stanford University Press, 1998.

Klineberg, Otto. "Notes on the Huichol." *American Anthropologist* 36, no. 3 (September 1934): 446–60.

Knowlton, Robert J. "Dealing in Real Estate in Mid-Nineteenth Century Jalisco: The Guadalajara Region." In *Liberals, the Church and Indian Peasants: Corporate Lands and the Challenge of Reform in Nineteenth-Century Spanish America*, edited by Robert H. Jackson, 13–36. Albuquerque: University of New Mexico Press, 1997.

Kourí, Emilio H. "Interpreting the Expropriation of Indian Pueblo Lands in Porfirian Mexico: The Unexamined Legacies of Andrés Molina Enríquez." *The Hispanic American Historical Review* 82, no. 1 (2002): 69–117.

Lázaro de Arregui, Domingo. *Descripción de la Nueva Galicia*. Seville: Talleres, 1946.

Leutenegger, Benedict, ed. *Nothingness Itself: Selected Writings of Ven. Fr. Antonio Margil, 1690–1724*. Chicago: Franciscan Herald Press, 1976.

Levi, Jerome. "A New Dawn or a Cycle Restored? Regional Dynamics and Cultural Politics in Indigenous Mexico, 1978–2001." In *The Politics of Ethnicity: Indigenous Peoples in Latin American States*, edited by David Maybury-Lewis, 3–49. Cambridge MA: Harvard University Press, 2002.

Lewis, Stephen E. "Mexico's National Indigenist Institute and the Negotiation of Applied Anthropology in Highland Chiapas, 1951–1954." *Ethnohistory* 55, no. 4 (2008): 609–32.

Liffman, Paul. *Huichol Territory and the Mexican Nation: Indigenous Ritual, Land Conflict, and Sovereignty Claims*. Tucson: University of Arizona Press, 2011.

López, Eucario. *Algunos documentos de Nayarit: los publica el Padre Eucario López*. Guadalajara: Libreria Font, 1978.

Lumholtz, Carl. "Explorations in Mexico." *The Geographical Journal* 21, no. 2 (February 1903): 126–39.

———. "The Huichol Indians of Mexico." *Bulletin of the American Geographical Society* 35, no. 1 (1903): 79–93.

———. *Unknown Mexico; a Record of Five Years' Exploration Among the Tribes of the Western Sierra Madre; in the Tierra Caliente of Tepic and Jalisco; and Among the Tarascos of Michoacan*. Vol. 2. 2 vols. New York: Charles Scribner's Sons, 1902.

Lutes, Steven V. "Yaqui Indian Enclavement: The Effects of Experimental Indian Policy in Northwestern Mexico." In *Ejidos and Regions of Refuge in Northwestern Mexico*, edited by N. Ross Crumrine and Phil C. Weigand, 11–20. Tucson: University of Arizona Press, 1987.

Lyon, G. F. *Journal of a Residence and Tour in the Republic of Mexico in the Year 1826 with Some Account of the Mines of That Country*. Vol. 1. London: J. Murray, 1828.

MacCormack, Sabine. *Religion in the Andes: Vision and Imagination in Early Colonial Peru*. Princeton NJ: Princeton University Press, 1991.

Mallon, Florencia E. "Reflections of the Ruins: Everyday Forms of State Formation in 19th Century Mexico." In *Everyday Forms of State Formation: Revolution and the Negotiation of Rule in Modern Mexico*, edited by Gilbert M. Joseph and Daniel C. Nugent, 69-106. Durham NC: Duke University Press, 1994.

Manero, Antonio. *Por el Honor y por La Gloria*. México DF: Imprenta T. Escalante, 1916.

Mata Torres, Ramón. *Matrimonio huichol: integración y cultura*. Guadalajara, Jalisco, México: Universidad de Guadalajara, 1982.

McCarty, Kieran, and Dan S. Matson. "Franciscan Report on the Indians of Nayarit, 1673." *Ethnohistory* 22, no. 3 (1975): 192–221.

Meyer, Jean. "Introducción: las misiones jesuitas del Gran Nayar, 1722–1767. Aculturación y predicación del evangelio." In *Visita de las misiones del Nayarit: 1768–1769*. México DF: Centro de Estudios Mexicanos y Centroamericanos: Instituto Nacional Indigenista, 1993.

Meyer, Jean A. *Atonalisco, Nayarit: una historia documental, 1695–1935*. México DF: Centro de Estudios Mexicanos y Centroamericanos; Instituto Nacional Indigenista, 1994.

———. *El Gran Nayar*. Guadalajara and México DF: Universidad de Guadalajara; Centre d'Etudes Mexicaines et Centraméricaines, 1989.

———. *Esperando a Lozada*. Zamora: El Colegio de Michoacán; México DF: CONACYT, 1984.

———. *La cristiada*. 3 vols. México DF: Siglo Veintiuno Editores, 2005.

———. *La tierra de Manuel Lozada*. Guadalajara and México DF: Universidad de Guadalajara; Centre d'Etudes Mexicaines et Centraméricaines, 1989.

Meyer, Michael C. *Huerta: A Political Portrait*. Lincoln: University of Nebraska Press, 1972.

Moksnes, Heidi. *Maya Exodus: Indigenous Struggle for Citizenship in Chiapas*. Norman: University of Oklahoma Press, 2012.

Myerhoff, Barbara G. *Peyote Hunt: The Sacred Journey of the Huichol Indians*. Ithaca NY: Cornell University Press, 1974.

———. "The Deer-Maize-Peyote Symbol Complex among the Huichol Indians of Mexico." *Anthropological Quarterly* 43, no. 2 (April 1970): 64–78.

Negrín, Juan. *Acercamiento histórico y subjetivo al huichol*. Guadalajara: Universidad de Guadalajara, 1985.

———. "The Huichol: Wixárika," n.p., 2003, http://wixarika.mediapark.net/en/assets/pdf/TheHuichol1.pdf.

Osorio, Rubén. "Villismo: Nationalism and Popular Mobilization in Northern Mexico." In *Rural Revolt in Mexico: US Intervention and the Domain of Subaltern Politics*, edited by Daniel Nugent, 89–106. Durham NC: Duke University Press, 1998.

Osnaya Velázquez, Salvador. *Los misioneros Josefinos en la Diócesis de Zacatecas: Sierra del Nayar y Santuario de Plateros (1901–1922)*. México DF: Ediciones Familia Josefina, 2007.

Palka, Joel W. *Unconquered Lacandon Maya: Ethnohistory and Archaeology of Indigenous Culture Change*. Gainesville FL: University Press of Florida, 2005.

Parry, J. H. *The Audiencia of New Galicia in the Sixteenth Century*. Cambridge: Cambridge University Press, 1948.

Peña, Guillermo de la. *Culturas indígenas de Jalisco*. Guadalajara: Secretaría de Cultura, Goberierno del Estado de Jalisco, 2006.

———. "Social and Cultural Policies Toward Indigenous Peoples: Perspectives from Latin America." *Annual Review of Anthropology* 23 (2005): 717–39.

Perlstein Pollard, Helen. *Taríacuri's Legacy: The Prehispanic Tarascan State*. Norman: University of Oklahoma Press, 1993.

Pimentel, Francisco. *Obras completas de D. Francisco Pimentel*. Vol. 3. 5 vols. México DF: Tipografía Económica, 1903.

Powell, T. G. "Mexican Intellectuals and the Indian Question, 1876–1911." *Hispanic American Historical Review* 48, no. 1 (1968): 19–36.

Preuss, Konrad Theodor. "A Ride through the Country of the Huichol Indians in the Mexican Sierra Madre: Fourth Report of the Travels of K. Th. Preuss." *Globus* 92, no. 10 (1907): 1–26.

———. "Die Hochzeit des Maises und andere Geschichten der Huichol-Indianer." *Globus* 91 (1907): 185–92.

———. "Die religiösen Gesänge un Mythen einiger Stämme der mexikanischen Sierra Madre." *Archiv für Religionswissenschaft* 2 (1908): 369–98.

———. *Fiesta, literatura y magia en el Nayarit: ensayos sobre coras, huicholes y mexicaneros de Konrad Theodor Preuss*. México DF: Instituto Nacional Indígenista, 1998.

P. Robles, Pbro. Francisco de, and Manuel Velasco. *Ensayo Catequístico En Castellano Y En Huichol Por El Pbro. Francisco de P. Robles*. Zacatecas: Sagrado Corazón de Jesus, 1906.

Purnell, Jennie. *Popular Movements and State Formation in Revolutionary Mexico: The Agraristas and Cristeros of Michoacán*. Durham NC: Duke University Press, 1999.

Reina, Leticia. *Las rebeliones campesinas en México, 1819–1906*. México DF: Siglo Veintiuno Editores, 1980.

Rojas, Beatriz, ed. *Los huicholes: documentos históricos*. Colonia Tlacopac: INI, 1992.

———. *Los huicholes en la historia*. México DF: Centro de Estudios Mexicanos y Centroamericanos, Instituto Nacional Indigenista, 1993.

Rugeley, Terry. *Rebellion Now and Forever: Mayas, Hispanics, and Caste War Violence in Yucatán, 1800–1880*. Stanford CA: Stanford University Press, 2009.

———. *Yucatán's Maya Peasantry and the Origins of the Caste War*. Austin: University of Texas Press, 1996.

Ruiz Medrano, Ethelia. *Mexico's Indigenous Communities: Their Lands and Histories, 1500–2010*. Boulder: University Press of Colorado, 2010.

Sahagún, Bernardino de. *General History of the Things of New Spain: Florentine Codex, Translated from the Aztec into English, with Notes and Illustrations*. Translated by Charles Dibble and Arthur J. O. Anderson. Vol. 10. Santa Fe NM: School of American Research, 1953.

Sandoval Godoy, Luís. *Un rincón de la suave patría: el Teúl, Zacatecas*. Zacatecas, 1980.

Santoscoy, Alberto. *Obras completas*. Vol. 2. Guadalajara: Unidad Editorial, 1986.

Schaefer, Stacy B. "Culture Summary: Huichol." HRAF, 2016. http://ehrafworldcultures.yale.edu.www.libproxy.wvu.edu/document?id=nu19-000 [requires user name and password].

———. "The Cosmos Contained: The Temple Where Sun and Moon Meet." In *People of the Peyote: Huichol Indian History, Religion, and Survival*, edited by Stacy B. Schaefer and Peter T. Furst, 332–73. Albuquerque: University of New Mexico Press, 1996.

Schaefer, Stacy B., and Peter T. Furst, eds. *People of the Peyote: Huichol Indian History, Religion, & Survival.* Albuquerque: University of New Mexico Press, 1996.

Scott, James C. *Seeing Like a State: How Certain Schemes to Improve the Human Condition Have Failed.* New Haven CT: Yale University Press, 1998.

Seler, Eduard. *Die Huichol-indianer des staates Jalisco in Mexico.* Wien: Im Selbstverlage der anthropologischen Gesellschaft, 1901.

———. "The Huichol Indians of the State of Jalisco in Mexico." In *Collected Works in Mesoamerican Linguistics and Archaeology*, edited by J. Eric S. Thompson and Francis B. Richardson, Vol. 4, 179–97. Culver City CA: Labyrinthos, 1993.

Shelton, Anthony Alan. "The Recollection of Times Past: Memory and Event in Huichol Narrative." *History and Anthropology* 2, no. 2 (1986): 355–78.

Sissons, Jeffrey. *First Peoples: Indigenous Cultures and Their Futures.* London: Reaktion Books, 2005.

Taylor, William B. "Banditry and Insurrection: Rural Unrest in Central Jalisco, 1790–1816." In *Riot, Rebellion, and Revolution: Rural Social Conflict in Mexico*, edited by Friedrich Katz, 205–46. Princeton NJ: Princeton University Press, 1988.

Tello, Antonio. *Crónica miscelánea de la Sancta Provincia de Xalisco. Libro III.* Edited by José Cornejo Franco. Guadalajara: Editorial Font, 1942.

Torres, Fray Francisco Mariano de. *Crónica de la Sancta Provincia de Xalisco.* Edited by Luis del Refugio de Palacio. Guadalajara: Instituto Jaliscience de Antropología e Historia, 1965.

Trigger, Bruce G. *The Cambridge History of the Native Peoples of the Americas.* Cambridge: Cambridge University Press, 2000.

Tuck, Jim. *The Holy War in Los Altos: A Regional Analysis of Mexico's Rebellion.* Tucson: University of Arizona Press, 1982.

Tutino, John. *From Insurrection to Revolution in Mexico: Social Bases of Agrarian Violence, 1750–1940.* Princeton NJ: Princeton University Press, 1986.

Vanderwood, Paul J. *The Power of God Against the Guns of Government: Religious Upheaval in Mexico at the Turn of the Nineteenth Century.* Stanford CA: Stanford University Press, 1998.

Van Oosterhout, K. Aaron. "Confraternities and Popular Conservatism on the Frontier: Mexico's Sierra Del Nayarit in the Nineteenth Century." *The Americas* 71, no. 1 (July 2014): 101–30.

Van Young, Eric. *Hacienda and Market in Eighteenth-Century Mexico: The Rural Economy of the Guadalajara Region, 1675–1820*. Berkeley: University of California Press, 1981.

———. "Moving toward Revolt: Agrarian Origins of the Hidalgo Rebellion in the Guadalajara Region." In *Riot, Rebellion, and Revolution: Rural Social Conflict in Mexico*, edited by Friedrich Katz, 176–204. Princeton NJ: Princeton University Press, 1988.

Velázquez, María del Carmen. *Colotlán: doble frontera contra los bárbaros*. México DF: Universidad Autónoma de México, 1961.

Weigand, Phil C. "Differential Acculturation Among the Huichol Indians." In *Themes of Indigenous Acculturation in Northwest Mexico*, edited by Thomas B. Hinton and Phil C. Weigand, 9–21. Tucson: University of Arizona Press, 1981.

———. *Ensayos sobre el Gran Nayar: entre coras, huicholes y tepehuanos*. México DF and Zamora: Centro de estudios Mexicanos y Centroamericanos de la Embajada de Francia en México; Instituto Nacional Indigenista; El Colegio de Michoacán, 1992.

———. *Los orígenes de los caxcanes y su relación con la guerra de los nayaritas: una hipótesis*. Zapopan: El Colegio de Jalisco, 1995.

———. "The Role of the Huichol Indians in the Revolutions of Western Mexico." *Proceedings of the Pacific Coast Council on Latin American Studies* 6 (1977): 167–76.

Weigand, Phil C., and Jay Fikes. "Sensacionalismo y etnografía: el caso de los huicholes de Jalisco." *Relaciones* 25, no. 98 (Primavera 2004): 50–68.

Weigand, Phil C., and Acelia García de Weigand. "Huichol Society Before the Arrival of the Spanish." *Journal of the Southwest* 42, no. 1 (2000): 12–36.

Zingg, Robert M. *Huichol Mythology*. Tucson: University of Arizona Press, 2004.

———. *Los huicholes: una tribu de artistas*. Vol. 1. 2 vols. México DF: Instituto Nacional Indigenista, 1982.

———. *Report of the Mr. and Mrs. Henry Pfeiffer Expedition for Huichol Ethnography: The Huichols, Primitive Artists*. Millwood NY: Kraus Repr. Co., 1977.

INDEX

CPSIA information can be obtained
at www.ICGtesting.com
Printed in the USA
LVOW11*0016070418
572542LV00004BA/10/P